T0318807

Bank Liquidity Creation and Financial Crises

Bank Liquidity Creation and Financial Crises

Allen N. Berger
Darla Moore School of Business, University of South Carolina
Wharton Financial Institutions Center
European Banking Center

Christa H.S. Bouwman
Mays Business School, Texas A&M University
Wharton Financial Institutions Center

ELSEVIER

AMSTERDAM • BOSTON • HEIDELBERG • LONDON
NEW YORK • OXFORD • PARIS • SAN DIEGO
SAN FRANCISCO • SINGAPORE • SYDNEY • TOKYO
Academic Press is an Imprint of Elsevier

Academic Press is an imprint of Elsevier
125, London Wall, EC2Y 5AS, UK
525 B Street, Suite 1800, San Diego, CA 92101-4495, USA
225 Wyman Street, Waltham, MA 02451, USA
The Boulevard, Langford Lane, Kidlington, Oxford OX5 1GB, UK

Notices
Knowledge and best practice in this field are constantly changing. As new research and experience broaden our understanding, changes in research methods, professional practices, or medical treatment may become necessary.

Practitioners and researchers must always rely on their own experience and knowledge in evaluating and using any information, methods, compounds, or experiments described herein. In using such information or methods they should be mindful of their own safety and the safety of others, including parties for whom they have a professional responsibility.

To the fullest extent of the law, neither the Publisher nor the authors, contributors, or editors, assume any liability for any injury and/or damage to persons or property as a matter of products liability, negligence or otherwise, or from any use or operation of any methods, products, instructions, or ideas contained in the material herein.

British Library Cataloguing-in-Publication Data
A catalogue record for this book is available from the British Library

Library of Congress Cataloging-in-Publication Data
A catalog record for this book is available from the Library of Congress

ISBN: 978-0-12-800233-9

For information on all Academic Press publications
visit our website at http://store.elsevier.com/

Working together
to grow libraries in
developing countries

www.elsevier.com • www.bookaid.org

Publisher: Nikki Levy
Acquisition Editor: J. Scott Bentley
Editorial Project Manager: Susan Ikeda
Production Project Manager: Nicky Carter
Designer: Alan Studholme

Typeset by Thomson Digital
Printed and bound in the USA

To Mindy Ring
Allen N. Berger

To My Parents, My Daughter Arya,
and My Mentors
Christa H.S. Bouwman

Contents

Part II
Liquidity Creation Measurement and Uses

5. **Using Liquidity Creation to Measure Bank Output**

6. **Using Liquidity Creation to Measure Bank Liquidity**

Part III
Financial Crises, Liquidity Creation, and their Links

Part IV
Causes and Consequences of Liquidity Creation

12. How Do Government Policies and Actions affect Bank Liquidity Creation during Normal Times and Financial Crises?

13. Bank Liquidity Creation: Value, Performance, and Persistence

Part V
Looking Toward the Future

Preface

We met in the summer of 2004 when Christa was a PhD student at the University of Michigan and Allen was a senior economist at the Federal Reserve Board in Washington. We were introduced via email by Arnoud Boot of the University of Amsterdam, who had been a former teacher of Christa and a professional colleague of Allen. Arnoud asked Allen if he would take on Christa as an intern for the summer and Allen agreed, and our long-term collaboration began. Eventually, Christa graduated, moved to Case Western Reserve University in Cleveland, and then went on to become an Associate Professor with Tenure and Republic Bank Research Fellow at Texas A&M University in College Station. Allen moved to the University of South Carolina in Columbia, where he is now H. Montague Osteen, Jr., Professor in Banking and Finance and Carolina Distinguished Professor.

Our first project, started in the early summer of 2004, was to test the theories of the effects of bank capital on liquidity creation. We quickly realized that there were no available measures of liquidity creation that incorporated the liquidity created or destroyed by all commercial bank assets, liabilities, and off-balance-sheet activities, so we developed our own measures of bank liquidity creation. Our preferred measure, "cat fat," classifies all bank financial activities as liquid, semiliquid, or illiquid. It uses categories for loans (the Call Report only allows classification by category or maturity, but not both) and both category and maturity for other assets, liabilities, and off-balance-sheet activities. We later found a contemporaneous working paper by Deep and Schaefer (2004) that measured bank liquidity transformation, but for reasons described in the book, did not suit our purposes. When we presented the paper the next May at the 2005 Federal Reserve Bank of Chicago Bank Structure and Competition conference, we were surprised that all of the attention and questions were on the liquidity creation measures, rather than on the tests of the effects of capital on liquidity creation. As a result, we flipped the order to focus first on the liquidity creation measures, eventually adjusted the title of the paper to be simply "Bank Liquidity Creation," and it was published in the *Review of Financial Studies* in 2009.

In early 2008, when the recent financial crisis was just underway, but well before the widespread panic of September 2008 when Lehman Brothers failed, we began work on financial crises. We developed a paper that linked financial crises with bank capital, liquidity creation, and monetary policy. We eventually separated it into two papers, one on bank capital and financial crises which was published in the *Journal of Financial Economics* in 2013, and one on liquidity creation, monetary policy, and financial crises, which is currently a revise-and-resubmit at another journal.

Since these papers, there has been a lot of research and policy interest in bank liquidity creation, financial crises, and their linkages. We contemplated writing a book on this topic and were therefore delighted when Elsevier approached us to do exactly that. In the book, we provide thorough reviews and integration of the existing research on these topics and run numerous new analyses using liquidity creation and financial crisis data. The new analyses use information on liquidity creation for virtually all individual commercial banks in the US on a quarterly basis for 31 years over the period 1984:Q1 – 2014:Q4.

The book's website (http://booksite.elsevier.com/9780128002339) makes the liquidity creation data used in the book available for benchmarking of bank performance, research, and policy work. This website also contains links to a number of other websites with U.S. data, documents, and other information relevant for such work. Regular data and website link updates will be posted there as well. It is our hope that readers find these to be helpful.

Acknowledgments

The authors thank Norah Barger, Cici Chiang, Yongqiang Chu, Andrew Cohen, Michael Gordy, Erik Heitfield, Burton Hollifield, Bjorn Imbierowicz, Dasol Kim, Sviatlana Phelan, Chris Rauch, Herman Saheruddin, Blake Sutter, Amine Tarazi, Holly Taylor, Anjan Thakor, Ahmet Tuncez, Liying Wang, Laurent Weill, Jason Wu, and Wei Wu for useful comments, and Malik Alatshan, Shradha Bindal, Darian Ennels, Xinming Li, and Raluca Roman for both useful comments and excellent research assistance. We also thank Han Hong, Jing-Zhi Huang, and Deming Wu for providing Basel III liquidity ratios estimated for U.S. banks.

Part I

Introductory Materials

Chapter 1

Introduction

This chapter gives the focus of the book: to inform readers about liquidity creation by commercial banks, financial crises, and their links. It also describes commercial banks and indicates how they differ from other financial institutions. Finally, it provides a brief overview of all the other chapters in the book. Specifically, it introduces liquidity creation theories and measurement; how liquidity creation may be used to measure bank output and bank liquidity; alternative approaches to defining and dating financial crises; links between bank liquidity creation and these crises; how much liquidity banks create during normal times and financial crises; the effects of bank capital, other bank characteristics, and government policies and actions on liquidity creation; and many more topics.

1.1 THE FOCUS OF THE BOOK

The purpose of the book is to inform bank executives, financial analysts, researchers (including academics and students), and policy makers (including legislators, regulators, and central bankers) about bank liquidity creation, financial crises, and the links between the two. The book explains that bank liquidity creation is a more comprehensive measure of a bank's output than traditional measures. It discusses that when a bank creates liquidity for the public, it makes itself illiquid in the process. It then shows how normalized liquidity creation (i.e., liquidity creation divided by assets) may be used as a direct measure of bank illiquidity, or an inverse measure of bank liquidity. The book describes how high levels of bank liquidity creation may cause or predict future financial crises, and how bank liquidity creation tends to fall during such crises. It reviews the existing theoretical and empirical literature, provides new econometric analyses using liquidity creation and financial crisis data, raises new questions to be addressed in future research, and provides links to websites with data and other materials to address these questions. The information in this book is generally not available in other banking textbooks (e.g., Freixas and Rochet, 2008; Saunders and Cornett 2014; and Greenbaum, Thakor, and Boot, 2016).

The book's website (http://booksite.elsevier.com/9780128002339) contains more than three decades of quarterly liquidity creation data on virtually every commercial bank in the United States. At the time of this writing, these data cover the period 1984:Q1–2014:Q4. It also provides links to other websites containing downloadable data, documents, and key information that are helpful for those interested in studying bank liquidity creation, financial crises, and many other important banking topics using US data. The liquidity creation data and the web links will be updated regularly in the future.

The main emphasis in the book is on commercial banks, although – as discussed in the book – liquidity creation may be measured and analyzed for other financial institutions and markets. Box 1.1 describes commercial banks and compares them with other types of financial institutions.

BOX 1.1 Different Types of Financial Institutions

The financial institutions discussed below are very common in the United States, but the array of institutions in other nations may differ.

Commercial banks are typically defined as institutions that make commercial loans and issue transactions deposits. They also have many other types of assets and liabilities and may engage in off-balance sheet activities, including financial guarantees (like loan commitments) and derivatives.[a] They are unique among financial institutions in having significant off-balance sheet activities, although most of these activities are concentrated in the largest commercial banks. Commercial banks are highly regulated.

Given their important role in the economy, they have access to a government safety net: a large part of their deposit funding tends to be covered by government deposit insurance (in the United States provided by the Federal Deposit Insurance Corporation (FDIC)) to avoid potentially disruptive bank runs by depositors, and they may have access to liquidity provided by the central bank (the Federal Reserve in the United States), also called the lender of last resort, when needed. In addition, the very largest commercial banks are typically thought to be too big to fail, meaning that the government would not allow these institutions to fail. All of these protections may lead to moral hazard incentives that cause banks to take excessive risks.[b] To curb such undue risk taking and to keep the banking sector healthy, regulators impose capital requirements and other prudential regulation and supervision (such as regular examinations to ensure that banks do not have excessively risky portfolios) on commercial banks.

Commercial banks in the United States are regulated and supervised by several authorities. The Federal Reserve and state banking authorities regulate state-chartered banks that choose to be members of the Federal Reserve System.[c] The FDIC and state banking authorities regulate state-chartered nonmember banks. The Office of the Comptroller of the Currency (OCC) charters, regulates, and supervises nationally chartered banks.

The four largest US commercial banks, each with well over $1 trillion in assets as of 2014:Q4, are JPMorgan Chase Bank, Bank of America, Wells Fargo Bank, and Citibank.

Bank holding companies (BHCs) are companies that own at least 25% of one or more commercial banks, although most own 100% of the banks. BHCs emerged in the early 1900s for two reasons.

First, they were a way around interstate and intrastate bank branching restrictions: BHCs could operate in multiple states, while banks were not allowed to do so, and often could only operate one office in their own state (so-called unit banking). To prevent BHCs from circumventing state bank branching restrictions, the Douglas Amendment to the Bank Holding Company Act of 1956 gave states the power to control whether and under what circumstances out-of-state BHCs could own and operate banks within their state. No state gave such permission for 22 years, except in unusual circumstances.[d] In the period 1978–1994, states started allowing BHCs to own commercial banks across state lines (with Maine being the first to grant such permission), and the Riegle-Neal Act of 1994 allowed national bank holding companies to cross state lines and consolidate their commercial banks in different states into a single bank.

The second reason why BHCs emerged in the early 1900s is that banks were prohibited from engaging in certain activities, while BHCs were allowed to own commercial firms, such as retail, transportation, or manufacturing firms. This raised the concern that deposits from their bank subsidiaries would be used to make loans to their other operations, giving them an unfair advantage. The Bank Holding Company Act of 1956 addressed this and specified a limited set of financial activities in which multibank BHCs could engage, and the 1970 amendments to the act extended these rules to one-bank BHCs.[e]

Currently, there are three main advantages of forming a BHC. First, as mentioned earlier, BHCs may engage in various activities not permitted by commercial banks. Second, BHCs may have enhanced access to capital markets: besides issuing equity, a BHC can raise debt and inject that as capital into a subsidiary bank. Third, there may be greater ease of acquiring another bank: a BHC can merge a bank into its subsidiary bank or decide to operate as a multibank BHC; it can even own another BHC. The company at the top of the ownership chain is called the top holder. Disadvantages to forming a BHC include increased costs related to supervision and reporting requirements by the Federal Reserve, and additional governance requirements.

Under the Gramm-Leach-Bliley Act of 1999, a BHC may register as a **financial holding company (FHC)**, which allows it to engage in activities such as securities underwriting and dealing, and insurance underwriting. An FHC has both bank and nonbank subsidiaries. Its stakes in its nonbank subsidiaries have to be separately capitalized, that is, they cannot be part of the bank subsidiaries.

The Federal Reserve is currently the umbrella supervisor over all US BHCs, including FHCs. Their subsidiaries are overseen by functional supervisors that specialize in that type of institution (e.g., commercial banking, investment banking, and insurance), although the Federal Reserve retains back-up examination authority.

The four largest US BHCs, with well over $1 trillion in assets as of 2014:Q4, are JPMorgan Chase & Co., Bank of America Corporation, Citigroup Inc., and Wells Fargo & Company.[f] These BHCs bear names that are similar to those of the four largest commercial banks, which is not surprising since they own those banks.

Thrifts, also known as **savings associations** or **savings and loan associations (S&Ls)**, are institutions that generally focus on making real estate loans and issuing

(Continued)

savings accounts. However, the distinction between thrifts and commercial banks has blurred over time. Many thrifts have commercial loans and transactions deposits similar to those of commercial banks, but in the United States by law, they cannot have more than 20% of their lending in commercial loans, and they must pass a qualified thrift lender test that assures that at least 65% of their assets are in residential mortgages or mortgage-backed securities. This makes them especially vulnerable to downturns in the housing market. Thrifts are also prudentially regulated and supervised to curb moral hazard and keep them safe. They are regulated and supervised by the OCC or state agencies, depending on whether they are nationally or state chartered, respectively.

Most thrifts are small relative to the largest commercial banks. However, there are some large ones. Similar to commercial banks, the largest thrifts are generally in holding companies. The largest public thrift holding companies in the United States, each with assets over $10 billion as of 2014:Q4, are New York Community Bancorp (owns New York Community Bank), Hudson City Bancorp Inc. (owns Hudson City Savings Bank), EverBank Financial Corp. (owns EverBank), Investors Bancorp Inc. (owns Investors Bank), Astoria Financial Corp. (owns Astoria Bank), and TFS Financial Corp. (owns Third Federal Savings and Loan Association of Cleveland). Some of the large depository institutions that failed during the subprime lending crisis of 2007:Q3–2009:Q4 were thrifts, including IndyMac Bank and Washington Mutual.

Credit unions make loans and issue deposits much like commercial banks. However, they are run in a very different way. Credit unions in the United States are not-for-profit institutions owned by their deposit account holders, called members, who also often take out consumer loans and home mortgages. Some credit unions also provide restricted quantities of member business loans. All members are required to have a common bond with each other, which typically means they work for the same employer and/or live in the same geographical area. Credit unions do not pay taxes, and any profits earned may be re-invested, paid out as dividends, or used to improve deposit and loan rates to its members. Many credit unions provide services aimed at community development. Credit unions are overseen by the National Credit Union Administration (NCUA), which also provides them deposit insurance.

Credit unions are typically much smaller than commercial banks in terms of assets, but there are a few large ones. The largest credit unions in the United States, each with over $10 billion in assets as of 2014:Q4, are Navy Federal Credit Union, State Employees' Credit Union (North Carolina), Pentagon Federal Credit Union, Boeing Employees Credit Union, and SchoolsFirst Federal Credit Union (California).

Finance companies are financial firms that make loans like commercial banks, but do not issue deposits. Instead they issue short- and long-term debt, such as commercial paper[8] and bonds, as well as equity to finance the loans. Finance companies are typically less highly levered than commercial banks because they do not have insured deposit funding and must rely on more equity to signal solvency to potential creditors. Finance companies may specialize in commercial or consumer loans. Some specialize in making loans to customers of a particular retailer or manufacturer. Finance companies are less regulated than deposit-taking institutions in part because they are not subject to the moral hazard incentives created by deposit insurance and other elements of the government safety net, such as access to the Federal Reserve's liquidity facilities and too-big-to-fail protection.

An example of a finance company that makes loans to customers of a particular firm is Ford Motor Credit Company. A finance company that makes consumer loans is J.G. Wentworth and a finance company that makes commercial loans is Nations Equipment Finance, LLC.

Investment banks are financial firms that typically aid nonfinancial and other financial firms in issuing publicly traded equity and debt in cooperation with financial markets. They also often assist firms involved in mergers and acquisitions (M&As), and may provide additional services including market making (i.e., facilitating trading in certain securities by quoting firm buy and sell prices for these securities) and the trading of derivatives.

Investment banks have traditionally not been regulated as much as depository institutions and have not had access to the government safety net (deposit insurance, access to the Federal Reserve's liquidity facilities, and too-big-to-fail protection). During the subprime lending crisis (2007:Q3–2009:Q4), out of the five largest investment banks, one failed (Lehman Brothers) and two were bought out (Bear Stearns and Merrill Lynch). Two investment banks (Goldman Sachs and Morgan Stanley) were granted access to liquidity from the Federal Reserve and received capital support from the US Treasury. Since the crisis, both have given up their independence and are now subsidiaries of financial holding companies that also own commercial banks. The main advantage to them is that they can now access liquidity through insured deposits and from the Federal Reserve when needed, the main cost is that they are now subject to bank holding company regulations and supervision.

Some of the largest US investment banks are Goldman Sachs and Morgan Stanley, which as noted are subsidiaries of financial holding companies that also own banks, as well as the largest BHCs' investment bank subsidiaries (J.P. Morgan, Bank of America Merrill Lynch, Citi, and Wells Fargo Securities).[h]

Mutual funds, **insurance companies**, and **pension funds** are often collectively referred to as **institutional investors**. Mutual funds are institutions that invest in many different stocks, bonds, and/or money market instruments, and issue shares in their portfolios to investors. Mutual funds thus give small investors access to diversified portfolios of various securities that would be hard to create by these investors individually. Shares in the mutual funds may be redeemed by investors at virtually any time in virtually any quantity. Insurance companies are financial firms that typically invest in securities and issue insurance policies that pay off policy holders when insured events occur. Pension funds similarly invest employees' savings in securities and pay these employees when they retire.

Examples of large mutual funds, insurance companies, and pension funds are The Vanguard Group (Vanguard), Prudential Financial Inc. (Prudential), and California Public Employees' Retirement System (CalPERS), respectively.

(Continued)

Shadow banks are financial institutions that engage in the same or similar activities as commercial banks, but are not highly regulated depository institutions such as commercial banks, thrifts, or credit unions. They include the finance companies, investment banks, mutual funds, insurance companies, and pension funds already discussed, as well as **hedge funds**, **private equity funds**, and other financial firms.[i] Shadow banks are usually only lightly regulated and supervised or unregulated and unsupervised because they do not accept traditional deposits. As a result, many shadow banks do not have regulatory-imposed capital requirements and are riskier. Since the subprime lending crisis of 2007:Q3–2009:Q4, shadow banks have come under increased scrutiny and regulation. For example, a few shadow banks in the United States are now classified as systemically important financial institutions (SIFIs), and are now prudentially regulated and supervised by the Federal Reserve.[j]

---

a. Readers who are not very familiar with the financial statements of commercial banks will find Chapter 3 helpful. It compares the financial statements of a large nonfinancial firm, a large commercial bank, and a small commercial bank.

b. Moral hazard occurs when a party takes more risk because another party bears some of the costs if things go badly. The term comes from the insurance industry. Insurance companies worry that those who purchase insurance will behave in riskier ways. For example, purchasers of car insurance may stop wearing seat belts.

c. All national banks are members of the Federal Reserve as well as state-chartered banks that choose such membership. As of 2015, 38% of commercial banks in the United States are members of the Federal Reserve System. Members, particularly the national banks, are typically larger and have more branch locations.

d. Unusual circumstances often included the purchase of troubled banks. In 1987, before Texas and New York allowed cross-state penetration, Chemical Bank from New York was allowed to acquire the troubled bank Texas Commerce.

e. Another issue concerns the definition of a bank. The Bank Holding Company Act of 1956 defined a bank to be an institution that takes deposits and makes loans. The 1970 Amendments altered this, requiring an institution to accept demand deposits and make commercial (as opposed to personal) loans. This motivated some commercial firms to engage in either activity, thus avoiding classification as a bank. It inspired others to acquire FDIC-insured nonbank banks, which took demand deposits and made consumer (rather than commercial) loans, effectively giving them access to cheap funding. This nonbank bank issue was addressed in the Competitive Equality Banking Act of 1987, which redefined a bank to be either an FDIC-insured institution (whether or not it accepts demand deposits or makes commercial loans) or an institution that accepts demand deposits and makes commercial loans.

f. The National Information Center, a repository of financial data and institution characteristics collected by the Federal Reserve System provides a list with the names, location, and size of all holding companies with assets over $10 billion at http://www.ffiec.gov/nicpubweb/nicweb/top50form.aspx.

g. Commercial paper is a security issued by large firms to obtain funds to meet short-term obligations. It is unsecured, meaning that it is not backed by collateral. It typically has a maturity up to 270 days, since short maturities avoid complications associated with registering the security with the Securities and Exchange Commission (SEC), the US agency in charge of protecting investors and maintaining fair, orderly, and efficient securities markets.

h. The largest investment banks active in the United States also contain several foreign banks: Barclays, Deutsche Bank, Credit Suisse, Union Bank of Switzerland (UBS), and Hongkong & Shanghai Banking Corp. (HSBC).

i. A hedge fund aims to generate high returns in a short period of time for high net worth individuals by investing in a wide range of primarily liquid securities and other instruments. A private equity fund uses funds from high net worth individuals to buy equity in private firms (or in public firms that it then takes private) over a longer time period (3–10 years).

j. Chapter 12 elaborates on SIFIs and provides a list of institutions designated as such as of 2014:Q4. They include nonbanks MetLife, Inc., American International Group (AIG), Inc., General Electric (GE) Capital Corp, Inc., and Prudential Financial, Inc.

1.2 LIQUIDITY CREATION THEORIES

Chapter 2 discusses that liquidity creation is one of the most important roles that banks play in the economy, and this is formally recognized by modern financial intermediation theory. Banks create liquidity on the balance sheet by transforming illiquid assets like business loans into liquid liabilities like transactions deposits. The theory also recognizes that banks create liquidity off the balance sheet through loan commitments and similar claims to liquid funds, whereby customers can draw funds from the bank under predetermined conditions.

1.3 UNDERSTANDING FINANCIAL STATEMENTS

The measurement of liquidity creation requires the use of detailed financial statement data with which many readers may not be very familiar. For this reason, Chapter 3 examines differences among the financial statements of a large nonfinancial firm, a large commercial bank, and a small commercial bank.

1.4 MEASUREMENT OF BANK LIQUIDITY CREATION

Chapter 4 explains that until recently, bank liquidity creation was mainly a theoretical concept and was not measured or used in empirical studies. Berger and Bouwman (2009) provide several alternative liquidity creation measures, discussed in depth in the chapter. Their preferred "cat fat" measure is the first comprehensive liquidity creation measure that takes into account the contributions to bank liquidity creation of all bank activities (assets, liabilities, equity, and off-balance sheet activities). To give an initial flavor of the methodology, Box 1.2 briefly summarizes the three-step approach to calculate this measure.

BOX 1.2 Brief Summary of the Three-Step Approach to Measure "Cat Fat" Liquidity Creation

Step 1: All bank activities are classified as liquid, semiliquid, or illiquid.

Step 2: A weighting scheme is applied to these activities. The weights are based on liquidity creation theory and judgments about the liquidity of each item. Since the theories argue that liquidity is created when banks transform illiquid assets (e.g., business loans) into liquid liabilities (e.g., transactions deposits), positive weights are given to both illiquid assets and liquid liabilities. Similarly, banks destroy liquidity when they transform liquid assets (e.g., marketable securities) into illiquid liabilities (e.g., subordinated debt) or equity, so negative weights are assigned to liquid assets, illiquid liabilities, and equity. Off-balance sheet activities (e.g., loan commitments and derivatives) receive weights consistent with those assigned to functionally similar on-balance sheet activities. Loan commitments are given positive weights because they are illiquid (like business loans) to the bank and liquid (like transactions deposits) for the customers.

Step 3: The dollar amount of liquidity creation by a bank is calculated as the weighted sum of all activities.

1.5 USING LIQUIDITY CREATION TO MEASURE BANK OUTPUT

Chapter 5 discusses that bank liquidity creation may be viewed as a measure of the output of a bank. Virtually every empirical study in banking uses a measure of assets or lending as its main measure of bank output. As explained in the chapter, the preferred "cat fat" liquidity creation measure is a superior output measure because it takes into account all bank activities (all assets, liabilities, equity, and off-balance sheet activities). In addition, it gives better weights to different assets than these other measures. For example, "cat fat" assigns a negative weight to marketable securities held by a bank because holding such securities takes something liquid away from the public, reducing the output of the bank. In contrast, these securities are given a positive weight when assets are used to measure output, and a zero weight when lending is used.

1.6 USING LIQUIDITY CREATION TO MEASURE BANK LIQUIDITY

Chapter 6 explains that bank liquidity creation differs from, but is related to, the concept of bank liquidity. Traditional bank liquidity indicators measure how liquid a bank is. They are usually simple ratios that use only a few of the bank's assets and/or liabilities. In contrast, bank liquidity creation measures how much liquidity the bank creates for its customers, making the bank illiquid in the process. Thus, liquidity creation divided by assets (i.e., normalized liquidity creation) is a direct measure of a bank's illiquidity and an inverse measure of its liquidity. Normalized "cat fat" liquidity creation is a more comprehensive measure of bank liquidity than traditional indicators since it uses information on all assets, liabilities, equity, and off-balance sheet activities. The chapter discusses that liquidity creation is also related to more complex liquidity measures, such as the Basel III liquidity ratios and the Liquidity Mismatch Index. Correlations between the "cat fat" measure of liquidity creation and the Basel III liquidity ratios are examined. Differences between measures of bank liquidity and market measures of the liquidity of publicly traded bank equity and debt are explained.

1.7 DEFINING AND DATING FINANCIAL CRISES

Chapter 7 indicates that there are many approaches to defining and dating financial crises in the literature, and argues that there is not one that fully dominates the others. Financial crises may feature credit crunches, that is, significant reductions in the supply of credit by financial institutions, such as the one that occurred in 1990:Q1–1992:Q4 in the United States. They may also involve frozen credit markets, such as happened for the commercial paper and interbank lending markets[1] during the subprime lending crisis of 2007:Q3–2009:Q4. Financial crises can have severe consequences for the real economy. For example, the subprime lending crisis led to a major recession in the United States and spread to other nations as well.

Much of the literature focuses on defining and dating crises that happened over different time periods around the world. The empirical analyses in this book focus on five financial crises that occurred in the United States over the 31-year period from 1984:Q1 to 2014:Q4. They include two banking crises (crises that originate in the banking sector) and three market crises (those that originate in financial markets).

1.8   HOW MUCH LIQUIDITY DO BANKS CREATE DURING NORMAL TIMES AND FINANCIAL CRISES?

Chapter 8 shows how much liquidity US banks created quarterly over the 31-year period from 1984:Q1–2014:Q4 for different size classes of banks. It does so using the preferred liquidity creation measure and its on- and off-balance sheet components, both in levels and normalized by assets. It also shows how alternative measures of liquidity creation and bank output evolved over time. It discusses reasons why liquidity creation has grown so dramatically, and it compares liquidity creation during normal times and during financial crises.

1.9   THE LINKS BETWEEN BANK LIQUIDITY CREATION AND FUTURE FINANCIAL CRISES

Chapter 9 links the two main topics of the book – bank liquidity creation and financial crises. Aggregate bank liquidity creation may directly affect the probability that a future financial crisis occurs, or at least help in predicting such crises. Some research suggests that abnormally high aggregate liquidity creation on the balance sheet may lead to an asset price bubble that subsequently bursts and causes a financial crisis, and that excessive aggregate liquidity creation off the balance sheet may precede financial crises as well. Other research suggests that banks may make correlated on- and off-balance sheet portfolio choices when bank liquidity creation is high. Such correlated choices can induce systemic risk and increase the probability of a financial crisis.[2] Consistent with these arguments, empirical research finds that aggregate liquidity creation in excess of the trend increases the probability of a financial crisis.

---

1. In interbank lending markets, banks extend loans to each other at the interbank rate, known as the federal funds rate in the United States. The vast majority of such loans are overnight. Banks that do not have sufficient liquid assets to meet their liquidity needs or require reserves borrow in the interbank market to cover the shortfalls. Banks that have excess liquid assets lend money in this market.

2. Systemic risk is the risk of serious damage to or collapse of the entire financial system, rather than the breakdown of an individual entity or component of the financial system. Systemic risk refers to the risks caused by interdependencies and interlinkages in the financial system, where the failure of one entity or component can have ripple effects, which can cause the entire financial system to break down.

1.10 DO BETTER CAPITALIZED BANKS CREATE MORE OR LESS LIQUIDITY?

Chapter 10 reviews the theory and empirical evidence on the effects of bank capital on liquidity creation. Some theories suggest that banks with higher capital ratios create less liquidity because capital reduces banks' ability to monitor its clients or because capital "crowds out" deposits. Other theories suggest that higher capital improves banks' ability to absorb risk and hence their ability to create liquidity. Empirical evidence from the United States and other countries is reviewed. The US evidence suggests a positive effect of capital on liquidity creation for large banks, and a negative effect for small banks. Limited evidence from Europe and the rest of the world is broadly consistent with the US evidence, although the effect on liquidity creation by large bank seems to be weaker, perhaps because large banks in other nations have few off-balance sheet activities.

1.11 WHICH BANKS CREATE THE MOST AND LEAST LIQUIDITY?

Chapter 11 identifies the large, medium, and small banks that create the most and least liquidity (in dollar terms and normalized by assets) in 1984:Q1 and in 2014:Q4. It distinguishes between each bank's "cat fat" liquidity creation and its on- and off-balance sheet components. It also examines important characteristics of banks – size, capital, portfolio risk, regulator identity, and bank holding company status – and relates these to normalized liquidity creation.

1.12 HOW DO GOVERNMENT POLICIES AND ACTIONS AFFECT BANK LIQUIDITY CREATION DURING NORMAL TIMES AND FINANCIAL CRISES?

Chapter 12 discusses the effects of government policies and actions on bank liquidity creation. This includes the effects of capital and liquidity requirements (including Basel III), stress tests, capital support or bailouts, regulatory interventions, central bank funding, and monetary policy in various nations. These government policies and actions are described is some detail and existing evidence is discussed. The evidence suggests that some of these policies and actions may have significant effects on bank liquidity creation that differ during normal times and financial crises.

1.13 BANK LIQUIDITY CREATION: VALUE, PERFORMANCE, AND PERSISTENCE

Chapter 13 examines the effects of bank liquidity creation on value and performance and the extent to which liquidity creation is persistent. It reviews the existing literature on the relation between liquidity creation and bank performance. It also provides new empirical analyses on the relations between bank liquidity creation normalized by assets and several key bank performance measures.

These analyses distinguish "cat fat" liquidity creation and its on- and off-balance sheet components.

1.14   HOW CAN BANK EXECUTIVES, FINANCIAL ANALYSTS, RESEARCHERS (INCLUDING ACADEMICS AND STUDENTS), AND POLICY MAKERS (INCLUDING LEGISLATORS, REGULATORS, AND CENTRAL BANKERS) USE BANK LIQUIDITY CREATION DATA TO THEIR ADVANTAGES?

Chapter 14 is devoted to explaining how bank executives, financial analysts, researchers, and policy makers may use bank liquidity creation data, which are available free of charge to the readers on the book's website (http://booksite.elsevier.com/9780128002339). It discusses how liquidity creation may be used to benchmark the performance of a bank against that of its peers and against its own past liquidity creation, to predict financial crises, to assess risk taking, and to predict failure of individual banks. The chapter also indicates that the liquidity creation data may be used to further address issues discussed in earlier chapters, as well as conduct research on open questions such as those identified in the next chapter.

1.15   WHERE WE STAND NOW AND THE OPEN RESEARCH AND POLICY QUESTIONS

Chapter 15 briefly looks back at the topics that have been addressed in the existing literature and then looks forward to some of the important open research questions. These include the measurement of bank liquidity creation, its causes and consequences in more nations around the world. It is also important to understand how liquidity creation is affected by mergers and acquisitions, competition and market power, deregulation, deposit insurance, and corporate governance (ownership, executive compensation, and board and management structure). Furthermore, it is useful to understand how liquidity creation relates to risk and affects economic activity. Further topics to be researched include whether there is an optimal scale of bank liquidity creation for the industry and for individual banks, the dynamics of liquidity creation, and how liquidity creation differs in different financial and legal systems. Finally, liquidity creation by other types of financial institutions and markets should be measured and their interactions with bank liquidity creation should be investigated.

1.16   LINKS TO WEBSITES CONTAINING DATA, DOCUMENTS, AND OTHER INFORMATION USEFUL FOR US BANK PERFORMANCE BENCHMARKING, RESEARCH, AND POLICY WORK

Chapter 16 gives links to numerous websites containing US data and other useful information for benchmarking bank performance and conducting banking research and policy work on bank liquidity creation, financial crises, and a broad range of other banking topics. These links are also available on the book's website (http://booksite.elsevier.com/9780128002339), where they will be updated when necessary. The sources provide: liquidity creation data, bank Call Report data, bank reporting forms, bank holding company (BHC) data, BHC reporting forms, the Micro Data Reference Manual, bank structure and geographical data, Summary of Deposits data, bank and BHC mergers and acquisitions data, bank failures data, the Senior Loan Officer Survey, aggregate data on the banking sector, FRED economic data, CRSP data and EDGAR financial statement data on listed banks and BHCs, the Federal Reserve's monetary policy tools, capital support provided through the Treasury's Troubled Asset Relief Program (TARP), Home Mortgage Disclosure Act (HMDA) data, Dealscan syndicated loan data, the Survey of Small Business Finances data, the Kauffman Firm Survey data, and the Survey of Consumer Finances data.

1.17 SUMMARY

This introductory chapter describes the purpose of this book: To inform readers about bank liquidity creation, financial crises, and the links between the two. It explains that the book covers extant theoretical and empirical literature, contains evidence from around the world, and includes new empirical analyses focused on the United States. The book uses quarterly data on virtually all US commercial banks from 1984:Q1 to 2014:Q4. The liquidity creation data are provided for free on the book's website (http://booksite.elsevier.com/9780128002339), and will be updated regularly. The remainder of the chapters is also introduced. The key takeaways from this chapter are the importance of bank liquidity creation, financial crises, and their links; and encouragement to perform further analysis, research, and policy work on topics discussed in the book including the open questions that are introduced.

Chapter 2

Liquidity Creation Theories

This chapter briefly describes in intuitive terms the theories of liquidity creation. Liquidity creation is one of the most important roles that banks play in the economy. The concept goes far back in time. Claims that bank liquidity creation is vital for economic growth date back at least to Smith (1776).[1] The contemporary theories of liquidity creation (see below) suggest that banks create liquidity on and off the balance sheet. Examples are given to show how banks do both. Finally, extensions to other financial institutions and markets are discussed.

2.1 LIQUIDITY CREATION ON THE BALANCE SHEET

Contemporary financial intermediation theories focus on bank liquidity creation on the balance sheet (e.g., Bryant, 1980; and Diamond and Dybvig, 1983). In these models, the emphasis is on the liability side of the bank's balance sheet, with liquidity creation being viewed as the provision of improved risk sharing for depositors subject to uncertainty about their preference for the timing of consumption. Banks are passive on the asset side in the sense that they simply invest in projects with given payoffs. That is, banks create liquidity by giving depositors the right to withdraw on demand. A recent theory emphasizes the importance of both the asset and liability sides for liquidity creation (Donaldson, Piacentino, and Thakor, 2015). In their model, banks are active on the asset side in that bank lending increases aggregate investment in the economy, and the more illiquid the assets are, the more liquidity is created. This approach is closest in spirit to the on-balance-sheet liquidity creation concept embraced in Berger and Bouwman (2009) and used in this book.[2]

---

1. Smith (Book II, Chapter II, 1776) highlights the importance of liquidity creation by banks and describes how it helped commerce in Scotland.

2. The modern theory of financial intermediation identifies risk transformation as another main role of banks. According to the risk transformation theories, banks transform risk by issuing riskless deposits to finance risky loans (e.g., Diamond, 1984; Ramakrishnan and Thakor, 1984; and Boyd and Prescott, 1986). The risk transformation role is well studied and beyond the scope of this book. Importantly, while risk transformation may coincide with liquidity creation (e.g., when banks issue riskless liquid deposits to finance risky illiquid loans), the two do not move in perfect tandem – the amount of liquidity created may vary considerably for a given amount of risk transformed. It is therefore essential to study both roles of banks and to distinguish between them.

Bank Liquidity Creation and Financial Crises

To see how on-balance-sheet liquidity creation works, consider the example in Box 2.1.

BOX 2.1 How Banks Create Liquidity on the Balance Sheet – Steel Mill Example

To understand how banks create liquidity on the balance sheet, picture a steel company with a mill in need of financing. Suppose it needs a $10 million, 10-year loan.

In a world without banks, the steel company would have to raise such financing directly from the nonbank public, who would have to hold a very illiquid claim against the steel company and would only be able to get its funds back in full after 10 years. In contrast, in a world with banks, a bank provides the financing to the steel company, and the public can simply deposit their funds at the bank. The bank holds the illiquid claim against the steel company; the public holds very liquid claims against the bank, and is able to retrieve its funds any time.

The reason why the bank can give the public liquid claims even though it holds an illiquid claim itself has to do with diversification. In practice, the bank will not just provide one loan to the steel company, but it will have a diversified loan portfolio containing many loans with imperfectly correlated prospects that pay off at different times. This enables the bank to issue deposits, knowing that depositors generally access their funds at different times as well. The bank in this example has transformed something very illiquid (a large, long-term loan) into things that are very liquid (small, short-term transactions deposits), thereby creating liquidity for the public.

2.2 LIQUIDITY CREATION OFF THE BALANCE SHEET

More recently, it has been recognized that banks also create liquidity off the balance sheet through loan commitments and similar claims to liquid funds (e.g., Boot, Greenbaum, and Thakor, 1993; Holmstrom and Tirole, 1998; and Kashyap, Rajan, and Stein, 2002). From the bank's perspective, loan commitments are very similar to illiquid loans in that the bank is essentially required to provide the funding when requested. From the customer's perspective, a loan commitment is similar to a transactions deposit because it allows the customer to draw down liquid funds up to the specified limit at any time, albeit only over the life of the commitment.[3] Thus, a loan commitment requires the bank to hold something illiquid and give the public something liquid, creating liquidity.

Most banks create liquidity off the balance sheet primarily via loan commitments and similar claims to liquid funds. The recent literature that explicitly

---

3. An important difference between a loan commitment and a transactions deposit is that a bank can escape its obligation to lend on a formal commitment if the borrower's condition has suffered a 'material adverse change' (MAC), or if the borrower has violated some other covenant in the commitment contract. While MAC clauses are somewhat vague, banks may nevertheless honor commitments to borrowers to whom they would otherwise refuse credit or charge a higher rate in order to maintain the bank's reputation for future commitments or to avoid legal costs (Boot, Greenbaum, and Thakor, 1993). If banks did not honor their commitment under adverse circumstances or rationed credit, then commitments would lose much of their insurance value and firms would not purchase them for protection from a decline in firm-specific or market conditions (Avery and Berger, 1991).

acknowledges this builds on an earlier loan commitments literature in which the creation of liquidity is more implicitly recognized. This earlier literature explains the existence of bank loan commitments as providing a mechanism for optimal risk sharing (Ho and Saunders, 1983; and Campbell, 1978), reducing credit rationing (James, 1981; Blackwell and Santomero, 1982; Morgan, 1994; and Thakor, 2005), and ameliorating informational frictions between the borrower and the bank (Boot, Thakor, and Udell, 1987; Boot, Thakor, and Udell, 1991; and Berkovitch and Greenbaum, 1991). Melnik and Plaut (1986), Shockley and Thakor (1997), and Sufi (2009) provide detailed overviews of the contractual features of loan commitments and lines of credit.

Off-balance-sheet liquidity creation is important. As shown in Chapter 8, it accounts for about half of all bank liquidity creation in the United States, with most of the off-balance-sheet liquidity creation due to loan commitments. Furthermore, as discussed in Chapter 9, banks may create too much liquidity off the balance sheet through loan commitments, and this can sow the seeds of a future crisis.

2.3 LIQUIDITY CREATED BY OTHER TYPES OF FINANCIAL INSTITUTIONS AND MARKETS

To our knowledge, liquidity creation theory is confined to banks, and has not been formally extended to other types of financial institutions and markets. However, it seems clear that the theory can be extended to these parties.

Thrift institutions create liquidity in much the same way as commercial banks do, on the balance sheet by transforming mostly real-estate loans into savings accounts or by securitizing such loans and creating mortgage-backed securities that trade in markets, often with the assistance of government-sponsored enterprises like Fannie Mae and Freddie Mac.[4] Credit unions create liquidity by transforming consumer loans and mortgages into deposits. Investment banks, with the help of financial markets, create liquidity by transforming previously illiquid nontraded shares into traded securities via initial public offerings and seasoned equity offerings, taking something illiquid from the public and giving it something liquid. Mutual funds create liquidity because the shares they issue provide investors access to small denomination claims against diversified baskets of securities, and hence provide access at lower transactions costs to investors than if they had to invest in the individual securities themselves. Insurance companies likely destroy liquidity on net because they often invest in liquid assets and issue relatively illiquid insurance policies, although they do provide valuable risk-reduction services to their policyholders. Other shadow banks, such as hedge funds, private equity funds, and other financial firms that

---

4. Securitization generally means that a number of similar loans are bundled together and securities are issued with payoffs that depend on the cash flows from those loans. Mortgage-backed securities are examples of securitization based on bundles of mortgages.

engage in bank-like activities likely create liquidity in a manner similar to commercial banks to the extent that they provide services similar to those provided by banks. Stock, bond, and other capital markets create liquidity by providing platforms for relatively illiquid claims on companies and governments to be traded and become liquid.

2.4 SUMMARY

This chapter briefly reviews still-evolving liquidity creation theories and provides the intuition behind how banks create liquidity both on and off the balance sheet. On the balance sheet, banks create liquidity by financing illiquid assets (e.g., business loans) with liquid liabilities (e.g., transactions deposits); an example illustrates this. Off the balance sheet, banks create liquidity primarily through loan commitments and similar claims to liquid funds. While existing theories focus on liquidity creation by commercial banks, these theories can be extended to include other types of financial institutions and markets, which also create and destroy liquidity.

The key takeaways are that the theories suggest that banks create liquidity on and off the balance sheet, and that while no theories exist, such theories may be extended to other types of financial institutions and markets.

Chapter 3

Understanding Financial Statements

A basic understanding of the financial statements of commercial banks is essential to understand the liquidity creation measures developed in Chapter 4. This chapter first compares the financial statements of a large nonfinancial firm with those of a large commercial bank. To illustrate how different large and small commercial banks are, it also compares the financial statements of the same large commercial bank and a small commercial bank.

3.1 FINANCIAL STATEMENTS OF A LARGE NONFINANCIAL FIRM VERSUS A LARGE COMMERCIAL BANK

This section compares the financial statements of a large publicly traded nonfinancial firm with those of a large commercial bank. It is standard to use the 10-K for a publicly traded nonfinancial firm. The Consolidated Reports of Condition and Income, generally referred to as the Call Report, is typically used for a commercial bank. The Call Report has to be used if the bank is private and not part of a listed BHC since the 10-K is not available in this case. If the bank is listed (uncommon) or part of a listed BHC, Call Report information at the commercial bank level is often preferred to 10-K data of the listed institution for two reasons: (1) it has more detailed information; and (2) it avoids confounding commercial bank data with those of investment banks, insurance companies, and other noncommercial bank affiliates that may also be in the BHC. An added advantage of using Call Report data is that, unlike 10-Ks, Call Reports are available for all banks, not just publicly traded entities.

Table 3.1 Panel A shows financial statement data obtained from the 10-K of a large nonfinancial firm, Exxon Mobil Corp. (ticker symbol: XOM). Panel B shows Call Report data of a large commercial bank, JPMorgan Chase Bank, National Association. Both companies' books are as of 12/31/2014. Chapter 16 Sections 15 and 2.3), respectively, explain how these data can be downloaded from the web.

For both companies, the balance sheet balances: total assets equals total liabilities and equity combined, since what the firm owns must equal the financial claims on the firm. Each on- and off-balance sheet item in Table 3.1 is presented two ways: the value as reported in $ million and as a percent of total assets,

19

TABLE 3.1 Examples Comparing a Large Nonfinancial Firm, a Large Commercial Bank, and a Small Commercial Bank

Panel A: Exxon Mobil Corp. (ticker symbol: XOM)

10-K Balance Sheet 12/31/2014

Assets	$ million	% of total assets	Liabilities	$ million	% of total assets
Cash and cash equivalents (including bank deposits)	4,658	1.3	Accounts payable	47,165	13.5
Accounts receivable	28,009	8.0	Short-term debt	17,468	5.0
Inventory	16,678	4.8	Other current liabilities	0	0.0
Other current assets	3,565	1.0	Total current liabilities	64,633	18.5
Total current assets	52,910	15.1			
Long-term investments	35,239	10.1	Long-term debt	16,978	4.9
Property, plant, and equipment	252,668	72.3	Other long-term liabilities	93,483	26.7
Other long-term assets	8,676	2.5			
			Equity	174,399	49.9
Total assets	349,493	100.0	Total liabilities and equity	349,493	100.0

Off-balance sheet commitments	$ million	% of total assets
Short-term lines of credit	6,300	1.8

Panel B: JPMorgan Chase Bank, National Association

Call Report Balance Sheet 12/31/2014

Assets	$ million	% of total assets	Liabilities	$ million	% of total assets
Cash and balances due from depository institutions	500,146	24.1	Transactions deposits	270,886	13.1
Securities	608,509	29.3	Time deposits	73,831	3.6
Federal funds sold and repos	173,329	8.4	Savings deposits	769,462	37.1
			Foreign deposits	325,225	15.7
Residential real estate (RRE)	206,876	10.0	Total deposits	1,439,404	69.4
Commercial real estate (CRE)	82,781	4.0			
Commercial and industrial (C&I) loans	126,031	6.1	Federal funds purchased and repos	94,325	4.5
Consumer loans	93,429	4.5	Subordinated debt	9,893	0.5
Other loans	143,036	6.9	Other liabilities	345,122	16.6
Gross loans	652,153	31.4			
− Allowance for loan and lease losses (ALL)	11,352	0.5	Equity	186,208	9.0
− Allocated transfer risk reserve (ATRR)	0	0.0			
Net loans	640,801	30.9			
Premises and fixed assets	11,028	0.5			
Other assets	141,139	6.8			
Total assets	2,074,952	100.0	Total liabilities and equity	2,074,952	100.0
Memo: gross loans split into:					
Short-term loans	141,326	6.8			
Long-term loans	510,827	24.6			

(Continued)

TABLE 3.1 Examples Comparing a Large Nonfinancial Firm, a Large Commercial Bank, and a Small Commercial Bank (*Cont.*)

Panel B: JPMorgan Chase Bank, National Association

Off-balance sheet activities	$ million	% of total assets
Loan commitments	431,476	20.8
Net financial and performance standby letters of credit	95,129	4.6
Other off-balance sheet guarantees	99,951	4.8
Derivatives (notional value)	63,683,309	3,069.1
Derivatives (sum of gross fair values)	14,322	0.7

Panel C: Community Bank of El Dorado Springs

Call Report Balance Sheet 12/31/2014

Assets	$ million	% of total assets
Cash and balances due from depository institutions	8.0	7.8
Securities	49.0	48.0
Federal funds sold and repos	3.5	3.5
Residential real estate (RRE)	8.6	8.4
Commercial real estate (CRE)	23.0	22.6
Commercial and industrial (C&I) loans	0.0	0.0

Liabilities	$ million	% of total assets
Transactions deposits	27.8	27.2
Time deposits	36.9	36.2
Savings deposits	21.5	21.1
Foreign deposits	0.0	0.0
Total deposits	86.2	84.5
Federal funds purchased and repos	0.0	0.0
Subordinated debt	0.0	0.0

	$ million	% of total assets
Consumer loans	3.3	3.2
Other loans	6.4	6.2
Gross loans	41.3	40.5
– Allowance for loan and lease losses (ALLL)	1.1	1.0
– Allocated transfer risk reserve (ATRR)	0.0	0.0
Net loans	40.2	39.4
Premises and fixed assets	0.1	0.1
Other assets	1.2	1.2
Total assets	101.9	100.0
Memo: gross loans split into:		
Short-term loans	21.5	21.1
Long-term loans	19.7	19.4
Other liabilities	0.2	0.2
Equity	15.6	15.3
Total liabilities and equity	101.9	100.0

Off-balance-sheet activities	$ million	% of total assets
Loan commitments	2.3	2.2
Net financial and performance standby letters of credit	0.0	0.0
Other off-balance sheet guarantees	0.0	0.0
Derivatives (notional value)	0.0	0.0
Derivatives (sum of gross fair values)	0.0	0.0

This table compares the financial statements of a large nonfinancial firm (Exxon Mobil Corp. – Panel A), a large commercial bank (JPMorgan Chase Bank, National Association – Panel B), and a small commercial bank (Community Bank of El Dorado Springs – Panel C).

although liabilities, equity, and off-balance sheet activities are not parts of assets. In addition, derivatives are reported in terms of their notional values and their gross fair values, both in $ million. The notional value of a derivative contract is the underlying amount (also called the contractual or principal amount) specified at the inception of the contract upon which the exchange of funds is based.[1] To understand the gross fair value of derivatives, it is important to realize that a derivative can be an asset derivative or a liability derivative. The fair value of a derivative contract is "the amount at which an asset (liability) could be bought (incurred) or sold (settled) in a current transaction between willing parties, that is, other than in a forced or liquidation sale" (Financial Accounting Standards Board (FASB) Statement 133, paragraph 540).[2] Call Reports present gross fair values, meaning that offsetting positions are not netted out.

As illustrated in the table, the financial statements of nonfinancial firm Exxon Mobil and commercial bank JPMorgan Chase are very different in a number of dimensions.

First, bank deposits and loans appear on the balance sheets of both, but in very different places. Bank deposits are assets of nonfinancial firms: the money those firms own and have deposited at a commercial bank are similar to those firms' cash holdings and are included for Exxon Mobil in cash and cash equivalents. In contrast, these deposits are liabilities of banks: when firms and/ or individuals deposit money at banks, they provide financing to those banks. Analogously, bank loans are liabilities of nonfinancial firms, providing an important source of financing for most firms. These appear as parts of short-term debt and long-term debt for Exxon Mobil. In contrast, loans are assets of banks: once banks have extended loans to firms and individuals, the loans become part of what the banks own. As shown in Table 3.1, deposits and gross loans are very substantial relative to JPMorgan Chase's assets, 69.4% and 31.4%, respectively, reflecting that these are main business lines of a commercial bank, whereas they are much smaller relative to assets, less than 1.3% and (5.0% + 4.9% =) 9.9%, respectively, for Exxon Mobil.

Second, a large portion of the assets of Exxon Mobil, 72.3%, are tied up in property, plant, and equipment, as opposed to just 0.5% in premises and fixed assets for JPMorgan Chase. Since commercial banks can expand easily without major investments in buildings and fixed assets, they are able to grow much larger than nonfinancial firms, in particular those that have to invest considerable funds in additional buildings and fixed assets in order to expand. Of course, this does not mean that every commercial bank is larger than every nonfinancial firm, but the largest commercial banks are generally much larger than the larg-

---

1. For example, in an interest rate swap, if the parties are exchanging the difference between a fixed and floating rate on a stated notional amount of $1 million, then $1 million is the notional value of this derivative contract.

2. If a quoted market price is available, the fair value equals the number of trading units times the quoted market price. If a quoted market price is not available, the estimate of fair value is based on the best information available.

est nonfinancial firms. As shown in the table, JPMorgan Chase has more than $2 trillion in total assets, almost six times as many total assets as Exxon Mobil.

Third, cash and cash equivalents amount to a mere 1.3% of Exxon Mobil's assets. In contrast, JPMorgan Chase holds 24.1% of its assets in cash and balances due from other depository institutions, and 29.3% in securities. Part of the reason for so much cash and balances due from other depository institutions is likely that JPMorgan Chase is a large trading bank, with significant presence in both the loan sales and derivative markets. For example, when it sells loans to another institution, it either receives cash right away or it will have a balance due from the buying institution. The large investments in securities as well as cash and due from may also be due to the need for JPMorgan Chase to be liquid, as demands for liquidity from depositors and off-balance sheet counterparties may be substantial.

Fourth, for JPMorgan Chase, off-balance sheet activities are even larger than on-balance sheet assets. Off-balance sheet loan commitments – which account for a sizeable portion of bank liquidity creation as shown in Chapter 8 – are 20.8% of on-balance sheet total assets and about two-thirds of the size of on-balance sheet loans. Thus, if all commitments were taken down immediately, the loan portfolio (and hence total assets) would go up very substantially, and have to be financed on the balance sheet by issuing new liabilities or equity or selling other assets. Other off-balance sheet activities, particularly the notional value of derivative contracts, are much larger than the bank's on-balance sheet assets. The notional value of JPMorgan Chase's derivatives alone are almost $64 trillion, more than 30 times its on-balance sheet assets of about $2.1 trillion. In contrast, the sum of the gross fair values of its derivative contracts are a mere $14.3 billion or 0.7% of its on-balance sheet assets, reflecting the fact that gross positive and negative fair values of derivatives tend to offset each other because most banks operate with nearly matched books. In comparison, Exxon Mobil's off-balance sheet commitments are in the form of short-term lines of credit and equal a mere 1.8% of on-balance sheet total assets.

A few other facts about JPMorgan Chase will help to understand the measurement of liquidity creation in Chapter 4 and other indicators of bank output in Chapter 5. The existing literature typically focuses on assets and/or lending to measure bank output. Some measure assets by total assets (TA), which includes all of the assets except the allocation for loan and lease losses (ALLL), an accounting item for expected losses, and the allocated transfer risk reserve (ATRR), a reserve for certain troubled foreign loans for which there has been a protracted inability by the borrowers to make payments.[3] Others measure assets by gross total assets (GTA), which adds the ALLL and ATRR to TA. The ALLL and ATRR are also the difference between gross loans and net loans. Thus, an advantage of GTA over TA is that it includes the full value of all of the assets,

---

3. The details of ATRR requirements are specified in Title 12 of the Code of Federal Regulations of the United States of America, Part 122, Section 43: https://www.fdic.gov/regulations/laws/rules/7500-1100.html.

including the full value of the loans originally financed by the bank. Of the ALLL and the ATRR, the ALLL is the more important item by far – the ATRR is zero for the vast majority of banks, including for JPMorgan Chase.[4]

In addition, the balance sheet of JPMorgan Chase shown here reports loans by category (residential real estate, commercial real estate, etc.). Below the balance sheet, these loans are also shown by maturity, distinguishing short-term loans with maturities up to one year from long-term loans with maturities over 1 year. Maturities are not available in the Call Report for loans split by loan category. As shown in Chapter 4, some of the liquidity creation measures therefore classify loans entirely based on loan category ("cat"), while others classify them entirely based on loan maturity ("mat").

3.2 FINANCIAL STATEMENTS OF A LARGE COMMERCIAL BANK VERSUS A SMALL COMMERCIAL BANK

The empirical analyses in this book cover virtually all commercial banks in the United States, the vast majority of which are community banks, typically defined as commercial banks with up to $1 billion in assets. Many of these have less than $100 million in assets. It is interesting to also show the financial statements of a community bank, since they are generally very different from those of large banks like JPMorgan Chase in more dimensions than just size.

Table 3.1 Panel C presents the financial statements taken from the Call Report of Community Bank of El Dorado Springs in El Dorado Springs, Missouri as of 12/31/2014. Chapter 16 Section 2.3 explains how these data can be downloaded from the web. Community Bank of El Dorado Springs has $101.9 million in assets. Note that JPMorgan Chase is more than 20,000 times larger with over $2 trillion in assets. Like JPMorgan Chase, Community Bank of El Dorado Springs has largely financial assets like loans and securities and is funded mostly by deposits. But several important differences are apparent, and illustrative of typical differences between very large and very small commercial banks.

First, there are several striking differences in the loan portfolios. Commercial real estate loans make up over five times the percentage of assets for Community Bank of El Dorado Springs than for JPMorgan Chase, 22.6% versus 4.0%; Community Bank of El Dorado Springs has virtually no commercial and industrial loans, 0.0% of assets, relative to 6.1% of assets for JPMorgan Chase; and more than half of Community Bank of El Dorado Springs' loans are short-term, whereas the vast majority of JPMorgan Chase's loans are long-term.

Second, Community Bank of El Dorado Springs has a higher percentage of deposits than JPMorgan Chase, 84.5% versus 69.4%. This reflects the greater retail orientation of the small bank.

---

4. Over all quarterly observations of US commercial banks from 1984:Q1 to 2014:Q4, over 99.9% record zero for ATRR, and the nonzero observations total only about 1/3 of one percent of gross loans on average.

Third, like JPMorgan Chase, Community Bank of El Dorado Springs holds over 50% of its assets in cash and balances due from other depository institutions and securities, but the composition is very different. Community Bank of El Dorado Springs holds 7.8% of its assets in cash and balances due from other depository institutions, considerably less than JPMorgan Chase's 24.1%. In contrast, it holds far more in securities (48.0% versus 29.3%). The smaller cash and due from percentage is likely because Community Bank of El Dorado Springs is not a trading bank. The higher securities percentage may be due in part to limited lending opportunities in its local retail market (dealing with individuals and smaller firms) and lack of access to wholesale loan markets (dealing with large corporate customers).

Fourth, not surprisingly, Community Bank of El Dorado Springs has a much higher Equity/Assets ratio, 15.3% versus 9.0% for JPMorgan Chase. This is typical for small banks for several reasons. It is more difficult for them to diversify their portfolios, so they may hold more capital to offset the higher credit risk. They are also often closely held, and their owners may be relatively risk averse and hold more capital as protection against failure. Unlike some large banks, they are not perceived to be too big to fail and hence need more capital, since they are less likely to be bailed out in case of significant problems. It is also generally harder for small banks to raise capital quickly because they do not have access to public markets.

Fifth, off-balance sheet activities are far smaller for Community Bank of El Dorado Springs. Its loan commitments are very small compared to its loans, its other off-balance sheet guarantees such as standby letters of credit are so small that they round to $0.0 million, and both the notional and the gross fair values of its derivative contracts are exactly zero.[5] These statistics are not unusual for community banks – most have very few off-balance sheet guarantees and do not have any derivatives.

3.3 SUMMARY

A basic understanding of bank financial statements is needed to understand the measurement of bank liquidity creation. This chapter highlights the differences among the financial statements of a large nonfinancial firm, a large commercial bank, and a small commercial bank. The key takeaway is an understanding of how financial statements differ across types of firms, so that the liquidity creation measures, which use data from these statements, become intuitive and easier to comprehend.

---

5. A standby letter of credit acts as a financial guarantee. It obliges the bank to pay a third-party beneficiary when a customer (the buyer of the letter of credit) fails to perform on a contractual obligation. It is often used to back up commercial paper, to protect the commercial paper holder against default by the issuer.

Part II

Liquidity Creation Measurement and Uses

Chapter 4

Measurement of Bank Liquidity Creation

This chapter explores the measurement of bank liquidity creation. The preferred "cat fat" measure of liquidity creation used in the analyses in this book is introduced and compared to several alternative measures of liquidity creation.

4.1 PREFERRED "CAT FAT" MEASURE OF LIQUIDITY CREATION

The preferred "cat fat" measure of bank liquidity creation is directly inspired by financial intermediation theories. The theories argue that banks create liquidity on the balance sheet by financing relatively illiquid assets with relatively liquid liabilities, and off the balance sheet through loan commitments and similar claims to liquid funds.

Berger and Bouwman (2009) construct several alternative liquidity creation measures that try to capture the spirit of these theories, but acknowledge that banks in the real world are more complex than those pictured in the theories. Their "cat fat" liquidity creation measure is the closest in spirit to the theories and is therefore their preferred measure. It is constructed using a three-step procedure.

In Step 1, all bank assets, liabilities, equity, and off-balance sheet activities are classified as liquid, semiliquid, or illiquid. In Step 2, weights are assigned to the activities classified in Step 1. In Step 3, the "cat fat" liquidity creation measure is constructed by combining the activities as classified in Step 1 and as weighted in Step 2. The preferred "cat fat" measure classifies loans by product category alone ("cat") due to data availability issues explained in Step 1 in the next section. It also includes the amount of liquidity banks create off the balance sheet ("fat").

Table 4.1 Panel A illustrates the construction of the "cat fat" liquidity creation measure using a simplified version of Step 2. This simplified version only includes one or two asset-side, liability-side and off-balance sheet items that are classified as liquid, semiliquid, or illiquid to drive home the concept and gain an intuitive understanding of liquidity creation. Panel B illustrates the construction of the "cat fat" measure using a detailed version of Step 2, which helps the reader to gain a deeper understanding of the "cat fat" measure, and is also helpful for those who want to construct this measure themselves for banks or other institutions or markets in the United States or other countries.

Bank Liquidity Creation and Financial Crises

TABLE 4.1 Constructing Berger and Bouwman's (2009) Preferred "Cat Fat" Liquidity Creation Measure

Panel A: Understanding the "cat fat" measure using a *simplified* overview of Step 2

Step 1: Classify all bank activities as liquid, semiliquid, or illiquid. For activities other than loans, combine information on product category and maturity. Due to data limitations, classify loans entirely by product category ("cat"). Include off-balance sheet activities ("fat").

Step 2: Assign weights to the activities classified in **Step 1**. This panel only displays one or two asset-side, liability-side, and off-balance sheet items for simplicity.

(weight = ½)	*(weight = 0)*	*(weight = -½)*
Illiquid assets	*Semiliquid assets*	*Liquid assets*
E.g., business loans	E.g., residential mortgages	E.g., securities
Liquid liabilities	*Semiliquid liabilities*	*Illiquid liabilities + equity*
E.g., transactions deposits	E.g., time deposits	E.g., subordinated debt, equity
Illiquid guarantees	*Semiliquid guarantees*	*Liquid guarantees*
E.g., loan commitments	E.g., net credit derivatives	E.g., net participations acquired
		Liquid derivatives
		E.g., interest rate derivatives

Step 3: Combine bank activities as classified in Step 1 and as weighted in Step 2.

cat fat = +½ × illiquid assets	+0 × semiliquid assets	-½ × liquid assets
+½ × liquid liabilities	+0 × semiliquid liabilities	-½ × illiquid liabilities
+½ × liquid derivatives	-½ × liquid derivatives	-½ × equity
+½ × illiquid guarantees	+0 × semiliquid guarantees	-½ × liquid guarantees

Panel B: Understanding the "cat fat" measure using a *detailed* overview of Step 2

Step 1: Classify all bank activities as liquid, semiliquid, or illiquid. For activities other than loans, combine information on product category and maturity. Due to data limitations, classify loans entirely by product category ("cat"). Include off-balance sheet activities ("fat").

Step 2: Assign weights to the activities classified in **Step 1**.

Assets:

Illiquid assets (weight = ½)	*Semiliquid assets (weight = 0)*	*Liquid assets (weight = –½)*
Commercial real estate loans (CRE)	Residential real estate loans (RRE)	Cash and due from other institutions
Loans to finance agricultural production	Consumer loans	All securities (regardless of maturity)
Commercial and industrial loans (C&I)	Loans to depository institutions	Trading assets
Other loans and lease financing receivables	Loans to state and local governments	Overnight and term federal funds sold
Other real estate owned (OREO)	Loans to foreign governments	
Customers' liability on bankers acceptances		
Investment in unconsolidated subsidiaries		
Intangible assets		
Premises		
Other assets		

Liabilities plus equity:

Liquid liabilities (weight = ½)	*Semiliquid liabilities (weight = 0)*	*Illiquid liabilities plus equity (weight = –½)*
Transactions deposits	Time deposits	Bank's liability on bankers acceptances
Savings deposits	Other borrowed money (including term federal funds purchased)	Subordinated debt
Overnight federal funds purchased		Other liabilities
Trading liabilities		Equity

(Continued)

TABLE 4.1 Constructing Berger and Bouwman's (2009) Preferred "Cat Fat" Liquidity Creation Measure (cont.)

Step 2: Assign weights to the activities classified in **Step 1**. (cont.)

Off-balance sheet guarantees (notional values):

Illiquid guarantees (weight = ½)	Semiliquid guarantees (weight = 0)	Liquid guarantees (weight = −½)
Unused commitments	Net credit derivatives	Net participations acquired
Net standby letters of credit	Net securities lent	
Commercial and similar letters of credit		
All other off-balance sheet liabilities		

Off-balance sheet derivatives (gross fair values):

		Liquid derivatives (weight = −½)
		Interest rate derivatives
		Foreign exchange derivatives
		Equity and commodity derivatives

Step 3: Combine bank activities as classified in **Step 1** and as weighted in **Step 2**.

cat fat = +½ × illiquid assets	+0 × semiliquid assets	−½ × liquid assets
+½ × liquid liabilities	+0 × semiliquid liabilities	−½ × illiquid liabilities
+½ × illiquid guarantees	−½ × liquid guarantees	−½ × equity
+½ × illiquid guarantees	+0 × semiliquid guarantees	−½ × liquid guarantees

This table explains the construction in the "cat fat" measure using a simplified overview of Step 2 (Panel A) and using a detailed overview of Step 2 (Panel B).
Source: Adapted from Berger and Bouwman (2009, Table 1).

The three steps, adapted from Berger and Bouwman (2009), are now discussed in detail.

4.1.1   Step 1 – Classifying Activities as Liquid, Semiliquid, or Illiquid

In Step 1, all assets are classified as liquid, semiliquid, or illiquid based on the ease, cost, and time for banks to dispose of their obligations to obtain liquid funds to meet customers' demands. Bank liabilities and equity are similarly classified to obtain liquid funds from the bank. Off-balance sheet guarantees and derivatives are classified consistently with treatments of functionally similar on-balance sheet items.

Ideally, information on both product category and maturity would be used to classify all bank activities. For example, business loans are generally more illiquid than residential mortgages, as the latter can often be more easily securitized and sold to meet liquidity demands. Within each category, shorter-maturity items are more liquid than longer-maturity items because they self-liquidate sooner without effort or cost.

For bank activities other than loans, Call Reports provide sufficient detail on category and maturity, so our classification of those activities incorporates both aspects. Unfortunately, this is not the case for loans. Call Reports split loans into various loan categories and into different maturity classes, but do not provide maturity information for individual loan categories. The preferred "cat fat" liquidity creation measure classifies loans entirely by category ("cat"). This is done primarily because what matters to liquidity creation on the asset side is the ease, cost, and time for banks to dispose of their obligations to obtain liquid funds. The ease, cost, and time with which a particular loan category can be securitized is closer to this concept than the time until self-liquidation – for example, a 30-year residential mortgage may be securitized relatively quickly at a relatively small cost, even though it is a long-term loan. Hence, it is classified as semiliquid. In contrast, a commercial and industrial (C&I) loan of any maturity normally is hard to securitize and is not fully repaid until maturity.[1] Hence, it is classified as illiquid.

The Step 1 classifications of bank activities are shown in Box 4.1.

4.1.2   Step 2 – Assigning Weights to the Activities Classified in Step 1

In Step 2, weights are assigned to all of the bank activities classified in Step 1. That is, weights are assigned to the classes of liquid, semiliquid, and illiquid assets, liabilities, equity, and off-balance sheet guarantees and derivatives shown in Table 4.1.

---

1. Large syndicated C&I loans are an exception since they can be sold relatively quickly. However, Call Reports do not break out these loans.

BOX 4.1 Step 1 Classifications of Activities on the Asset Side, Liability Side, and Off the Balance Sheet

Assets

- *Classifying loans:* Business loans and leases of any type (e.g., C&I, commercial real estate, and agricultural) are classified as illiquid assets because they typically cannot be sold quickly without incurring a major loss. Residential mortgages and consumer loans are generally relatively easy to securitize, and loans to depositories and governments are likely to be comparatively easy to sell or otherwise dispose of because the counterparties are relatively large and informationally transparent. These loan categories are classified as semiliquid assets.

- *Classifying assets other than loans:* Premises and investments in unconsolidated subsidiaries are classified as illiquid assets because typically these items cannot be sold quickly without incurring major losses. Cash, securities, and other marketable assets that the bank can use to meet liquidity needs quickly without incurring major losses are classified as liquid assets.

Liabilities and Equity

- *Classifying liabilities:* Funds that can be quickly withdrawn without penalty by customers – such as transactions deposits, savings deposits, and overnight federal funds purchased – are counted as liquid liabilities. Deposits that can be withdrawn with more difficulty or a sizeable penalty are classified as semiliquid. This includes all time deposits regardless of maturity, since all time deposits can be borrowed against with a sizeable penalty regardless of maturity. The balance sheet item "other borrowed money," which contains other short- and medium-maturities with terms longer than overnight, such as term federal funds, repurchase agreements, and borrowings from Federal Reserve Banks and Federal Home Loan Banks,[a] are also classified as semiliquid. Long-term liabilities that generally cannot be withdrawn easily or quickly, such as subordinated debt, are classified as illiquid.

- *Classifying equity:* Equity is classified as illiquid because investors cannot demand liquid funds from the bank. Although the equity of some banks is publicly traded and may therefore be sold relatively easily, the investors are able to retrieve liquid funds through the capital market, not from the bank. Thus, while traded equity may be liquid from an individual investor's point of view, such liquidity is created by the capital market, rather than by the bank.[b]

Off-balance sheet activities

- *Classifying guarantees:* Loan commitments and (standby and commercial) letters of credit are classified as illiquid guarantees.[c] These items are functionally similar to on-balance sheet business loans in that they are obligations that are illiquid from the point of view of the bank – except in very unusual circumstances, the bank must provide the funds to the customer when contract conditions are met. As well, in most cases, the bank cannot sell or participate these items.[d,e] Net credit derivatives (i.e., the amount guaranteed minus the beneficiary amount)[f] and net securities lent (i.e., the amount lent minus the amount borrowed) are classified as semiliquid guarantees since they can potentially be sold or participated, analogous to semiliquid on-balance sheet residential mortgages and consumer loans. Net participations acquired from other institutions (i.e., the amount acquired

minus the amount conveyed to others) are treated as liquid guarantees, since they are functionally similar to on-balance sheet liquid securities.
- *Classifying derivatives:* All derivatives (other than credit derivatives which are classified earlier as guarantees) – interest rate, foreign exchange, and equity and commodity derivatives – are classified as liquid because they can be bought and sold easily and are functionally similar to liquid securities. Gross fair values of these derivatives are used, which measure how much liquidity the bank is absorbing from the public (in the case of positive gross fair values) or providing to the public (in the case of negative gross fair values).

a. There are eleven Federal Home Loan Banks (FHLBs) in the United States. These are government-sponsored banks that provide stable, low-cost funds to financial institutions that are members of the FHLB System in order to promote the financing of housing and community lending.
b. As argued in Chapter 15, it is an interesting topic for future research to examine how much liquidity is created by the capital market.
c. Call Reports provide some maturity information on loan commitments, so it may seem that loan commitments could also be classified by maturity with only the longest maturities being considered illiquid. However, this is not feasible because Call Reports only report original maturities, not remaining maturities of loan commitments.
d. As acknowledged in Chapter 2, banks could dispose of loan commitments by invoking the material adverse change (MAC) clause or enforcing a covenant violation, and the customer would not have access to the funds. However, failing to honor loan commitments is generally very rarely done due to legal and reputational concerns.
e. From the customer's point of view, loan commitments are functionally similar to liquid transactions deposits because the customer can draw down the funds almost at will. From the point of view of the bank, they are functionally similar to illiquid business loans because the bank cannot easily extricate itself from providing the funds. As will be shown in Step 2, transactions deposits, business loans, and loan commitments all receive the same weight. Hence, this classification is internally consistent.
f. Credit derivatives are instruments that transfer the credit risk of a loan or a bond from one party (the beneficiary) to another (the guarantor), implying that a party could lend without assuming credit risk or take on credit risk without making actual loans. A bank may be the guarantor in some transactions and the beneficiary in others. The net amount of credit derivatives then is the total amount guaranteed minus the total beneficiary amount.

The weights are based on liquidity creation theory, according to which banks create liquidity on the balance sheet when they transform illiquid assets into liquid liabilities, effectively holding illiquid items in place of the nonbank public, and giving the public liquid items. Therefore, positive weights are applied to both illiquid assets and liquid liabilities, so that liquidity is created when illiquid assets – such as business loans – are transformed into liquid liabilities – such as transactions deposits. Following similar logic, negative weights are applied to liquid assets, illiquid liabilities, and equity, so that when liquid assets – such as treasury securities – are transformed into illiquid liabilities or equity, liquidity is destroyed.[2]

2. Note that the negative weight on equity only captures the direct effect of capital on liquidity creation. Any indirect (positive or negative) effects on liquidity creation are attributed to the individual items that are affected. For example, if capital allows banks to extend more illiquid loans, this positive effect is captured by the positive weight applied to illiquid loans multiplied by the associated dollar increase in loans. The full effects, including both the direct and indirect effects, are investigated in Chapter 10, where the effects of bank capital on liquidity creation are investigated.

The magnitudes of the weights are based on simple dollar-for-dollar adding-up constraints, so that $1 of liquidity is created when banks transform $1 of illiquid assets into $1 of liquid liabilities. Similarly, $1 of liquidity is destroyed when banks transform $1 of liquid assets into $1 of illiquid liabilities. Based on these constraints, a weight of ½ is assigned to both illiquid assets and liquid liabilities and a weight of –½ is applied to both liquid assets and illiquid liabilities. The weights of ½ and –½ are intuitive, since the amount of liquidity created or destroyed is only "half" determined by the source or use of the funds alone. The intermediate weight of 0 is applied to semiliquid assets and liabilities, based on the assumption that semiliquid activities fall halfway between liquid and illiquid activities.

Box 4.2 provides numerical examples to further illustrate the weights.

BOX 4.2 Numerical Examples to Illustrate the Step 2 Weights

When a bank takes in $1 in transactions deposits to fund a $1 business loan, it creates liquidity of ½ × $1 + ½ × $1 = $1 (it creates liquidity on both the liability side and the asset side: maximum liquidity is created).

When a bank takes in $1 in transactions deposits to buy $1 in treasury securities, it creates liquidity of ½ × $1 + (–½) × $1 = $0 (while it creates liquidity on the liability side, it destroys liquidity on the asset side: it creates no liquidity on net).

When a bank takes in $1 in time deposits to buy $1 in residential mortgages, it creates liquidity of 0 × $1 + 0 × $1 = $0 (it creates no liquidity on the liability or asset sides of the balance sheet, creating zero liquidity on net).

When a bank issues $1 in equity to buy $1 in treasury securities, it creates liquidity of (–½) × $1 + (–½) × $1 = –$1 (it destroys liquidity on both the liability and asset sides: it destroys maximum liquidity).

Weights are applied to off-balance sheet guarantees and derivatives using the same principles, consistent with the functional similarities to on-balance sheet items discussed in Step 1. For example, illiquid off-balance sheet guarantees – such as loan commitments – are functionally similar to on-balance sheet illiquid assets – such as business loans – in that they are obligations of the bank to provide funds that cannot be easily sold or participated. Therefore the same weight of ½ is applied to illiquid guarantees as to illiquid assets. Similarly, the same weight of 0 is applied to semiliquid guarantees as to functionally similar semiliquid on-balance sheet assets, and the same weight of –½ is applied to liquid guarantees as to functionally similar on-balance sheet liquid assets.

Analogously, the gross fair values of derivatives are assigned the same weight of –½ as on-balance sheet liquid assets.[3] As discussed in Step 1, these

---

3. As discussed in Chapter 3, Call Reports report gross fair values, where "fair value" is defined as: "the amount at which an asset (liability) could be bought (incurred) or sold (settled) in a current transaction between willing parties, that is, other than in a forced or liquidation sale" (Financial Accounting Standards Board (FASB) Statement 133, paragraph 540). The fair value equals the quoted market price, if available. If a quoted market price is not available, the estimate of fair value is based on the best information available in the circumstances.

contracts can be bought and sold easily and are functionally similar to liquid securities. Like securities, derivatives with gross positive fair values reduce bank liquidity creation as the bank effectively holds a positively valued liquid asset in place of the public. Derivatives with gross negative fair values increase bank liquidity creation as the bank effectively holds a negatively valued liquid asset in place of the public. The Call Reports show contracts that have gross positive fair values with a positive sign and contracts that have gross negative fair values with a negative sign. Thus, these opposing effects on liquidity creation can be captured by simply applying weights of –½ (the same weight as that assigned to liquid securities) to the dollar values of both. While the gross positive and negative fair values of derivatives are often quite substantial, as seen in the example of JPMorgan Chase (see Section 3.1), these values tend to offset each other, yielding a small net contribution to liquidity creation because most banks operate with nearly matched books.

The columns that illustrate Step 2 in Table 4.1 are arranged such that all bank activities that contribute to liquidity creation are on the left, all those that subtract from liquidity creation are on the right, and all those with an approximately neutral effect on liquidity creation are in the center. Thus, those that are assigned a weight of ½ (illiquid assets, liquid liabilities, and illiquid guarantees) are grouped together on the left. Liquid assets, illiquid liabilities plus equity, and liquid guarantees and derivatives (which are assigned a weight of –½) are grouped on the right. Finally, semiliquid assets, liabilities, and guarantees with zero weights are grouped in the center.

4.1.3   Step 3 – Constructing the "Cat Fat" Liquidity Creation Measure by Combining Activities as Classified in Step 1 and as Weighted in Step 2

In Step 3, the "cat fat" liquidity creation measure is constructed by combining the activities as classified in Step 1 and weighted in Step 2. It classifies loans by category ("cat") and includes off-balance sheet activities ("fat"). The exact formula is shown at the bottom of Table 4.1. The bank activities that add to liquidity creation are again arranged on the left, those that subtract from liquidity creation on the right, and those with an approximately neutral effect in the center.

The weights of ½, –½, or 0, respectively, are multiplied times the dollar amounts of the corresponding bank activities and the weighted dollar amounts are then added to arrive at the total dollar value of liquidity creation of a particular bank. Liquidity creation of individual banks may be summed across all banks to obtain the total dollar value of liquidity created by the entire industry. Similarly, it can be summed across all banks in a particular size class, by bank type, by location, etc., to gauge how much liquidity a subset of banks create.

Box 4.3 explains why the "cat fat" liquidity creation measure uses only three liquidity classes and three weights.

BOX 4.3 Why Use Three Liquidity Classes and Three Weights?

The "cat fat" liquidity creation measure calculates the amount of liquidity created by a bank while classifying all bank activities as liquid, semiliquid, or illiquid, and applying only three weights, ½, 0, and –½, to them. Differences in liquidity obviously exist within each of the three classifications, but the data generally do not allow for much finer distinctions, and there are no other unambiguous weights to apply. The use of ½, –½, and 0 are the clear demarcations of full liquidity, full illiquidity, and neutrality, respectively, and no other clear choices present themselves.

4.2 OTHER MAIN MEASURES OF LIQUIDITY CREATION

Berger and Bouwman (2009) also introduce three other main measures of liquidity creation. "Mat fat," "cat nonfat," and "mat nonfat" use the same basic methodology as "cat fat," but with slightly different assumptions.

Box 4.4 explains these three acronyms and how they differ from the "cat fat" measure.

BOX 4.4 "Cat fat" and Other Acronyms Explained

The "cat fat," "cat nonfat," "mat fat," and "mat nonfat" measures differ in that loans are alternatively classified by product category only or maturity only ("cat" vs. "mat") due to data availability issues explained in Step 1, while all other activities are classified using information on both dimensions. The measures also alternatively include or exclude off-balance sheet activities ("fat" vs. "nonfat"). The table gives a simple overview of the four main measures.

Activities other than loans are classified using both product category and maturity while loans are classified by:	Off-balance sheet activities are:	
	Included	Excluded
– Product category	"cat fat"	"cat nonfat"
– Maturity	"mat fat"	"mat nonfat"

Table 4.2 highlights in a detailed manner how the three measures ("cat nonfat," "mat fat," and "mat nonfat") differ from the preferred "cat fat" measure, described in this section and shown in Table 4.1.

"Mat fat" uses the maturity dimension of loans in place of the category of loans used in "cat fat." All loans and leases with remaining maturities greater than 1 year are considered to be illiquid assets and are assigned a weight of ½, and all loans and leases with remaining maturities of up to 1 year are considered to be

TABLE 4.2 Constructing Berger and Bouwman's (2009) Three Alternative Main Liquidity Creation Measures

Panel A: Constructing the "cat nonfat" liquidity creation measure (using a *simplified* overview of Step 2)

Step 1: Classify all bank activities as liquid, semiliquid, or illiquid. For activities other than loans, combine information on product category and maturity. Due to data limitations, classify loans entirely by product category ("cat"). Exclude off-balance sheet activities ("nonfat").

Step 2: Assign weights to the activities classified in **Step 1**. This panel only displays one or two asset-side, liability-side and off-balance sheet items for simplicity.

(weight = ½)	*(weight = 0)*	*(weight = −½)*
Illiquid assets	*Semiliquid assets*	*Liquid assets*
E.g., business loans	E.g., residential mortgages	E.g., securities
Liquid liabilities	*Semiliquid liabilities*	*Illiquid liabilities + equity*
E.g., transactions deposits	E.g., time deposits	E.g., subordinated debt, equity
Illiquid guarantees	*Semiliquid guarantees*	*Liquid guarantees*
E.g., loan commitments	E.g., net credit derivatives	E.g., net participations acquired
		Liquid derivatives
		E.g., interest rate derivatives

Step 3: Combine bank activities as classified in **Step 1** and as weighted in **Step 2**.

cat nonfat =	+½ × illiquid assets	+0 × semiliquid assets	−½ × liquid assets
	+½ × liquid liabilities	+0 × semiliquid liabilities	−½ × illiquid liabilities
			−½ × equity
	+½ × illiquid guarantees	+0 × semiliquid guarantees	−½ × liquid guarantees
			−½ × liquid derivatives

(Continued)

TABLE 4.2 Constructing Berger and Bouwman's (2009) Three Alternative Main Liquidity Creation Measures *(cont.)*

Panel B: Constructing the *"mat fat"* liquidity creation measure (using a *simplified* overview of Step 2)

Step 1: Classify all bank activities as liquid, semiliquid, or illiquid. For activities other than loans, combine information on product category and maturity. Due to data limitations, classify loans entirely by maturity ("mat"). Include off-balance sheet activities ("fat").

Step 2: Assign weights to the activities classified in **Step 1**. This panel only displays one or two asset-side, liability-side and off-balance sheet items for simplicity.

(weight = ½)	*(weight = 0)*	*(weight = −½)*
Illiquid assets	*Semiliquid assets*	*Liquid assets*
E.g., business loans	E.g., residential mortgages	E.g., securities
E.g., long-term loans	E.g., short-term loans	
Liquid liabilities	*Semiliquid liabilities*	*Illiquid liabilities + equity*
E.g., transactions deposits	E.g., time deposits	E.g., subordinated debt, equity
Illiquid guarantees	*Semiliquid guarantees*	*Liquid guarantees*
E.g., loan commitments	E.g., net credit derivatives	E.g., net participations acquired
		Liquid derivatives
		E.g., interest rate derivatives

Step 3: Combine bank activities as classified in **Step 1** and as weighted in **Step 2**.

mat fat = +½ × illiquid assets	+0 × semiliquid assets	−½ × liquid assets
+½ × liquid liabilities	+0 × semiliquid liabilities	−½ × illiquid liabilities
		−½ × equity
+½ × illiquid guarantees	+0 × semiliquid guarantees	−½ × liquid guarantees
		−½ × liquid derivatives

Panel C: Constructing the "*mat nonfat*" liquidity creation measure (using a *simplified* overview of Step 2)

Step 1: Classify all bank activities as liquid, semiliquid, or illiquid. For activities other than loans, combine information on product category and maturity. For loans, classify loans entirely by maturity ("mat"). Exclude off-balance sheet activities ("nonfat").

Step 2: Assign weights to the activities classified in **Step 1**. This panel only displays one or two asset-side, liability-side and off-balance sheet items for simplicity.

(weight = ½)	*(weight = 0)*	*(weight = –½)*
Illiquid assets	*Semiliquid assets*	*Liquid assets*
E.g., business loans	E.g., residential mortgages	E.g., securities
E.g., long-term loans	E.g., short-term loans	
Liquid liabilities	*Semiliquid liabilities*	*Illiquid liabilities + equity*
E.g., transactions deposits	E.g., time deposits	E.g., subordinated debt, equity
Illiquid guarantees	*Semiliquid guarantees*	*Liquid guarantees*
E.g., loan commitments	E.g., net credit derivatives	E.g., net participations acquired
		Liquid derivatives
		E.g., interest rate derivatives

Step 3: Combine bank activities as classified in **Step 1** and as weighted in **Step 2.**

mat nonfat = +½ × illiquid assets   +0 × semiliquid assets   –½ × liquid assets

+½ × liquid liabilities   +0 × semiliquid liabilities   –½ × illiquid liabilities

    –½ × equity

+½ × illiquid guarantees   +0 × semiliquid guarantees   –½ × liquid guarantees

    –½ × liquid derivatives

This table explains the construction of three alternative main liquidity creation measures: "cat nonfat" (Panel A), "mat fat" (Panel B), and "mat nonfat" (Panel C) using a simplified overview of Step 2.
Source: Adapted from Berger and Bouwman (2009, Table 1).

semiliquid assets and are assigned a weight of 0. As noted in Section 4.1, "cat fat" is preferred to "mat fat" because the ease, cost, and time for banks to dispose of their obligations to obtain liquid funds is more closely related to category than maturity, particularly for residential mortgages, the largest category of bank loans.

"Cat nonfat" and "mat nonfat" are the same as "cat fat" and "mat fat," respectively, except that these measures exclude or put 0 weights on all off-balance sheet activities. The "fat" measures are strongly preferred to the "non-fat" measures because recent theory recognizes the contribution of off-balance sheet activities to the liquidity creation function of banks, and because these activities – as shown in Chapter 8 – make up about half of all bank liquidity creation in the United States using the preferred "cat fat" measure.

4.3   DEEP AND SCHAEFER'S (2004) LIQUIDITY TRANSFORMATION MEASURE

Deep and Schaefer's (2004) develop a liquidity transformation measure, which is related to the liquidity creation concept. Their measure is called the liquidity trans-formation gap or "LT gap," and is calculated as (liquid liabilities – liquid assets)/ total assets. This measure focuses to a large extent on loan maturities, and consid-ers all loans with maturity of 1 year or less to be liquid, and all longer-term loans as illiquid. Other assets and liabilities are classified as liquid or illiquid based on both product category and maturity. The "LT gap" explicitly excludes loan com-mitments and other off-balance sheet activities because of their contingent nature.

Deep and Schaefer's (2004) "LT gap" is conceptually close to the "mat nonfat" measure and may be viewed as a special case of it. If all assets and liabilities were classified as either liquid or illiquid (i.e., none as semiliquid), maturities were used for loan classification, off-balance sheet activities were ex-cluded, and total assets were used rather than gross total assets, the "mat nonfat" formula reduces to the "LT gap" formula.[4]

The "cat fat" liquidity creation measure is preferred to the "LT gap" measure for several reasons. First, the "LT gap" measures the liquidity of loans based on maturity ("mat") and thus ignores other factors that affect their liquidity. As discussed in Section 4.1, the preferred "cat fat" method classifies loans based on loan category ("cat"), which better takes into account the ease, cost, and time for banks to dispose of their assets and other obligations in order to meet customers' liquidity demands. For example, long-term residential mortgages can be relatively easily securitized by banks to raise liquid funds, while most short-term business loans cannot be easily sold or securitized by banks to raise liquid funds. The "LT gap" views the residential mortgages as illiquid and the

---

4. Applying these changes, the "mat nonfat" formula becomes [½ × illiquid assets – ½ × liquid assets + ½ × liquid liabilities – ½ × illiquid liabilities – ½ × equity]/total assets = [½ × (total assets – liquid assets) – ½ × liquid assets + ½ × liquid liabilities – ½ × (total assets – liquid li-abilities)]/total assets = [liquid liabilities – liquid assets]/total assets, which is the "LT gap" measure.

short-term business loans as liquid, whereas it seems more logical to treat the former as more liquid than the latter.

Second, the "LT gap" does not take into account the contribution of off-balance sheet activities to the liquidity creation function of banks. The liquidity creation theories suggest that banks do create liquidity off the balance sheet (Boot, Greenbaum, and Thakor, 1993; Holmstrom and Tirole, 1998; and Kashyap, Rajan, and Stein, 2002), and off-balance sheet activities make up about half of all US bank liquidity creation using the preferred "cat fat" measure.

Third, the "LT gap" considers only two classifications of assets and liabilities – liquid or illiquid – while the preferred "cat fat" approach uses three – liquid, semiliquid, and illiquid. The use of three buckets is preferred to two buckets since some assets and liabilities clearly fall in a classification between fully liquid and fully illiquid. For example, a bank time deposit cannot be accessed freely at each point in time so it is not liquid, but at the same time, it is not illiquid because it can be accessed quickly by paying a sizeable penalty. Thus, the ease, cost, and time to obtain liquid funds are not trivial, but neither are they large.

4.4 MODIFICATION OF THE "CAT FAT" MEASURE THAT TAKES INTO ACCOUNT TAKEDOWN PROBABILITIES OF OFF-BALANCE SHEET GUARANTEES

Berger and Bouwman (2009) also introduce two other modifications of the "cat fat" measure. The first incorporates the frequency with which customers obtain liquid funds through off-balance sheet guarantees, rather than the ease, cost, and time for customers to obtain liquid funds from the bank through these guarantees. This alternative liquidity creation measure is identical to the "cat fat" measure, except that the dollar amount of illiquid off-balance sheet guarantees is multiplied by 0.30, the observed frequency of drawdowns as documented in other research (Sufi, 2009). Thus, this measure is based in part on the extent to which customers avail themselves of the opportunity to obtain liquid funds.[5]

This measure is less desirable than the "cat fat" measure since the ability or option to obtain funds when needed or desired is more important than the actual drawdown frequency. This is also what the theories suggest – banks create liquidity through off-balance sheet guarantees because they give customers the option to draw down liquid funds when needed.

4.5 MODIFICATION OF THE "CAT FAT" MEASURE THAT TAKES INTO ACCOUNT SECURITIZATION FREQUENCIES

The second modified "cat fat" measure incorporates the frequencies with which banks securitize loans, recognizing that the ability to securitize different types of loans changes over time. This measure is identical to the "cat fat" measure,

---

5. In principle, this alternative concept could be expanded to measure how often depositors drawdown their funds as well, except that such information is generally not known.

except for the way that loans are classified. For each loan category, quarterly US Flow of Funds data are gathered on the total amount of loans outstanding and the total amount of loans securitized. These data are used to calculate the fraction of loans that have been securitized in the market in each year. Following Loutskina (2011), it is assumed that each bank can securitize that fraction of its own loans. For example, for 2014:Q4, \$9.9 trillion in residential real estate loans were outstanding in the market, and 22.1% of these loans were securitized. If a bank has \$10 million in residential and real estate loans in that year, then it is assumed that 22.1% thereof can be securitized, and hence, \$2.21 million of these loans are classified as semiliquid and the remainder as illiquid.

There are two problems with this alternative approach. First, it uses the actual amount of securitization, whereas the theories suggest that the ability to securitize matters for liquidity creation, not the amount securitized. Second, this alternative approach assumes that each bank securitizes the same fraction of loans in a particular category, even though in practice major differences may exist across banks. That is, when the US Flow of Funds data indicates that 22.1% of all residential real estate loans were securitized in 2014, it is assumed that every bank securitizes 22.1% of those loans in that year, even though one bank may have securitized virtually its entire residential real estate portfolio, while another bank may have securitized nothing.[6]

4.6 SUMMARY

This chapter introduces the preferred "cat fat" measure of bank liquidity creation that is used in the empirical analyses in this book. This measure classifies virtually all bank activities as liquid, semiliquid, or illiquid using information on product category and maturity, but classifies loans purely by category ("cat") due to data limitations, and includes off-balance sheet activities ("fat"). It also compares this measure to several alternative measures of liquidity creation that are based on loan maturity ("mat"), exclude off-balance sheet activities ("nonfat"), use only two liquidity buckets (liquid and illiquid), take into account takedown probabilities of off-balance sheet guarantees, take into account securitization frequencies, and discusses why the "cat fat" measure is preferred. The key takeaways are the method for calculating "cat fat" liquidity creation and the understanding that the "cat fat" measure is preferred because it is most consistent with the liquidity creation theories.

---

6. The second criticism is valid when one is interested in calculating how much liquidity an individual bank creates because the amount of liquidity creation will only be correct for a bank that securitizes 22.1% of residential real estate loans. The criticism does not hold when the goal is to calculate liquidity creation by the entire banking sector.

Chapter 5

Using Liquidity Creation to Measure Bank Output

This chapter explores the measurement of commercial bank output using liquidity creation versus traditional measures. Traditional approaches that measure bank output using assets or lending are discussed first. They are then compared to the preferred "cat fat" measure of liquidity creation. A detailed numerical example is provided to illustrate the differences.

5.1 TRADITIONAL APPROACHES TO MEASURING BANK OUTPUT AND WHAT IS MISSING

Many banking studies aim to quantify what banks do: some indicate they try to capture bank output, while others focus on bank size. Bank output and size are essentially the same thing, so the terms are used interchangeably here.

Three measures of bank output are generally used in the literature: total assets, gross total assets, and lending. These measures are discussed in turn.

1. **Total assets (TA)** captures the total size of the balance sheet by adding up all of the individual assets recorded on the balance sheet and subtracting off two loan- and lease-related factors highlighted in Chapter 3, the allocation for loan and lease losses (ALLL: an accounting item for expected losses), and the allocated transfer risk reserve (ATRR: a reserve for certain foreign loans). Thus, TA does not include gross loans (the actual amount of loans extended by the bank), but net loans. As discussed in Chapter 3, the ATRR is zero for virtually all banks. Indeed, in the example in Table 3.1 Panels B and C, the ATRR is zero for both JPMorgan Chase and Community Bank of El Dorado Springs, whereas the ALLL amounts to 0.5% of assets for JPMorgan Chase and 1% of assets for Community Bank of El Dorado Springs.
2. **Gross total assets (GTA)** includes these two allocations. GTA may be considered a better measure of output than TA because GTA includes gross loans, the actual amount of loans extended, and hence includes all activities that must be financed, while TA does not. In the rest of this book, TA and

GTA are often collectively referred to as "assets," but GTA is used as a measure of assets in the empirical analyses.[1,2]

Total assets and gross total assets are used in the vast majority of empirical banking studies as the main measure of bank output. As well, most empirical banking studies employ financial ratios with assets as the denominators. Assets are also used to divide banks into size classes, to define the size of community banks, and in policy rules for different treatments of banks of different sizes.

See Box 5.1 for examples of these in the literature.

BOX 5.1 Examples of Literature and Policies That Use Assets to Measure Bank Output or Size

How are assets used in empirical studies and in policy rules?	Topics	Studies
A. Included in regressions as a direct measure of bank output or size	Competition	• Shaffer (1993)
		• Berger and Bouwman (2013)
	Corporate governance	• Laeven and Levine (2009)
	Bank failure probabilities	• Cole and White (1995, 2012)
	Bank risk taking	• Demsetz and Strahan (1997)
	Small business lending and relationship lending	• Petersen and Rajan (1994) • Berger, Miller, Petersen, Rajan, and Stein (2005)
	Lending and pricing outcomes of bank mergers and acquisitions	• Berger, Saunders, Scalise, and Udell (1998) • Focarelli and Panetta (2003)
	Liquidity creation	• Berger and Bouwman (2009)
	Monetary policy transmission channels	• Kishan and Opiela (2012) • Jimenez, Ongena, Peydro, and Saurina (2014)
	Bank switching	• Ioannidou and Ongena (2010) • Degryse, Masschelein, and Mitchell (2011)
	Risk and lending outcomes of government interventions and bailouts	• Black and Hazelwood (2013) • Duchin and Sosyura (2014)

(Continued)

---

1. Historically, researchers also use other measures of bank output. For example, Alhadeff (1954) and Horvitz (1963) use earning assets as a measure of bank output. Greenbaum (1967) suggests using estimated income from lending plus observed nonlending operating income. See Hester (1967) for more discussion on these older measures of bank output.

2. Studies of bank scale efficiency (how close banks are to minimum average cost for their product mix) and X-efficiency (how close banks are to their minimum cost or maximum profit for a given scale and product mix) often use a vector of multiple products as measures of output, while the focus here is on single measures of output. This issue of bank scale efficiency is covered in Section 15.10 when discussing optimal levels of bank size.

How are assets used in empirical studies and in policy rules?	Topics	Studies
B. Included in regressions as a way to normalize financial statement items	The effect of the equity capital to assets ratio on bank failure	• Cole and Gunther (1995)
	The effect of the equity capital to assets ratio on bank risk taking	• Koehn and Santomero (1980)
	The effect of the equity capital to assets ratio on liquidity creation	• Berger and Bouwman (2009) • Horvath, Seidler, and Weill (2014)
	The effect of Troubled Asset Relief Program (TARP)[a] on competition	• Berger and Roman (forthcoming)
	The effect of regulation on risk taking	• Ongena, Popov, and Udell (2013)
	The effect of monetary policy on lending	• Kashyap and Stein (2000)
C. Used as a size cutoff	Define the size of community banks	• DeYoung, Hunter, and Udell (2004) • Federal Deposit Insurance Corporation (2012)
	Determine whether a bank poses systemic risks, is subject to stress tests, or has different capital rules	• Supervisory Capital Assessment Program (SCAP) of 2009 • Dodd Frank Act of 2010 • Comprehensive Capital Analysis and Review (CCAR) (from 2011 onward) • Federal Reserve Press Release, July 2, 2013

[a]TARP is discussed in more detail in Section 7.5.

Assets, defined as either TA or GTA, is not a particularly good measure of bank output for several reasons. First, it ignores off-balance-sheet activities, which are important outputs of some banks, in particular large US banks such as JPMorgan Chase, as discussed in Chapter 3. For example, bank customers are often able to use off-balance-sheet guarantees (like loan commitments and standby letters of credit) to plan their investments and other expenditures, and to back up other capital market financing (such as commercial paper), and derivatives to hedge their market risks. Second, these measures ignore all bank liabilities, such as the important output contribution of deposits and the payments services, which are associated with them, which are large for both JPMorgan Chase and Community Bank of El Dorado Springs discussed in Chapter 3. Third, these measures assume that all assets contribute positively to bank output. This does not seem correct since cash and marketable securities, while useful to the bank in terms of reducing liquidity risk, do not produce output to customers in a similar fashion to loans.

3. **Lending** has been used in some research as a more narrowly defined measure of bank output. At least three topics have been studied: the effects of low bank capital and regulatory capital minimums on bank lending during the credit crunch of 1990:Q1–1992:Q4; the effects of the subprime lending crisis of 2007:Q3–2009:Q4 and government interventions during this crisis on lending; and the effects of monetary policy on lending through the bank-lending channel.[3] These studies generally ignore differences in output contribution across different loan categories, as well as the important bank services associated with other assets, liabilities, equity, and off-balance-sheet activities.

See Box 5.2 for examples of some of these studies.

BOX 5.2 Examples of Literature That Use Lending to Measure Bank Output

How is lending used in empirical studies?	Studies
A. Effects of low bank capital and regulatory capital minimums on bank lending during the credit crunch of 1990:Q1–1992:Q4	• Berger and Udell (1994) • Hancock, Laing, and Wilcox (1995) • Peek and Rosengren (1995a, b) • Shrieves and Dahl (1995) • Thakor (1996)
B. Effects of the subprime lending crisis of 2007:Q3–2009:Q4 and government interventions on lending during this crisis	• Cornett, McNutt, Strahan, and Tehranian (2011) • Gambacorta and Marques-Ibanez (2011) • Dell'Ariccia, Igan, and Laeven (2012) • Berger, Black, Bouwman, and Dlugosz (2015)
C. Bank lending channel of monetary policy	• Kashyap and Stein (1994, 2000) • Bernanke and Gertler (1995) • Jimenez, Ongena, Peydro, and Saurina (2012)

---

3. The bank-lending channel is discussed in detail in Section 12.5.

5.2   WHY "CAT FAT" BANK LIQUIDITY CREATION IS A SUPERIOR MEASURE OF BANK OUTPUT

Liquidity creation is a superior measure of bank output to the alternative measures of assets or loans because it is more consistent with the banking theories discussed in Chapter 2. Liquidity creation takes into account all bank activities (all assets including different loan types, all liabilities plus equity capital, and all off-balance-sheet activities). It also recognizes that banks create liquidity when they engage in certain activities but destroy liquidity when they engage in other activities.

Assets only measures the total size of the asset-side of the balance sheet and lending focuses even more narrowly on just one asset class – loans. Both measures ignore output from off-balance-sheet activities. Loan commitments and standby letters of credit allow customers to obtain funds in critical circumstances to better plan their investments and purchases. Both assets and lending also ignore differences in composition on the liability side of the balance sheet. They thus do not recognize that transactions deposits increase bank output because they directly benefit the public with liquidity and payment services, whereas bank equity decreases it because the public's funds are tied up and cannot be easily withdrawn. Finally, assets and lending abstract from important differences in the composition of the asset side of the balance sheet. They ignore differences between the output contributions among loan categories. They also do not take into account that marketable securities reduce bank output by taking something liquid away from the public.

The "cat fat" liquidity creation measure deals with these issues in very different ways. It includes off-balance-sheet activities – in fact, they make up about half of "cat fat" liquidity creation in the United States as shown in Chapter 8. It also includes different loan categories with different weights, views transactions deposits as adding to liquidity creation, and bank equity and marketable securities as reducing liquidity creation. These different treatments, consistent with the theories, make "cat fat" liquidity creation a more appropriate measure of bank output than assets or loans.

Box 5.3 contains a numerical example to illustrate these points.

5.3   SUMMARY

This chapter explores the measurement of bank output using "cat fat" liquidity creation versus traditional measures (total assets, gross total assets, and lending), and explains that "cat fat" liquidity creation is superior to these measures because it is more consistent with the theory. A numerical example drives home these points. The key takeaway is that liquidity creation is superior to other measures of bank output.

BOX 5.3 Numerical Example to Show Why "Cat Fat" Liquidity Creation is a Superior Measure of Output

Consider two banks: Lazy Bank and Hardworking Bank. Lazy Bank has equity, subordinated debt, takes in deposits, and invests all those funds in treasuries. It does not extend any loans, nor does it provide any loan commitments to its customers. Hardworking Bank has the same amount of equity, no subordinated debt, and more deposits. It lends all those funds to its customers, and also provides them with loan commitments.

Lazy Bank				Hardworking Bank			
Treasuries	$10	Transactions		Treasuries	$0	Transactions	
Residential		deposits	$6	Residential		deposits	$8
mortgages	$0	Subordinated		mortgages	$6	Subordinated	
Business		debt	$2	Business		debt	$0
loans	$0	Equity	$2	loans	$4	Equity	$2
Total		Total liabilities		Total		Total liabilities	
assets	$10	and equity	$10	assets	$10	and equity	$10
Loan com-				Loan com-			
mitments	$0			mitments	$5		

In this simple example, the allowance for loan and lease losses (ALLL) and the allocated transfer risk reserve (ATRR) are assumed to be zero for simplicity, so total assets (TA) equals gross total assets (GTA), and net loans equals gross loans.[a]

Let us now compare the output of Lazy Bank and Hardworking Bank using assets, lending, and "cat fat" liquidity creation. All the calculations are shown in the table given below.

Using assets as a measure of bank output, the two banks produce the same output since both have assets of $10.

Using lending as a measure of bank output, Hardworking Bank shows higher output since it makes $6 in residential mortgages + $4 in business loans = $10 in loans, whereas Lazy Bank makes $0 in loans.

The "cat fat" liquidity creation measure takes into account off-balance-sheet activities, the output-increasing effect of transactions deposits, the output-decreasing effect of equity and marketable securities, and distinguishes between the effects on output of different loan categories. Using the "cat fat" liquidity creation measure, Hardworking Bank produces much more output: it creates $\frac{1}{2} \times \$4$ in business loans + $0 \times \$6$ in residential mortgages + $(-\frac{1}{2}) \times \$0$ in Treasuries = $2 in liquidity on the asset side; it creates $\frac{1}{2} \times \$8$ in transactions deposits + $(-\frac{1}{2}) \times \$2$ in equity = $3 of liquidity on the liability side; and it creates $\frac{1}{2} \times \$5$ in loan commitments = $2.5 of liquidity off the balance sheet; for a total liquidity creation of $2 + $3 + $2.5 = $7.5. In contrast, Lazy Bank creates $\frac{1}{2} \times \$0$ in business loans + $0 \times \$0$ in residential mortgages + $(-\frac{1}{2}) \times \$10$ in Treasuries = −$5 in liquidity on the asset side; it creates $\frac{1}{2} \times \$6$ in transactions deposits + $(-\frac{1}{2}) \times \$2$ in subordinated debt + $(-\frac{1}{2}) \times \$2$ in equity = $1 of liquidity on the liability side; and it creates $\frac{1}{2} \times \$0$ in loan commitments = $0 of liquidity off the balance sheet; for a total liquidity creation of −$5 + $1 + $0 = −$4, that is, it destroys $4 of liquidity.

Output measure	Lazy Bank	Hardworking Bank
Assets	$10	$10
Lending	$0	$6 + $4 = $10
Liquidity creation		
Asset-side	$\frac{1}{2} \times \$0 + 0 \times \$0$ $+ (-\frac{1}{2}) \times \$10 = -\$5$	$\frac{1}{2} \times \$4 + 0 \times \$6$ $+ (-\frac{1}{2}) \times \$0 = \$2$
Liability-side	$\frac{1}{2} \times \$6 + (-\frac{1}{2}) \times \$2$ $+ (-\frac{1}{2}) \times \$2 = \$1$	$\frac{1}{2} \times \$8 + (-\frac{1}{2}) \times \$2 = \$3$
Off-balance-sheet	$\frac{1}{2} \times \$0 = \$0$	$\frac{1}{2} \times \$5 = \$2.5$
Total	$-\$5 + \$1 + \$0 = -\$4$	$\$2 + \$3 + \$2.5 = \$7.5$

a. Recall that GTA = TA + ALLL + ATRR and gross loans = net loans + ALLL + ATRR.

Chapter 6

Using Liquidity Creation
to Measure Bank Liquidity

Bank liquidity differs from, but is related to bank liquidity creation. Bank liquidity creation is an indicator of how much liquidity a bank creates for the public. Bank liquidity is an indicator of the ease, cost, and time required for a bank to meet demands for liquidity from its liability, equity, and off-balance sheet customers, which can be done by reducing its assets (stored liquidity management) and/or increasing its liabilities (purchased liability management).[1] It is crucial to be able to measure bank liquidity because a liquid bank has reduced liquidity risk, one of the most important risks faced by banks. If a bank is illiquid and faces high demands for liquid funds, it has high liquidity risk: it may have to engage in "fire sales" (sell assets at heavily discounted prices) or forego profitable investment opportunities (including loans) to meet the demands for liquidity by its customers. In an extreme case (e.g., a run on a bank), liquidity risk may result in insolvency.

This chapter reviews simple measures of bank liquidity and then shows how a suitably normalized version of the "cat fat" liquidity creation measure is an indirect measure of bank liquidity that may be superior to the simple measures. The normalized liquidity creation measure is then compared to more complex measures of bank liquidity. Finally, market measures of liquidity are considered that may be used to calculate the liquidity of the publicly traded equity or debt of listed banks and BHCs.

6.1 SIMPLE MEASURES OF BANK LIQUIDITY

Bank liquidity is most often measured as the ratio of cash and sometimes other liquid assets to overall assets or deposits. See Box 6.1 for various examples of these in the literature.

These measures take into account only the liquidity of some of the bank's assets and liabilities and do not account for the different liquidity of all of the assets, liabilities, equity, and off-balance sheet activities.

---

1. It can reduce assets by drawing down cash or reserve balances at the Federal Reserve, selling securities, or not renewing loans. It can increase liabilities by issuing federal funds or other purchased funds such as negotiable certificates of deposit.

BOX 6.1 Examples of Literature That Use Simple Ratios to Measure Bank Liquidity

	Topics	Studies
A. Deposit growth rate	Impact of bank liquidity shocks	• Khwaja and Mian (2008) • Acharya and Mora (2015)
B. Ratio of cash to deposits	Effects of the Troubled Asset Relief Program (TARP)	• Li (2013) • Duchin and Sosyura (2014) • Berger and Roman (2015, forthcoming)
C. Ratio of cash to assets	Bank liquidity and crisis resolution	• Martinez Peria and Schmukler (2001) • Acharya, Shin, and Yorulmazer (2011)
D. Ratio of cash and liquid assets to total assets	Synergies between lending and deposits	• Kashyap, Rajan, and Stein (2002)
	Management of bank liquidity risk	• Gatev, Schuermann, and Strahan (2009)
	Effects of bank capital on performance	• Berger and Bouwman (2013) • Chu (forthcoming)
	Liquidity hoarding	• Berrospide (2013)
	Effects of bank taxes on bank capital structure	• Schandlbauer (2013)
	Transmission of liquidity shocks from BHCs to banks	• Allen, Hryckiewicz, Kowalewski, and Tumer-Alkan (2014)
	Effects of small bank market share on small businesses	• Berger, Cerquiero, and Penas (2015)
E. Ratio of securities to total assets	Effects of monetary policy	• Kashyap and Stein (2000)

6.2 USING NORMALIZED "CAT FAT" LIQUIDITY CREATION AS A DIRECT MEASURE OF BANK ILLIQUIDITY OR AN INDIRECT MEASURE OF BANK LIQUIDITY

While these balance sheet ratios measure a bank's liquidity directly, bank liquidity creation can be viewed as a direct measure of bank illiquidity or an inverse, and hence indirect, measure of bank liquidity. To see this, note first that when a bank creates liquidity, it provides liquidity to the public, and makes itself illiquid in the process. So when the bank creates more liquidity, it becomes more illiquid or less liquid. The ratio of liquidity creation to assets (either total assets TA or gross total assets GTA) measures the bank's illiquidity per unit of assets and can be used as a normalized inverse measure of the bank's liquidity, something that has been recognized in the literature. Since the publication of the liquidity creation measures in 2009, the ratio of "cat fat" liquidity creation to assets is used in several empirical banking studies as controls for bank liquidity or illiquidity (e.g., Distinguin, Roulet, and Tarazi, 2013; Berger, Goulding, and Rice, 2014; Horvath, Seidler, and Weill, 2014; Berger, Black, Bouwman, and Dlugosz, 2015; and Berger, Cerqueiro, and Penas, 2015).

An advantage of using the ratio of "cat fat" liquidity creation to assets instead of the simple bank liquidity ratios is that it includes all of the different sources and uses of liquidity in one measure. For example, business loans, transactions deposits, and loan commitments have positive weights in the measure of liquidity creation and they make the bank more illiquid, while cash, liquid assets, subordinated debt, and equity have negative weights and they make the bank more liquid.

6.3 THE BASEL III MEASURES OF BANK LIQUIDITY

Banks in the United States have had to meet liquidity requirements in the form of reserve requirements from the 1820s onward. These require that banks hold enough liquid funds to be able to meet expected deposit withdrawals. US banks currently have to hold required reserves in the form of vault cash or deposits at Federal Reserve Banks against their transactions deposits.[2] Banks in various other countries have to meet similar requirements. Banks have also been subject to scrutiny and rating of their liquidity during routine bank examinations in many countries.[3]

The subprime lending crisis of 2007:Q3–2009:Q4, however, made it clear that banks' liquidity positions had not received adequate attention since various institutions were facing significant liquidity problems. Discussions about the need to impose stricter liquidity requirements began and specific standards were included in Basel III. This Accord was drafted by the Basel Committee on Banking Regulations and Supervisory Practices, under the auspices of the Bank for International Settlements (BIS) in Basel, Switzerland, which historically focused only on imposing uniform capital requirements and had done so from 1988 onward. Box 12.1 in Chapter 12 explains more about the origins of the Basel Accords, while Box 12.2 discusses the Basel III capital requirements.

Basel III introduces two liquidity requirements. The Liquidity Coverage Ratio (LCR) specifies that a bank needs to have enough high-quality liquid assets to survive a 30-day standardized stress scenario. The Net Stable Funding Ratio (NSFR) specifies that to be able to survive an extended closure of wholesale

---

2. As of January 2015, the reserve requirement on transactions deposits between $0 and $14.5 million is 0%; between $14.5 million and $103.6 million is 3%; and over $103.6 million is 10%. There are no reserve requirements on nontransactions deposits. For a history on reserve requirements, see Feinman (1993) and Bouwman (2015).
3. Bank examinations in the United States and abroad use the CAMELS rating system, developed in the 1970s, to assess a bank's overall condition. The acronym stands for the components that are assessed: Capital adequacy, Asset quality, Management, Earnings, Liquidity, and Sensitivity to market risk (particularly interest rate risk). The ratings range from 1 (best) to 5 (worst). Each bank receives ratings on all six dimensions, as well as a composite rating.

funding markets, a bank has to operate with a minimum acceptable amount of "stable funding" based on the liquidity characteristics of the bank's assets and activities over a 1-year period. The LCR is currently being implemented in the United States and worldwide. The NSFR will be implemented in 2018. Box 6.2 provides further details on the LCR and NSFR. It also explains how the US implementation of the LCR differs from the original Basel proposal; such information is not yet known about the NSFR.

BOX 6.2 Basel III Liquidity Requirements

Basel III imposes two minimum liquidity requirements with complementary objectives.

1. The **Liquidity Coverage Ratio (LCR)** focuses on short-term resilience. It specifies that a bank needs to have enough high-quality liquid assets to survive a 30-day standardized stress scenario. Specifically, when fully implemented, the bank's unencumbered high-quality liquid assets (HQLA) must be sufficient to cover its projected net cash outflows (NCOF) over this 30-day period:

   $$LCR = \frac{HQLA}{NCOF} \geq 100\%.^{a}$$

   - The numerator, HQLA, includes two types of assets:
     - Level 1 assets comprise cash, central bank reserves, and certain marketable securities backed by sovereigns, public sector entities, and central banks. These assets can be included without limit and are not subject to a haircut.[b]
     - Level 2 assets comprise: Level 2A assets (certain government securities, and covered bonds and corporate debt securities rated AA- or higher), which are capped at 40% of HQLA after being subjected to a 15% haircut; and Level 2B assets (certain residential mortgage-backed securities, corporate debt securities rated between BBB- and A +, and common equity shares), which are capped at 15% after being subjected to haircuts of 25%–50%.
   - The denominator, NCOF, is defined as total expected cash outflows minus the minimum of (total expected cash inflows and 75% of total expected cash outflows) over the 30-day period used in the specified stress scenario. Total expected cash outflows are calculated as the outstanding balances of different types of liabilities and off-balance sheet commitments multiplied by the rates at which they are expected to run off or be drawn down. For example, unsecured interbank loans are assumed to run off fully if they come due during the stress scenario, while term deposits with less than 30 days maturity and transactions deposits are assumed to run off by 3%–10%.
   - The LCR was introduced internationally on January 1, 2015, with a minimum requirement of 60%, to be increased by 10% per year to 100% on January 1, 2019.
   - The Federal Reserve, Office of the Comptroller of the Currency (OCC), and the Federal Deposit Insurance Corporation (FDIC) issued a final rule about the implementation of the LCR in the United States in October 2014

(Department of the Treasury, Federal Reserve System, and Federal Deposit Insurance Corporation, 2014). Important differences include the following:

- The United States is implementing two versions: a full LCR (to be calculated each business day starting mid-2016) for large, internationally active banking organizations and some of their US bank subsidiaries; and a less stringent, modified LCR (to be calculated monthly starting early 2016) for large regional BHCs.[c] Smaller institutions are not subject to the LCR.
- The US definition of HQLAs is more stringent: HQLAs do not include securities issued or guaranteed by public sector entities, covered bonds, or residential mortgage-backed securities. Corporate debt securities are not included in Level 2A assets, but may qualify as Level 2B assets. Definitions of HQLAs do not reference external credit ratings since the Dodd-Frank Act prohibits their use.[d]
- Full LCR banks are subject to an additional peak net outflow day test, which ensures that the bank's HQLA are sufficient to meet expected outflows during a peak day (the day during the following 30 days on which the net cumulative cash outflows is expected to be the largest).
- The US implementation is faster: banking organizations subject to the full LCR must maintain a minimum LCR of 80% by January 1, 2015, while all banking organizations subject to the full or modified LCR have to maintain a minimum LCR of 90% by January 1, 2016, and 100% by January 1, 2017.

2. The **Net Stable Funding Ratio (NSFR)** focuses on long-run resilience. It specifies that to be able to survive an extended closure of wholesale funding markets, banks have to operate with a minimum acceptable amount of "stable funding" based on the liquidity characteristics of the bank's assets and activities over a one-year period.

- The NSFR requires that a bank's available stable funding (ASF) exceeds the required amount of stable funding (RSF) based on the liquidity characteristics of the bank's assets and activities over a one-year bank-specific stress scenario: $NSFR = \dfrac{ASF}{RSF} \geq 100\%$.
  - The numerator, ASF, includes equity, preferred stock with a maturity of at least one year, liabilities with effective maturities of at least one year, and demand deposits/term deposits/wholesale funding with maturities of less than one year that are expected to stay with the bank in case of idiosyncratic stress. The numerator is determined by assigning ASF factors (weights) to the amounts of stable funding the bank has. For example, Tier 1 capital and Tier 2 capital with a maturity exceeding one year receive an ASF factor of 100%, stable demand deposits and term deposits with residual maturity of less than one year receive an ASF factor of 90% or 95%, while less stable deposits are assigned an ASF factor of 50%.
  - The denominator, RSF, is calculated as the sum of the bank's assets and off-balance sheet activities multiplied by an RSF factor, which intends

(Continued)

to quantify the amount of an asset or off-balance sheet activity that has to be funded within one year without significant expense. Activities that are more liquid receive the lowest RSF factors (and require less stable funding) because they can act as a source of extended liquidity in case of stress. For example, cash is assigned an RSF factor of 0%, certain marketable securities and highly-rated corporate debt securities are assigned an RSF factor of 15%, residential mortgage-backed securities and lower-rated corporate debt securities are assigned a 50% RSF factor, loans to nonfinancial institutions with a remaining maturity of at least one year are weighted at 65%, physical traded commodities including gold receive an 85% RSF factor, while nonperforming loans with a residual maturity of at least one year are assigned a 100% RSF factor.

–   The Basel Committee announced in October 2014 that the NSFR will become a minimum standard by January 1, 2018 (BIS, 2014).

–   The US regulatory agencies anticipate issuing an NSFR implementation proposal after the Basel Committee adopts a final international version.

---

a. The LCR is expected to always be at least 100%. It may fall below 100% during times of idiosyncratic or systemic stress, but the banking organization should inform its regulator immediately when this occurs or is expected to happen.
b. A haircut is the percentage by which an asset's market value is reduced to provide an additional cushion.
c. Specifically, the full LCR applies to banking organizations with at least $250 billion in total consolidated assets or at least $10 billion in on-balance-sheet foreign exposure, and any consolidated bank or savings association subsidiary of one of these companies that, at the bank level, has total consolidated assets of at least $10 billion. The modified LCR applies to bank holding companies without significant insurance or commercial operations that have at least $50 billion in total consolidated assets but are not internationally active.
d. See Box 12.3 for more on the Dodd-Frank Act.

One key similarity between the Basel III liquidity ratios and the normalized "cat fat" measure is that they all have fixed weights. An important difference, however, is that the Basel III ratios focus only on what liquidity would be under stressful scenarios, whereas normalized "cat fat" liquidity creation is an inverse indicator of current liquidity. Another important difference is that publicly available data sources (such as Call reports for banks in the United States) do not have sufficient detail to compute the Basel III ratios, whereas they are sufficiently detailed to calculate "cat fat" liquidity creation.[4] The reason is that Basel III specifies rates of cash outflows and inflows during stressful scenarios

---

4. There are several studies of Basel III liquidity ratios that use data that are not publicly available. The Basel Committee on Banking Supervision (BIS 2010; 2012a,b) and the European Banking Authority (EBA 2012a,b) conduct five quantitative impact studies or monitoring exercises on the Basel III liquidity ratios using such data.

of certain asset and liability categories, while the Basel III classifications of these assets and liabilities differ from those in publicly available data sources. Thus, assumptions are needed to estimate the Basel III ratios using Call Report or other publicly available data sources.

The only research of which we are aware that makes assumptions and estimates Basel III ratios using publicly available data on banks in the United States is Hong, Huang, and Wu (2014). They use quarterly Call Report data on 8,349 banks of all sizes from 2001 to 2011. They start in 2001 because the Call Report was not sufficiently detailed before that year. They have two results which are of particular interest here. First, when examining how the Basel III ratios change over time, they find that these ratios increase significantly (indicating that banks became more liquid) throughout the subprime lending crisis and following it, consistent with arguments made elsewhere that banks hoarded liquidity during this crisis (e.g., Berrospide, 2013). Second, when running bank failure models, they find that the ratios have little explanatory power in predicting individual bank failure.

Dietrich, Hess, and Wanzenried (2014) make assumptions and estimate the NSFR using data from Bankscope for a sample of 921 large banks in Western Europe (Austria, Belgium, France, Germany, Luxembourg, Netherlands, and Switzerland) between 1996 and 2010.[5] They do not examine the LCR, arguing that Bankscope does not provide sufficiently detail to estimate it. Similar to Hong, Huang, and Wu (2014), they find that the NSFR generally increases during the subprime-lending crisis. They also find that this ratio is not statistically significant in explaining bank profitability.

Hong, Huang, and Wu (2014) graciously provided their estimated LCR and NSFR ratios quarterly from 2001:Q1 to 2012:Q4 to allow comparison with normalized "cat fat" liquidity creation over this time period.[6] Figure 6.1 Panels A and B show the correlations over time between normalized "cat fat" liquidity creation and their LCR and NSFR ratios, respectively, for small, medium, and large banks. As discussed further in Chapter 8, these size classes are used to indicate banks with GTA up to $1 billion, exceeding $1 billion and up to $3 billion, and exceeding $3 billion, respectively. The two financial crises during this period are demarcated with vertical dashed lines in the figure. The correlations are calculated quarterly and plotted over time because mixing time periods before calculating the correlations might confound the correlations with temporal factors.

Figure 6.1 Panel A shows that the correlations between normalized "cat fat" liquidity creation and the LCR are generally negative, as expected, but small

---

5. Bankscope has up to 16 years of data on over 30,000 banks worldwide and generally covers the largest banks in each country, typically including about 90% of banking assets. Bankscope requires a paid subscription.
6. They shared the following: the LCR ratio calculated based on the BIS' revised LCR standard issued in January 2013 (BIS, 2013) and the baseline assumptions contained therein; and the NSFR ratio calculated based on the BIS' revised NSFR standard issued in January 2014 and the baseline assumptions contained therein.

Panel A: Correlations over time between normalized "cat fat" liquidity creation and the LCR

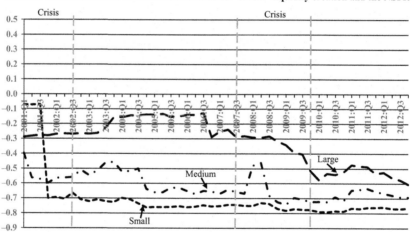

Panel B: Correlations over time between normalized "cat fat" liquidity creation and the NSFR

FIGURE 6.1 **Correlations over time between normalized "cat fat" liquidity creation and the Basel III liquidity ratios.** The figure shows correlations over time between "cat fat" liquidity creation normalized by gross total assets and the LCR in Panel A, and the NSFR in Panel B. "Cat fat" liquidity creation classifies bank activities other than loans based on maturity and product category combined, but classifies loans by category due to data limitations, and includes off-balance sheet activities. The LCR and NSFR focus on short- and long-term resilience, respectively.

in magnitude. The magnitudes are typically smallest for large banks, and they actually turn positive for these banks during the most severe part of the subprime lending crisis, 2008:Q4–2009:Q1, right after the Lehman Brothers bankruptcy. The lack of consistently large negative correlations suggest that the LCR and normalized "cat fat" liquidity creation are measuring significantly different things.

Panel A: Correlations over time between normalized on-balance sheet liquidity creation and the LCR

Panel B: Correlations over time between normalized on-balance sheet liquidity creation andthe NSFR

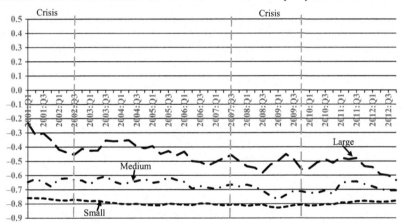

FIGURE 6.2 Correlations over time between normalized on-balance sheet liquidity creation and the Basel III liquidity ratios. The figure shows correlations over time between on-balance sheet liquidity creation normalized by gross total assets and the LCR in Panel A, and the NSFR in Panel B. On-balance sheet liquidity creation classifies bank activities other than loans based on maturity and product category combined, but classifies loans by category due to data limitations. The LCR and NSFR focus on short- and long-term resilience, respectively.

Figure 6.2 Panel A and Figure 6.3 Panel A, respectively, show these correlations separately for on- and off-balance sheet liquidity creation, and it is clear that the positive correlation during part of the crisis for large banks is due to off-balance sheet liquidity creation. The on-balance sheet correlations do not change significantly during the crisis, whereas the off-balance sheet correlations

Panel A: Correlations over time between normalized off-balance sheet liquidity creation and the LCR

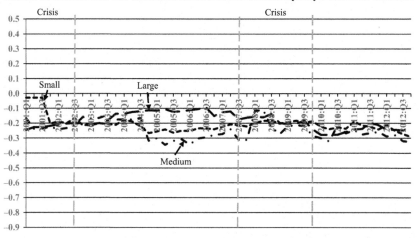

Panel B: Correlations over time between normalized off-balance sheet liquidity creation and the NSFR

FIGURE 6.3 **Correlations over time between normalized off-balance sheet liquidity creation and the Basel III liquidity ratios.** The figure shows correlations over time between off-balance sheet liquidity creation normalized by gross total assets and the LCR in Panel A, and the NSFR in Panel B. Off-balance sheet liquidity creation classifies bank activities based on maturity and product category combined. The LCR and NSFR focus on short- and long-term resilience, respectively.

turn positive. As discussed in Chapter 8, off-balance sheet liquidity creation fell precipitously in the subprime lending crisis due to reduced loan commitments. This finding does not seem to register well in the LCR – otherwise the correlations would have remained negative.

Figure 6.1 Panel B shows the correlations between normalized "cat fat" liquidity creation and the NSFR. The correlations are negative and sizeable for small and medium banks. The correlations are also negative, but much smaller in magnitude for large banks, in part because the correlations are relatively small for on-balance sheet liquidity creation (see Figure 6.2 Panel B), but mostly because the correlations are very small for off-balance sheet liquidity creation (see Figure 6.3 Panel B). This suggests that the NFSR is measuring something different for large banks, and is not capturing much of the large movements in off-balance sheet liquidity creation.

Overall, the correlations suggest that normalized "cat fat" liquidity creation, the LCR, and the NSFR capture different things. It is therefore important to measure all three and to conduct new research to see which are better at predicting future individual bank and banking industry performance.

6.4 THE LIQUIDITY MISMATCH INDEX (LMI) OF BANK LIQUIDITY

The final measure of liquidity considered here is the liquidity mismatch index (LMI), developed theoretically by Brunnermeier, Gorton, and Krishnamurthy (2011, 2014) and implemented empirically on US bank holding companies (BHCs) by Bai, Krishnamurthy, and Weymuller (2014). The LMI measures the mismatch between the market liquidity of an institution's assets and the funding liquidity of its (on- and off-balance sheet) liabilities.[7] The LMI aims to measure liquidity imbalances in the financial system and the amount of liquidity the Federal Reserve may have to provide to a BHC during a crisis.

The LMI is calculated by applying time-varying weights (i.e., weights that are adjusted for time-varying conditions in financial markets) to a BHC's assets and (on- and off-balance sheet) liabilities. Three-step procedures are used for assets and (on- and off-balance sheet) liabilities.

The first step to obtain the market liquidity of assets focuses on how easy it is to convert each asset into cash. It assigns weights ranging from 0 for items that are hard or time-consuming to sell (such as fixed assets) to 1 for items that are very liquid (such as cash and federal funds). The second step multiplies each initial weight by one minus the repo haircut of that asset class, arguing that the haircut measures how much cash can be borrowed against that asset, with average haircuts ranging from 0% (on cash) to 6.3% (on equities).[8] The third step multiplies the dollar amounts of each asset class with the haircut-adjusted weights. The market liquidity of the BHC's assets is the sum of these weighted dollar amounts.

The first step to get the funding liquidity of (on- and off-balance sheet) liabilities assesses how easy it is for financiers to withdraw funding. It does so by assigning to each funding source a maturity, ranging from 0 for overnight financing (such as federal funds) to 30 years for long-term financing (such as equity). The second step multiplies all the initial weights by a liquidity premium, measured as the spread between the overnight indexed swap (OIS) rate and the Treasury bill rate.[9] The third step multiplies the dollar amounts of each (on- and off-balance sheet) liability by a liability weight, which equals

---

7. The LMI incorporates four types of off-balance sheet contingent liabilities: loan commitments, credit lines, securities lent, and fair values of derivatives.

8. A haircut is the difference between an asset's collateral value and its sale price.

($-e^{-\text{maturity} \times \text{liquidity premium}}$). The funding liquidity of the BHC's (on- and off-balance sheet) liabilities is the sum of these weighted dollar amounts.

The LMI for a BHC then is the sum of the (positive) market liquidity of its assets and the (negative) funding liquidity of its on- and off-balance sheet liabilities.

There are two key differences between the LMI and "cat fat" liquidity creation. First, the LMI assigns only positive or zero (never negative) weights to assets and only negative or zero (never positive) weights to liabilities, whereas "cat fat" liquidity creation assigns positive, negative, and zero weights to different categories of both assets and liabilities, depending on their liquidity. The reason is that the LMI intends to measure the mismatch between the market liquidity of assets and the funding liquidity of liabilities, whereas "cat fat" liquidity creation aims to measure how much liquidity banks create for their customers.

Second, the weights in the LMI are time varying, depending on market conditions and repo haircuts, whereas the weights in the "cat fat" liquidity creation measure are fixed. The use of these time-varying weights makes the LMI challenging to compute: while "cat fat" liquidity creation can be calculated purely based on Call Report data, the LMI requires additional market and repo haircut information. Berger and Bouwman's (2009) securitization-adjusted measure does have time-varying weights for loans, but as explained in Section 4.5, "cat fat" is the preferred measure.

6.5 MARKET MEASURES OF THE LIQUIDITY OF PUBLICLY TRADED EQUITY AND DEBT OF LISTED BANKS AND BANK HOLDING COMPANIES (BHCs)

The discussions in this chapter have so far focused on measures of the liquidity of the bank itself. Those measures can be used for both unlisted banks and for listed banks and BHCs. For listed entities, there are also many market measures that focus on liquidity created by capital markets for the essentially illiquid equity and debt claims on banks and other firms. As explained in Chapter 4, bank equity and some debt are treated as illiquid for the purpose of computing liquidity creation because it is hard or costly for investors to demand liquid funds from the bank on these claims. However, in the case of listed banks and BHCs, investors can obtain liquid funds by selling publicly traded equity and debt. This liquidity is created by the capital markets, rather than the bank or BHC, and so it is not counted in bank liquidity creation or other measures of bank liquidity.

There are numerous market measures of the liquidity of publicly traded equity and debt of listed firms. All these measures try to capture the ease, cost, and time to convert a particular financial instrument into cash. However, there is no consensus in the literature on which of these measures captures market liquidity best. Box 6.3 explains several of these measures and mentions some studies that

---

9. Overnight index swaps (OIS) are interest rate swaps, financial instruments that enable financial institutions to exchange fixed rate interest payments for floating rate payments based on a specified principal amount. For swaps based on the US dollar, the floating rate is the daily effective federal funds rate. The T-Bill – OIS spread is sometimes used as a measure of financial intermediaries' funding conditions. It tends to be small during normal times and widen during financial crises.

BOX 6.3 Market Measures of Liquidity

Liquidity measure	Definition	Studies
Trading volume	The total volume per time interval. Some studies use the dollar volume, i.e., the number of units traded times the transaction price. Trading volume is an indirect but widely used measure of liquidity.	• Chordia, Roll, and Subrahmanyam (2001) • Hasbrouck and Seppi (2001) • Kamara and Koski (2001)
Turnover	Trading volume divided by the outstanding stock of equity or debt for the period. Higher turnover signals greater liquidity.	• Chordia, Roll, and Subrahmanyam (2001)
Depth	The sum of bid and ask volume at a particular point in time. This is also called quantity or volume depth. Some studies use the average depth, which is depth divided by two. Others express depth in dollar terms by multiplying the bid depth times the bid price and the ask depth times the ask price. Some use log depth, the sum of the logarithms of the best bid and ask volume, to improve distributional properties.	• Chordia, Roll, and Subrahmanyam (2001) • Huberman and Halka (2001) • Butler, Grullon, and Weston (2005)
Trading frequency	The total number of transactions per time interval. High trading frequency may indicate a more liquid market.	• Chordia, Roll, and Subrahmanyam (2001) • Hasbrouck and Seppi (2001) • Kamara and Koski (2001)
Quoted bid-ask spread	The difference between the lowest ask and the highest bid price associated with a transaction. This is also called the dollar spread. Some use the logarithm of the spread to improve distributional properties. This spread is often normalized by the midpoint of the quote ("relative spread"). A small spread indicates greater liquidity.	• Amihud and Mendelson (1986) • Christie and Schultz (1998) • Greene and Smart (1999) • Chordia, Roll, and Subrahmanyam (2001) • Hasbrouck and Saar (2002)

(Continued)

Liquidity measure	Definition	Studies
Effective bid-ask spread	The difference between the execution price and the midpoint of the prevailing bid-ask quote. This spread is sometimes multiplied by two to make it better comparable with other spread measures. This spread is sometimes normalized by the midpoint of the prevailing bid-ask quote. A small spread signals greater liquidity.	• Chordia, Roll, and Subrahmanyam (2001)
Roll measure	Roll shows that as prices bounce between bid and ask quotes, a negative return autocorrelation is induced. The Roll measure is the square root of minus one times the daily autocorrelation of returns. A high value denotes low liquidity.	• Roll (1984)
Gibbs measure	The Roll measure is not always well defined since the autocorrelation can be positive. Hasbrouck uses a Gibbs sampler estimate of the Roll measure to overcome this issue. This is called the Gibbs measure. A high value denotes low liquidity.	• Hasbrouck (2009)
Quote slope	The spread divided by log depth: a high value denotes low liquidity. Some studies use the log of the quote slope.	• Hasbrouck and Seppi (2001)
Amihud measure	The daily absolute price change induced by a one dollar trading volume, averaged over all positive-volume days in a time period. This measure is developed from the concept of Kyle's lambda (1985). (The ratio is undefined for zero volume days). Higher ratios signal greater illiquidity.	• Amihud (2002)
Amivest measure	The reciprocal of the Amihund measure. Higher ratios signal greater liquidity.	• Amihud, Mendelson, and Lauterbach (1997)
Pastor and Stambaugh gamma	The coefficient on signed volume (i.e., the sign of the daily return times volume on that day) obtained from regressing daily stock returns on lagged stock returns and lagged signed volume. This measure relies on the principle that volume-related return reversals are stronger when liquidity is lower.	• Pastor and Stambaugh (2003)
Fraction of no-trade days	The fraction of no-trade days, defined as days with zero daily returns, over a given time period. So this measure assumes there is no trading when prices do not move. Higher values signal greater illiquidity.	• Lesmond, Ogden, and Trzcinka (1999) • Bekaert, Harvey, and Lundblad (2007)

have used them. In principle, these can be applied to listed banks' and BHCs' traded equity and debt.

It would be very interesting to examine how the liquidity of listed banks and BHCs relates to the market liquidity of their publicly traded equity and debt. It may be hypothesized that more liquid banks and BHCs would have higher market liquidity for their traded claims because liquid banks and BHCs are less likely to experience problems during a liquidity-related financial crisis. Thus, for example, normalized "cat fat" liquidity creation (which is an inverse measure of bank or BHC liquidity) may be negatively correlated with market liquidity measures because banks and BHCs that create more liquidity per unit of assets are less liquid and are more likely to experience liquidity-related difficulties.

6.6 SUMMARY

This chapter first shows some simple bank liquidity measures used in the literature. It then discusses that "cat fat" liquidity creation normalized by assets may be used as an inverse measure of bank liquidity. It explains the advantages over the simple measures. Normalized liquidity creation is also compared to more complex liquidity measures, the Basel III ratios (the LCR and the NSFR) and the LMI. Finally, market measures of the liquidity of publicly traded equity and debt of listed banks and BHCs are considered. The key takeaways are that normalized "cat fat" liquidity creation can be used as an inverse measure of bank liquidity, that it has advantages over the simple measures of bank liquidity, that it provides different information from the Basel III ratios and the LMI, and that it may be related to market measures of the liquidity of listed banks' and BHCs' equity and debt.

Part III

Financial Crises, Liquidity Creation, and their Links

Chapter 7

Defining and Dating Financial Crises

The focus now turns to the other main topic of the book, financial crises. Many studies define and date financial crises around the world, too many studies to include here. Each of the studies seems to have a different definition of what constitutes a crisis. Allen and Gale (2007) argue that there is no such thing as "THE" theory of crises: "crises are complex phenomena in practice [...] there is no one theory that can explain all aspects of the phenomena of interest" (Allen and Gale, 2007, p. 24). The best way of defining and dating crises depends upon the task at hand and requires some judgment.

This chapter focuses on five important studies, several of which base their definitions and dates at least in part on other studies. Rather than trying to integrate those studies, this chapter discusses these contributions one by one. While there are commonalities among the studies, it will become clear that there are many differences in both the approaches taken to define crises and the actual crisis dates found by each study. For this reason, this chapter includes one table for each study that shows some or all of its crisis dates. The crises defined and dated by the last study are used in the new empirical analyses in this book.

7.1 DEMIRGUC-KUNT AND DETRAGIACHE'S (1998) ANALYSIS OF WORLDWIDE BANKING CRISES FROM 1980 TO 1994

Demirguc-Kunt and Detragiache (1998) analyze the determinants of banking crises in developed and developing countries around the world from 1980 to 1994. They base their classifications of banking crises primarily on five other studies (Drees and Pazarbasioglu, 1995; Sheng, 1995; Caprio and Klingebiel, 1996; Kaminsky and Reinhart, 1996; Lindgren, Garcia, and Saal, 1996), arguing that these studies form a complete survey of "fragility episodes" (periods of bank distress) that took place in the banking sector around the world. They split the 546 fragility episodes identified in those papers into systemic banking crises versus general fragility and localized crises. A fragility episode is defined to be a systemic banking crisis if at least one of the following four conditions holds:

1. "The ratio of nonperforming assets to total assets in the banking system exceeded 10%.
2. The cost of the rescue operation was at least 2% of GDP.
3. Banking sector problems resulted in a large-scale nationalization of banks.
4. Extensive bank runs took place or emergency measures such as deposit freezes, prolonged bank holidays, or generalized deposit guarantees were enacted by the government in response to the crisis."[1] (Demirguc-Kunt and Detragiache, 1998, p. 91)

When none of the conditions holds, they view the fragility episode to be localized and/or minor.

Demirguc-Kunt and Detragiache (1998) apply their definition to 65 countries over the period 1980–1994 and find 31 episodes of systemic banking crises out of the 546 total fragility episodes. Of these, 23 occurred in developing countries (7 in Africa, 7 in Asia, 6 in Latin America, and 3 in the Middle East) and 8 in developed countries, as shown in Table 7.1. Interestingly, for the United States, they find one banking crisis that lasts from 1981 to 1992. They appear to have effectively merged the savings and loan crisis of the 1980s with the bank credit crunch of 1990:Q1–1992:Q4.[2]

Their regression analyses suggest that banking crises are more likely when the macroeconomic environment is weak (low GDP growth and high inflation), real interest rates are high, and in some cases after balance of payments,

---

1. When depositors fear that their bank is (or may become) insolvent, they may try to withdraw their funds. A bank run occurs when a large number of depositors withdraw funds. In such a situation, the bank may be forced to liquidate assets at "fire sale" prices or forego profitable investment opportunities and the bank may fail, even if the fear was unfounded. To prevent this, bank regulators may declare an emergency bank holiday, that is, closure of the bank until it was determined to be solvent. In the United States, the first bank holiday was declared by President Franklin D. Roosevelt shortly after taking office in an attempt to curb bank failures during the Great Depression.

2. The bank credit crunch of 1990:Q1–1992:Q4 is discussed in detail in Section 7.5. The savings and loan (S&L) crisis of the 1980s is discussed here. This crisis was triggered in part by historically high short-term interest rates caused by tight monetary policy from October 1979 to August 1982 that was intended to curb inflation. This caused interest rate risk losses for S&Ls who by law had to hold fixed-rate mortgages. When interest rates went up, the existing stock of these mortgages lost value and wiped out the industry's net worth. The S&Ls also started to have operating losses because they were paying high short-term interest rates on deposits, while receiving low interest rates on long-term fixed-rate mortgages. Eventually, they suffered additional losses as many of the S&Ls engaged in "gambling for resurrection" and took on very risky projects, many of which lost money. Regulators did not have enough resources to close insolvent S&Ls. They engaged in "capital forbearance," relaxing the capital requirements for S&Ls (e.g., by allowing them to count as capital goodwill created when acquiring insolvent institutions), and failing to close S&Ls with little or negative capital. The S&L crisis was essentially ended when the 1989 Financial Institutions Reform, Recovery, and Enforcement Act (FIRREA) was passed to deal with these problems.

TABLE 7.1 Systemic Banking Crises by Country as Defined and Dated by Demirguc-Kunt and Detragiache (1998)

Countries	Banking crisis date	Countries	Banking crisis date
Columbia	1982–1985	Nepal	1988–1994
Finland	1991–1994	Philippines	1981–1987
Guyana	1993–1995	Papua New Guinea	1989–1994
India	1991–1994	Portugal	1986–1989
Indonesia	1992–1994	Senegal	1983–1988
Israel	1983–1984	South Africa	1985
Italy	1990–1994	Sri Lanka	1989–1993
Japan	1992–1994	Sweden	1990–1993
Jordan	1989–1990	Tanzania	1988–1994
Kenya	1993	Turkey	1991, 1994
Mexico	1982, 1994	Uganda	1990–1994
Mali	1987–1989	United States	1981–1992
Malaysia	1985–1988	Uruguay	1981–1985
Nigeria	1991–1994	Venezuela	1993–1994
Norway	1987–1993		

This table shows the 31 systemic banking crises that took place in developing and developed countries around the world between 1980 and 1994 as defined and dated by Demirguc-Kunt and Detragiache (1998).
Source: Table 1 from Demirguc-Kunt and Detragiache (1998).

problems have occurred.[3] They also find that countries with explicit deposit insurance schemes are more vulnerable to banking crises, consistent with the exploitation of moral hazard associated with such schemes.[4]

---

3. A country's balance of payments is a record of all transactions between that country's residents and the rest of the world in a particular period. These transactions include payments for its imports and exports of goods, services, financial capital, and financial transfers. The overall balance of payments will always balance, but imbalances generally exist on individual elements, such as the current account or the capital account. For example, when a country imports more than it exports, its current account balance (which includes its trade balance) will show a deficit. Funding of a current account deficit requires capital inflows or a drawdown in foreign currency reserves. Balance of payments problems may arise when a country operates with an unsustainable current account deficit and rising foreign debt.
4. Explicit deposit insurance schemes have laws that provide deposit guarantees, and specify details such as coverage limits, how depositors are paid in case of bank failure, and the types of deposits and institutions eligible for protection. In contrast, implicit deposit insurance schemes have no formal laws regarding depositor compensation in case of bank failure. The form of protection and reimbursement amounts are discretionary and ad hoc.

7.2   REINHART AND ROGOFF'S (2009) ANALYSIS OF WORLDWIDE FINANCIAL CRISES OVER NEARLY EIGHT CENTURIES

Reinhart and Rogoff (2009) empirically analyze financial crises over nearly eight centuries. For their main analysis, they focus on 66 countries over the period from 1800 or independence to 2008. They take a broad perspective and use two distinct approaches to define crises.

Approach I: Define crises using strict quantitative thresholds:

- Inflation crises (annual inflation exceeding 20%).
- Currency crashes (annual depreciation exceeding 15%).
- Currency debasement (a reduction in the metallic content of coins in circulation of at least 5%).
- The bursting of asset pricing bubbles.

Approach II: Define crises by events:

- Banking crises: defined as one of two types of events:
  - "Bank runs that lead to the closure, merging, or takeover by the public sector of one or more financial institutions (as in Venezuela in 1993 or Argentina in 2001) and
  - If there are no runs, the closure, merging, takeover, or large-scale government assistance of an important financial institution (or group of institutions) that marks the start of a string of similar outcomes for other financial institutions (as in Thailand from 1996 to 1997)." (Reinhart and Rogoff, 2009, p. 10)
- External debt crises (sovereign default, i.e., government's failure to service its debt)
- Domestic debt crises (sovereign default, i.e., government's failure to service its debt, plus bank deposits being frozen and/or being converted into local currency)

For the purpose of this book, their banking crises are most relevant. Reinhart and Rogoff (2009) indicate that they considered alternative approaches to dating banking crises. They argue that banking crises cannot be dated using Approach I since long-run time series data are lacking. For example, it is not possible to use bank stock price data since many banks are private. Dating banking crises using data on bank runs is not feasible either: while it would work well in the 1800s, recent banking crises did not start with problems on the liability side, but with worsening asset quality (e.g., due to dropping real estate prices) or with increased bankruptcies in the nonfinancial sector, and data on nonperforming loans and business failures are often not available.

They therefore use Approach II to date banking crises, but do not view this approach to be perfect for several reasons that they state. It is possible that the actual starting date is earlier than the assigned one since financial problems typically start prior to a bank being closed or merged. It is also possible that the actual starting date is later since the most severe part of a crisis may come later. It is also often not possible to accurately date the end of a crisis.

Table 7.2 Panel A shows that banking crises are common to all the countries in Reinhart and Rogoff's (2009) dataset from 1800 or a country's independence to 2008, and that they often cover substantial portions of the entire time period studied. The lowest percentage of years in banking crises is 1.0% for Russia and the highest is 38.8% for the Central African Republic (see Table 7.2, second column). The percentage for the United States is 13.0%, although the United States has had only two banking crises since 1945. Table 7.2 Panel B dates banking crises using the Reinhart and Rogoff (2009) methodology. For brevity, the sample period is restricted here from 1970 to 2008.

TABLE 7.2 Banking Crises as Defined and Dated by Reinhart and Rogoff (2009)

Panel A: Frequency of banking crises since independence or 1800[a]

Countries	Year of independence (if after 1800)	Percent of years in a banking crisis since independence or 1800	Number of banking crises since independence or 1800	Number of banking crises since independence or 1945
Algeria	1962	6.4	1	1
Angola	1975	17.6	1	1
Argentina	1816	8.8	9	4
Australia	1901	5.7	3	2
Austria		1.9	3	1
Belgium	1830	7.3	10	1
Bolivia	1825	4.3	3	3
Brazil	1822	9.1	11	3
Canada	1867	8.5	8	1
Central African Republic	1960	38.8	2	2
Chile	1818	5.3	7	2
China		9.1	10	1
Colombia	1819	3.7	2	2
Costa Rica	1821	2.7	2	2
Cote d'Ivoire	1960	8.2	1	1
Denmark		7.2	10	1
Dominican Republic	1845	1.2	2	2

(Continued)

TABLE 7.2 Banking Crises as Defined and Dated by Reinhart and Rogoff (2009) *(cont.)*

Panel A: Frequency of banking crises since independence or 1800[a] *(cont.)*

Countries	Year of independence (if after 1800)	Percent of years in a banking crisis since independence or 1800	Number of banking crises since independence or 1800	Number of banking crises since independence or 1945
Ecuador	1830	5.6	2	2
Egypt	1831	5.6	3	2
El Salvador	1821	1.1	2	2
Finland	1917	8.7	5	1
France		11.5	15	1
Germany		6.2	8	2
Greece	1829	4.4	2	1
Guatemala	1821	1.6	3	2
Honduras	1821	1.1	1	1
Hungary	1918	6.6	2	2
India	1947	8.6	6	1
Indonesia	1949	13.3	3	3
Italy		8.7	11	1
Japan		8.1	8	2
Kenya	1963	19.6	2	2
Korea	1945	17.2	3	3
Malaysia	1957	17.3	2	2
Mauritius	1968	2.4	1	1
Mexico	1821	9.7	7	2
Morocco	1956	3.8	1	1
Myanmar	1948	13.1	1	1
Netherlands		1.9	4	1
New Zealand	1907	4.0	1	1
Nicaragua	1821	5.4	1	1
Nigeria	1960	10.2	1	1
Norway	1905	15.7	6	1
Panama	1903	1.9	1	1

TABLE 7.2 Banking Crises as Defined and Dated by Reinhart
and Rogoff (2009) *(cont.)*

Panel A: Frequency of banking crises since independence or 1800[a] *(cont.)*

Countries	Year of independence (if after 1800)	Percent of years in a banking crisis since independence or 1800	Number of banking crises since independence or 1800	Number of banking crises since independence or 1945
Paraguay	1811	3.1	2	1
Peru	1821	4.3	3	1
Philippines	1947	19.0	2	2
Poland	1918	5.6	1	1
Portugal		2.4	5	0
Romania	1878	7.8	1	1
Russia		1.0	2	2
Singapore	1965	2.3	1	1
South Africa	1910	6.3	6	2
Spain		8.1	8	2
Sri Lanka[b]	1948	8.2	1	1
Sweden		4.8	5	1
Taiwan	1949	11.7	5	3
Thailand		6.7	2	2
Tunisia	1957	9.6	1	1
Turkey		2.4	2	2
United Kingdom		9.2	12	4
United States		13.0	13	2
Uruguay	1811	3.1	5	2
Venezuela	1830	6.2	2	2
Zambia	1964	2.2	1	1
Zimbabwe	1965	27.3	1	1

Panel B: Dating of banking crises 1970–2008[c]

Countries	Banking crisis date	Countries	Banking crisis date
Albania	1992	Angola	1992–1996
Algeria	1990–1992	Argentina	Mar 1980–1982

(Continued)

TABLE 7.2 Banking Crises as Defined and Dated by Reinhart and Rogoff (2009) *(cont.)*

Panel B: Dating of banking crises 1970–2008[c] *(cont.)*

Countries	Banking crisis date	Countries	Banking crisis date
Argentina	May 1985	Chile	1976
Argentina	1989–1990	Chile	1980
Argentina	1995	China	1997–1999
Argentina	Mar 2001	Colombia	Jul 1982–1987
Armenia	Aug 1994–1996	Columbia	Apr 1998
Australia	1989–1992	Congo, Dem. Rep. of	1982
Austria		Congo, Dem. Rep. of	1991–1992
Azerbaijan	1995	Congo, Dem. Rep. of	1994–?
Bangladesh	1987–1996	Congo, Rep. of	1992–?
Belarus	1995	Costa Rica	1987
Belgium		Costa Rica	1994–1997
Benin	1988–1990	Cote d'Ivoire	1988–1991
Bolivia	Oct 1987–1988	Croatia	1996
Bolivia	1994	Czech Republic	1991–?
Bolivia	1999	Denmark	Mar 1987–1992
Bosnia and Herzegovina	1992–?	Djibouti	1991–1993
Botswana	1994–1995	Dominican Republic	1996
Brazil	Nov 1985		
Brazil	1990	Dominican Republic	2003
Brazil	Jul 1994–1996		
Brunei	1986	Ecuador	1981
Bulgaria	1995–1997	Ecuador	1994
Burkina Faso	1988–1994	Ecuador	1996
Burundi	1994–1995	Ecuador	Apr 1998–1999
Cameroon	1987–1993	Egypt	Jan 1980–1981
Cameroon	1995–1998	Egypt	Jan 1990–1995
Canada	1983–1985	El Salvador	1989
Cape Verde	1993	El Salvador	1998
Central African Rep	1976–1982	Equatorial Guinea	1983–1985
Central African Rep	1988–1999	Eritrea	1993
Chad	1980s	Estonia	1992–1995
Chad	1992	Estonia	1994

TABLE 7.2 Banking Crises as Defined and Dated by Reinhart and Rogoff (2009) *(cont.)*

Panel B: Dating of banking crises 1970–2008[c] *(cont.)*

Countries	Banking crisis date	Countries	Banking crisis date
Estonia	1998	Israel	Oct 1983
Ethiopia	1994–1995	Italy	1990–1995
Finland	Sept 1991–1994	Jamaica	1994–1997
France	1994–1995	Jamaica	1995–2000
Gabon	1995	Japan	1992–1997
Gambia	1985–1992	Jordan	Aug 1989–1990
Georgia	1991	Kenya	1985–1989
Germany	1977	Kenya	1992
Ghana	1982–1989	Kenya	1993–1995
Ghana	1997	Kenya	1996
Greece	1991–1995	Korea	Jan 1986
Guatemala	1991	Korea	Jul 1997
Guatemala	2001	Kuwait	1983
Guatemala	2006	Kyrgyz Republic	1993
Guinea	1985	Lao People's Dem Rep	Early 1990s
Guinea	1993–1994		
Guinea-Bissau	1995	Latvia	1994–1999
Honduras	2001	Lebanon	1988–1990
Honduras	2002	Lesotho	1988
Honduras	1999	Liberia	1991–1995
Hong Kong	1982	Lithuania	1995–1996
Hong Kong	1983–1986	Macedonia	1993–1994
Hong Kong	1998	Madagascar	1988
Hungary	1991–1995	Malaysia	Jul 1985–1988
Iceland	1985–1986	Malaysia	Sept 1997
Iceland	1993	Mali	1987–1989
India	1993–1996	Mauritania	1984–1993
Indonesia	Nov 1992	Mauritius	1997
Indonesia	1994	Mexico	1981–1982
Indonesia	1997–2002	Mexico	Sept 1982–1991
Ireland		Mexico	Oct 1992
Israel	1977–1983	Mexico	1994–1997

(Continued)

TABLE 7.2 Banking Crises as Defined and Dated by Reinhart and Rogoff (2009) *(cont.)*

Panel B: Dating of banking crises 1970–2008[c] *(cont.)*

Countries	Banking crisis date	Countries	Banking crisis date
Morocco	1983	Slovakia	1991
Mozambique	1987–1995	Slovenia	1993–1994
Myanmar	1996–?	South Africa	Dec 1977–1978
Nepal	1988	South Africa	1989
Netherlands		Spain	1977–1985
New Zealand	1987–1990	Sri Lanka	1989–1993
Nicaragua	1987–1996	Swaziland	1995
Nicaragua	2000–2002	Sweden	Nov 1991–1994
Niger	1983–?	Switzerland	
Nigeria	1992–1995	Taiwan	1997–1998
Nigeria	1997	Taiwan	1983–1984
Norway	1987–1993	Taiwan	Jul 1995
Panama	1988–1989	Tajikistan	1996–?
Papua New Guinea	1989–?	Tanzania	1987
Paraguay	1995–1999	Thailand	Mar 1979
Paraguay	2002	Thailand	Oct 1983–1987
Peru	Apr 1983–1990	Thailand	May 1996
Peru	1999	Togo	1993–1995
Philippines	Jan 1981–1987	Trinidad and Tobago	1982–1993
Philippines	Jul 1997–1998	Tunisia	1991–1995
Poland	1991	Turkey	1982–1985
Portugal		Turkey	Jan 1991
Romania	1990	Turkey	Apr 1994
Russia	Aug 1995	Turkey	2000
Russia	1998–1999	Uganda	1994–2002
Rwanda	1991	Ukraine	1997–1998
Santo Domingo		United Kingdom	1974–1976
Scotland		United Kingdom	1984
Sao Tome and Principe	1991	United Kingdom	1991
Senegal	1988–1991	United Kingdom	1995
Sierra Leone	1990	United States	1984–1991
Singapore	1982	Uruguay	Mar 1971

TABLE 7.2 Banking Crises as Defined and Dated by Reinhart and Rogoff (2009) *(cont.)*

Panel B: Dating of banking crises 1970–2008[c] *(cont.)*

Countries	Banking crisis date	Countries	Banking crisis date
Uruguay	Mar 1981–1984	Vietnam	1997–?
Uruguay	2002	Yemen	1996–?
Venezuela	1978–1986	Zambia	1995
Venezuela	Oct 1993–1995	Zimbabwe	1995

This table focuses on the banking crises experienced in 66 countries since 1800 or a country's independence as defined and dated by Reinhart and Rogoff (2009). Panel A shows the year in which each of the 66 countries became independent (if after 1800), the share of years each country spent in a banking crisis since independence or 1800; the number of banking crises experienced by each country since independence or 1800; and the number of banking crises each country lived through since independence or 1945. Panel B dates the banking crises from 1970 to 2008.

[a]Source: Reinhart and Rogoff (2009): Year of independence – Table 3.1 Column 1; Share of years in default or rescheduling since independence or 1800 – Table 10.1 Column 2; Number of banking crises since independence or 1800 – Tables 10.3 and 10.4 Column 1; Number of banking crises since independence or 1945 – Tables 10.3 and 10.4 Column 2.

[b]Sri Lanka's year of independence does not appear in Table 3.1 in Reinhart and Rogoff (2009). This book's authors added this info.

[c]Source: Reinhart and Rogoff (2009): Data Appendix Table A.4.1.

After reflecting on all the crises, they indicate that it is "certainly clear that again and again, countries, banks, individuals, and firms take on excessive debt in good times without enough awareness of the risks that will follow when the inevitable recession hits" (Reinhart and Rogoff, 2009, p. xxxiii). They argue that government and government-guaranteed debt (implicitly including bank debt due to deposit insurance) causes the most problems because it can accumulate on a grand scale without being monitored by markets. This theme is discussed in Chapter 9, which focuses on the ability of excessive liquidity creation to predict financial crises.

7.3   LAEVEN AND VALENCIA'S (2013) ANALYSIS OF WORLDWIDE FINANCIAL CRISES FROM 1970 TO 2011

Laeven and Valencia (2013) present a comprehensive database on banking crises, sovereign debt crises, and currency crises around the world from 1970 to 2011.[5] They find 147 banking crises, of which 13 are borderline events, over this period, as well as 66 sovereign crises and 211 currency crises. They find that banking crises and sovereign crises are the most costly, followed by currency crises. The discussion here focuses on their banking crises, which is also their main emphasis.

---

5. A sovereign debt crisis refers to the problems caused by a country's actual or perceived inability to pay its public debt. A currency crisis is a situation in which market participants doubt that a country's central bank has enough foreign exchange reserves to maintain the country's fixed exchange rate, causing speculation that may eventually trigger devaluation.

They indicate that the dating of banking crises is often based on the definitions of "events" or subjective criteria, as for example, in Reinhart and Rogoff (2009). They argue that such an approach is flexible, but may be arbitrary. In an attempt to come up with an approach that is less subject to such criticism, they define a banking crisis as an event that meets two conditions:

1. "Significant signs of financial distress in the banking system (as indicated by significant bank runs, losses in the banking system, and/or bank liquidations).
2. Significant banking policy intervention measures in response to significant losses in the banking system." (Laeven and Valencia, 2013, p. 228).

To make sure that a crisis is dated at the first sign of major problems, the first year in which these criteria are met is defined to be the year the crisis became systemic.

Laeven and Valencia (2013) argue that the first condition is in principle sufficient since a banking crisis without policy interventions can cause the fall of the banking sector, but acknowledge that it at times fails to measure distress in a timely and precise way. They therefore add the second condition that focuses on policy interventions as an indirect measure of distress. They consider condition (2) to be sufficient to classify banking crises provided the interventions in the banking sector are significant, that is, when at least three out of the following six interventions are used:

1. "Deposit freezes and/or bank holidays (authorities impose a deposit freeze or declare a bank holiday).
2. Significant bank nationalizations (the government takes over systemically important financial firms, including instances in which it obtains a majority equity stake in these institutions).
3. Bank restructuring gross costs (gross fiscal outlays, including recapitalization costs but excluding liquidity and asset purchases, aimed at restructuring the banking sector are at least 3% of GDP).
4. Extensive liquidity support (exceeds 5% of deposits and liabilities to nonresidents, and equals more than two times its precrisis level).
5. Significant guarantees (the government issues full protection of liabilities or extends guarantees to nondeposit liabilities).
6. Significant asset purchases (the government buys assets totaling at least 5% of GDP)." (Laeven and Valencia, 2013, p. 229).

If there are only two policy interventions, the event is considered to be borderline.[6] In their methodology, the end date of a crisis is the year before both real GDP growth and real credit growth are positive for at least two consecutive years.

Table 7.3 Panel A replicates their Table 1, which focuses on the most recent period from 2007 to 2011. It shows the 17 systemic banking crises and 8 borderline

---

6. There are exceptions when only two interventions are used, a crisis episode is considered to be systemic if the country intervenes on a large scale. This holds if (1) the banking sector's nonperforming loans exceed 20% or bank closures involve at least 20% of the banking sector's assets; or (2) the banking sector's fiscal restructuring costs exceed 5% of GDP.

TABLE 7.3 Systemic Banking Crises 1970–2011 as Defined and Dated by Laeven and Valencia (2013)

Panel A: 17 systemic banking crises and 8 borderline cases from 2007 to 2011[a]

Countries	Start of crisis	Date when systemic	Extensive liquidity support	Significant guarantees on liabilities	Significant restructuring costs	Significant asset purchases	Significant nationalizations
Systemic cases							
Austria	2008	2008	✓	✓	✓		✓
Belgium	2008	2008	✓	✓	✓		✓
Denmark	2008	2009	✓	✓			✓
Germany	2008	2009	✓	✓			✓
Greece	2008	2009	✓	✓	✓		
Iceland	2008	2008	✓	✓	✓		✓
Ireland	2008	2009	✓	✓	✓	✓	✓
Kazakhstan	2008	2010	✓		✓		✓
Latvia	2008	2008	✓	✓	✓		✓
Luxembourg	2008	2008	✓	✓	✓		✓
Mongolia	2008	2009	✓	✓	✓		✓
Netherlands	2008	2008	✓	✓	✓	✓	✓
Nigeria	2009	2011	✓	✓	✓		
Spain	2008	2011	✓	✓	✓		
Ukraine	2008	2009	✓		✓		✓

(Continued)

TABLE 7.3 Systemic Banking Crises 1970–2011 as Defined and Dated by Laeven and Valencia (2013) (cont.)

Panel A: 17 systemic banking crises and 8 borderline cases from 2007 to 2011[a] (cont.)

Countries	Start of crisis	Date when systemic	Extensive liquidity support	Significant guarantees on liabilities	Significant restructuring costs	Significant asset purchases	Significant nationalizations
United Kingdom	2007	2008	✓	✓	✓	✓	✓
United States	2007	2008	✓	✓	✓	✓	✓
Borderline cases							
France	2008		✓	✓			
Hungary	2008		✓	✓			
Italy	2008		✓	✓			
Portugal	2008		✓	✓			
Russia	2008		✓	✓			
Slovenia	2008		✓	✓			
Sweden	2008		✓	✓			
Switzerland	2008		✓			✓	

Panel B: 147 systemic banking crises from 1970 to 2011[b]

Countries	Start	End	Output loss	Countries	Start	End	Output loss
Albania	1994	1994	–	Argentina	1989	1991	12.6
Algeria	1990	1994	41.4	Argentina	1995	1995	0.0
Argentina	1980	1982	58.2	Argentina	2001	2003	70.9

Country				Country			
Armenia	1994	1994	–	Chile	1976	1976	19.9
Austria	2008	–	13.8	Chile	1981	1985	8.6
Azerbaijan	1995	1995	–	China, Mainland	1998	1998	19.5
Bangladesh	1987	1987	0.0	Columbia	1982	1982	47.0
Belarus	1995	1995	–	Columbia	1998	2000	43.9
Belgium	2008	–	19.1	Congo, Dem. Rep. of	1983	1983	1.4
Benin	1988	1992	14.9	Congo, Dem. Rep. of	1991	1994	129.5
Bolivia	1986	1986	49.2	Congo, Dem. Rep. of	1994	1998	79.0
Bolivia	1994	1994	0.0	Congo, Dem. Rep. of	1992	1994	47.4
Bosnia and Herzegovina	1992	1996	–	Costa Rica	1987	1991	0.0
Brazil	1990	1994	62.3	Costa Rica	1994	1995	0.0
Brazil	1994	1998	0.0	Cote d'Ivoire	1988	1992	44.8
Bulgaria	1996	1997	63.1	Croatia	1998	1999	–
Burkina Faso	1990	1994	–	Czech Republic	1996	2000	–
Burundi	1994	1998	121.2	Denmark	2008	–	36.3
Cameroon	1987	1991	105.5	Djibouti	1991	1995	0.0
Cameroon	1995	1997	8.1	Dominican Republic	2003	2004	–
Cape Verde	1993	1993	0.0	Ecuador	1982	1986	98.2
Central African Republic	1976	1976	0.0	Ecuador	1998	2002	23.3
Central African Republic	1995	1996	1.6	Egypt	1980	1980	0.9
Chad	1983	1983	0.0	El Salvador	1989	1990	0.0
Chad	1992	1996	0.0	Equatorial Guinea	1983	1983	0.0

(Continued)

TABLE 7.3 Systemic Banking Crises 1970–2011 as Defined and Dated by Laeven and Valencia (2013) (cont.)

Panel B: 147 systemic banking crises from 1970 to 2011[b] (cont.)

Countries	Start	End	Output loss	Countries	Start	End	Output loss
Eritrea	1993	1993	–	Ireland	2008	–	105.3
Estonia	1992	1994	–	Israel	1977	1977	76.0
Finland	1991	1995	67.3	Italy	2008	–	33.2
France	2008	–	23.6	Jamaica	1996	1998	32.2
Georgia	1991	1995	–	Japan	1997	2001	45.0
Germany	2008	–	12.1	Jordan	1989	1991	106.4
Ghana	1982	1983	14.1	Kazakhstan	2008	–	0.0
Greece	2008	–	43.1	Kenya	1985	1985	23.7
Guinea	1985	1985	0.0	Kenya	1992	1994	50.3
Guinea	1993	1993	0.0	Korea	1997	1998	56.1
Guinea-Bissau	1995	1998	15.7	Kuwait	1982	1985	143.4
Guyana	1993	1993	0.0	Kyrgyz Republic	1995	1999	–
Haiti	1994	1998	37.5	Latvia	1995	1996	–
Hungary	1991	1995	–	Latvia	2008	–	106.2
Hungary	2008	–	39.9	Lebanon	1990	1993	102.2
Iceland	2008	–	41.9	Liberia	1991	1995	–
India	1993	1993	0.0	Lithuania	1995	1996	–
Indonesia	1997	2001	69.0	Luxembourg	2008	–	36.4

Country			
Macedonia, FYR	1993	1995	—
Madagascar	1988	1988	0.0
Malaysia	1997	1999	31.4
Mali	1987	1991	0.0
Mauritania	1984	1984	7.5
Mexico	1981	1985	26.6
Mexico	1994	1996	10.2
Mongolia	2008	—	0.0
Morocco	1980	1984	21.9
Mozambique	1987	1991	0.0
Nepal	1988	1988	0.0
Netherlands	2008	—	23.0
Nicaragua	1990	1993	11.4
Nicaragua	2000	2001	0.0
Niger	1983	1985	97.2
Nigeria	1991	1995	0.0
Nigeria	2009	—	0.0
Norway	1991	1993	5.1
Panama	1988	1989	85.0
Paraguay	1995	1995	15.3
Peru	1983	1983	55.2
Philippines	1983	1986	91.7
Philippines	1997	2001	0.0
Poland	1992	1994	—
Portugal	2008	—	36.8
Romania	1990	1992	—
Russia	1998	1998	—
Russia	2008	—	0.0
Sao Tomé& Principe	1992	1992	1.9
Senegal	1988	1991	5.6
Sierra Leone	1990	1994	34.5
Slovak Republic	1998	2002	44.2
Slovenia	1992	1992	—
Slovenia	2008	—	38.0
Spain	1977	1981	58.5
Spain	2008	—	38.7
Sri Lanka	1989	1991	19.6
Swaziland	1995	1999	45.7
Sweden	1991	1995	31.6
Sweden	2008	—	25.5
Switzerland	2008	—	0.0
Tanzania	1987	1988	0.0
Thailand	1983	1983	24.8
Thailand	1997	2000	109.3
Togo	1993	1994	38.5
Tunisia	1991	1991	1.3

(Continued)

TABLE 7.3 Systemic Banking Crises 1970–2011 as Defined and Dated by Laeven and Valencia (2013) (cont.)

Panel B: 147 systemic banking crises from 1970 to 2011[b] (cont.)

Countries	Start	End	Output loss	Countries	Start	End	Output loss
Turkey	1982	1984	35.0	Uruguay	1981	1985	38.1
Turkey	2000	2001	37.0	Uruguay	2002	2005	66.1
Uganda	1994	1994	0.0	Venezuela	1994	1998	1.2
Ukraine	1998	1999	0.0	Vietnam	1997	1997	0.0
Ukraine	2008	–	0.0	Yemen	1996	1996	12.2
United Kingdom	2007	–	25.6	Zambia	1995	1998	31.6
United States	1988	1988	0.0	Zimbabwe	1995	1999	10.4
United States	2007	–	30.6				

This table shows systemic banking crises that took place worldwide between 1970 and 2011 as defined and dated by Laeven and Valencia (2013). Panel A focuses on the 17 systemic banking crises and 8 borderline cases that occurred between 2007 and 2011. Systemic banking crises (borderline cases) are situations where at least three (exactly two) out of six interventions occurred. The interventions include the following. Extensive liquidity support: liquidity support greater than 5% of deposits and foreign liabilities and at least two times the precrisis levels. Significant guarantees on liabilities: the government issues full protection of liabilities or extends guarantees to nondeposit liabilities. Significant restructuring costs: gross fiscal outlays, including recapitalization costs but excluding liquidity and asset purchases, aimed at restructuring the banking sector exceeding 3% of GDP and excluding liquidity and asset purchases. Significant asset purchases: those exceeding 5% of GDP. Significant nationalizations: the government takes over systemically important financial firms. Deposit freezes and bank holidays: this column is left out as in Laeven and Valencia (2013) as there were no bank holidays and only one deposit freeze from 2007 to 2011. Panel B shows the start year, end year, and output loss of 119 systemic banking crises that occurred from 1970 to 2011. Output loss is the cumulative sum of the differences between actual real GDP and trend real GDP from [T, T+3] as a percent of trend real GDP, with T being the start of the crisis.

[a]Source: Table 1 of Laeven and Valencia (2013).
[b]Source: Table A1 (first four columns only) of Laeven and Valencia (2013).

cases from 2007 to 2011, including the year the crises began, the year they became systemic (i.e., when at least 3 policy interventions were undertaken), and which policy interventions were taken. As in Laeven and Valencia (2013), Panel A does not include a column for measure (1), deposit freezes and bank holidays, since there were no bank holidays during the late 2000s and there was only one deposit freeze (for Parex bank in Latvia). It also does not include crisis end dates, since the condition for a crisis to end had not yet been met in any country by 2011, the sample end year.

Table 7.3 Panel B shows the first four columns of Laeven and Valencia's (2013) Table A1, which covers their full time period, 1970–2011. It lists a total of 147 banking crises. Using their methodology, the United States experienced two banking crises during this time period: a borderline case in 1988 and a systemic banking crisis that lasted from 2007 to at least the end of 2011. Three things are noteworthy. First, their classification does not view the credit crunch of 1990:Q1–1992:Q4 to be a banking crisis. Second, their methodology considers the subprime lending crisis to last at least until 2011, the last year of their sample period. Third, column four shows the output loss caused by each crisis and reveals that the 1988 banking crisis resulted in an output loss of 0.0% of GDP whereas the subprime lending crisis caused a massive output loss of 30.6% of GDP.

7.4   VON HAGEN AND HO'S (2007) 1980–2007 WORLDWIDE BANKING CRISES

Von Hagen and Ho (2007) indicate that the definition of crisis events is a common challenge in empirical studies on banking crises. The literature typically uses the events method, which focuses on visible policy interventions, such as forced mergers, closures, or bailouts. They argue against this method on several grounds, including that sometimes policy interventions are not in response to crises, it is difficult to decide when an intervention is major enough to be called a crisis, and interventions often take place considerably after the crisis is underway. They show that studies that use the events method often yield very different banking crisis dates, even when data sources overlap.

Table 7.4 Panel A reproduces the banking crisis dates from seven studies highlighted by them that use the events method: Lindgren, Garcia, and Saal (1996), Caprio and Klingebiel (1996), Demirguc-Kunt and Detragiache (1998), Glick and Hutchison (2001), Kaminsky and Reinhart (1999), Bordo and Schwartz (2000), and Bordo, Eichengreen, Klingebiel, and Martinez-Peria (2001).

Von Hagen and Ho (2007) use an alternative approach inspired by the literature on currency crises. They argue that a banking crisis occurs when the banking sector's demand for central bank reserves increases dramatically due to: (1) a major drop in loan quality and/or an increase in nonperforming loans; (2) unexpected deposit withdrawals; and (3) a drying up of interbank

TABLE 7.4 Von Hagen and Ho's (2007) Comparison of Banking Crisis Dates of Selected Studies and Their Own Crisis Dates

Panel A: Comparison of banking crises dates of selected studies[a]

	Lindgren, Garcia, and Saal (1996)	Caprio and Klingebiel (1996)	Demirguc-Kunt and Detragiache (1998)	Click and Hutchison (2001)	Kaminsky and Reinhart (1999) (beginning)	Kaminsky and Reinhart (1999) (peak)	Bordo and Schwartz (2000)	Bordo, Eichengreen, Klingebiel, and Martinez-Peria (2001)
Covered period	1980–1996	Late 1970s–1995	1980–1994	1975–1997	1970–1995	1970–1995	1973–1999	1972–1998
Argentina	1980–1982 1989–1990 1995	1980–1982 1989/1990 1995		1980–1982 1989–1990 1995–1997	Mar 1980 May 1985 Dec 1994	Jul 1982 Jun 1989 Mar 1995	1980 1985 1989 1995	1980 1985 1989 1995
Bolivia	1986–1987 1994–present	1986–1987		1986–1987 1994–1997	Oct 1987	Jun 1988	1985	
Brazil	1994–present	1994/1995		1990 1994–1997	Nov 1985 Dec 1994	Nov 1985 Mar 1996	1990 1994	1990 1994
Cameroon	1989–1993 1995–present	1987–		1987–1993 1995–1997				
Chile	1981–1987	1976	No	1976 1981–1983	Sept 1981	Mar 1983	1976 1981	1976 1981
Colombia	1982–1985	1982–1987	1982–1985	1982–1987	Jul 1982	Jun 1985	1982	1982
Cote d'Ivoire	1988–1990	1988–1991						

Country								
Denmark	1987–1992		No	1987–1992	Mar 1987	Jun 1990		1987
Ecuador	1995–present	Early 1980s	No	1980–1982			1981	1981
Egypt	1991–1995	Early 1980s	No	1996–1997				1981
	1993	1990–1991		1980–1985				1990
Finland	1991–1994	1991–1993	1991–1994	1991–1995	Sept 1991	Jun 1992		1991
France	1991–1995	1994/1995	No	1991–1994				1994
Germany	1990–1993	Late 1970s	No	1994–1995				1977
Ghana	1983–1989	1982–1989		1978–1979				
				1982–1989				
Greece	1991–1995		No	1997				
				1991–1995				
Iceland	1985–1986			1985–1986				
	1993			1993				
India	1991–present	1994/1995	1991–1994	1993–1997				
Indonesia	1992–present	1994	1992–1994	1994	Nov 1992	Nov 1992	1992	
				1997			1997	
Ireland	1985		No	No				
Israel	1983–1984	1977–1983	1983–1984	1990–1995	Oct 1983	Jun 1984	1977	
Italy	1990–1995		1990–1994	1994–1997				
Jamaica	1994–present		No					
Japan	1992–present	1990s	1992–1994	1992–1997				1992
Kenya	1993	1985–1989	1993	1985–1989				

(Continued)

TABLE 7.4 Von Hagen and Ho's (2007) Comparison of Banking Crisis Dates of Selected Studies and Their Own Crisis Dates (cont.)

Panel A: Comparison of banking crises dates of selected studies[a] (cont.)

	Lindgren, Garcia, and Saal (1996)	Caprio and Klingebiel (1996)	Demirguc-Kunt and Detragiache (1998)	Glick and Hutchison (2001)	Kaminsky and Reinhart (1999) (beginning)	Kaminsky and Reinhart (1999) (peak)	Bordo and Schwartz (2000)	Bordo, Eichengreen, Klingebiel, and Martinez-Peria (2001)
Covered period	1980–1996	Late 1970s–1995	1980–1994	1975–1997	1970–1995	1970–1995	1973–1999	1972–1998
Kenya		1992		1992–1997				
		1993–1995						
Malaysia	1985–1988	1985–1988	1985–1988	1985–1988	Jul 1985	Aug 1986	1985	1985
				1997				1998
Mexico	1982	1981/1982	1982	1981–1991	Sept 1982	Jun 1984	1981	1981
	1994–present	1995	1994	1995–1997	Oct 1992	Mar 1996	1994	1994
Nepal	Late 1980s to present	1988	1988–1994	1988–1994				
New Zealand	1989–1990	1987–1990	No	1987–1990			1987	1987
Nigeria	1991–1995	1990s	1991–1994	1993–1997				1991
Norway	1987–1993	1987–1989	1987–1993	1987–1993	Nov 1998	Oct 1991		1987
Paraguay	1995–present	1995	No	1995–1997			1995	1995
Peru	1983–1990		No	1983–1990	Mar 1983	Apr 1983	1983	1983
Philippines	1981–1987	1981–1987	1981–1987	1981–1987	Jan 1981	Jun 1985	1981	1981
				1997				1998

Country								
Portugal	1983–1988			1986–1989				No
Senegal		1988–1991	1983–1988	1986–1989			1982	1982
Singapore	1985	1982	No	1982			1977	1977
South Africa	1989–present	1977	1985	1977				1985
				1985				
				1989				
Spain	1977–1985	1977–1985		1977–1985	Nov 1978	Jan 1983		1977
Sweden	1990–1993	1991	1990–1993	1990–1993	Nov 1991	Sept 1992		
Thailand	1983–1987	1983–1987	No	1983–1987	Mar 1979	Mar 1979	1983	
				1997	Oct 1983	Jun 1985	1997	
Turkey	1982	1982–1985		1982–1985	Jan 1991	Mar 1991	1982	
1991	1991		1991	1991			1991	
1994	1994		1994				1994	
Uganda	1990–present	1994	1990–1994	1994–1995				
UK		1974–1976	No	1994–1997				
				1975–1976				
				1984				
US	1980–1992	1984–1991	1981–1992	1981–1984	Mar 1971	Dec 1971	1981	
Uruguay	1981–1985	1981–1984	1981–1985	1978–1986	Mar 1981	Jun 1985	1980	
Venezuela	1994–present	1980–?	1993–1994	1994–1997	Oct 1993	Aug 1994	1993	
		1994/1995						

(Continued)

TABLE 7.4 Von Hagen and Ho's (2007) Comparison of Banking Crisis Dates of Selected Studies and Their Own Crisis Dates (*cont.*)

Panel B: Banking crisis dates of 47 countries[b]

Countries	Window width = 8Q	Countries	Window width = 8Q
Austria	No crisis	Mexico	1989Q2
Burundi	1998Q4	Nepal	No crisis
Chile	1984Q4	Netherlands	1986Q4
Cyprus	1986Q1	New Zealand	1983Q1
Denmark	1993Q1	Niger	1982Q3
Ecuador	1984Q2	Nigeria	1996Q3
Egypt	1990Q4	Papua New Guinea	1981Q2
El Salvador	1987Q4	Peru	1990Q2
Finland	1989Q4	Portugal	1985Q3
France	1981Q3	Senegal	1995Q4
Germany	1988Q4	Seychelles	1982Q2
Greece	1981Q2	South Africa	1990Q1
Guatemala	1991Q4	Spain	1983Q3
Honduras	1985Q4	Sri Lanka	1983Q3
India	1999Q4	Swaziland	1982Q1
Indonesia	1998Q1	Sweden	1992Q3
Ireland	1992Q4	Switzerland	1998Q4
Israel	1984Q3	Thailand	1998Q1

Italy	1992Q3		Togo	1980Q3
Jamaica	1997Q1		Turkey	2001Q1
Japan	1998Q3		Uganda	1989Q3
Kenya	1993Q2		United States	1981Q3
Korea	1998Q1		Uruguay	1983Q1
			Venezuela	1997Q4

This table shows two panels that contain tables from Von Hagen and Ho (2007). Panel A compares banking crisis dates of seven studies that use the events method, which focuses on visible policy interventions, such as forced mergers, closures, or bailouts. The studies include Lindgren, Garcia, and Saal (1996), Caprio and Klingebiel (1996), Demirguc-Kunt and Detragiache (1998), Glick and Hutchison (2001), Kaminsky and Reinhart (1999), Bordo and Schwartz (2000), and Bordo, Eichengreen, Klingebiel, and Martinez-Peria (2001). A blank indicates that the study did not assess crises in that country and a "No" indicates that the study did assess that country and found no crises. Panel B contains the dates of 47 banking crises as identified by Von Hagen and Ho's index of money market pressure, IMP, a weighted average of the changes in the ratio of reserves to bank deposits and changes in the short-term real interest rate, between 1980 and 2001.
aSource: Table 1 of Von Hagen and Ho (2007).
bSource: Table 8 of Von Hagen and Ho (2007).

lending.[7] The central bank can respond by: (i) increasing the short-term interest rate; and/or (ii) injecting more reserves into the banking system. Building on this, they develop an index of money market pressure, IMP, which is a weighted average of changes in the ratio of reserves to bank deposits and changes in the short-term real interest rate. They determine the beginning of a banking crisis in a country as the period in which the IMP is higher than the 98.5th percentile of the sample distribution of that country's IMP and the IMP increased by at least 5% since the last period. Thus, only exceptional events are classified as crises. They use data from 47 countries from 1980 to 2001 to classify banking crises (see Table 7.4 Panel B) and show that major recessions, high inflation, large fiscal deficits, overvalued currency, and explicit deposit insurance help to predict such crises.

7.5   BERGER AND BOUWMAN'S (2013) FINANCIAL CRISES IN THE UNITED STATES FROM 1984:Q1 TO 2010:Q4

Berger and Bouwman (2013) focus on financial crises in the United States from 1984:Q1 to 2010:Q4 to study the effect of bank capital on performance during financial crises and normal times. They recognize that not all financial crises are alike. A crisis that originates in the banking sector could differ in impact from one that originates in the capital markets. They classify two banking crises (crises that originate in the banking sector): the credit crunch of the early 1990s (1990:Q1–1992:Q4) and the subprime lending crisis (2007:Q3–2009:Q4). They also classify three market crises (crises that originate outside banking in financial markets): the 1987 stock market crash (1987:Q4); the Russian debt crisis and Long-Term Capital Management (LTCM) bailout of 1998 (1998:Q3–1998:Q4); and the bursting of the dot.com bubble and the September 11 terrorist attacks of the early 2000s (2000:Q2–2002:Q3).[8]

---

7. In a theoretical study, Flannery (1996) similarly focuses on bank liquidity shocks. He analyzes the operation of a large-value payment system during normal times and financial crises. Such systems almost necessarily involve interbank credit, and therefore the possibility of systemic risk during a financial crisis. He defines a financial crisis as one with two important features, (1) "at least a few large banks (and/or perhaps many small ones) experience a liquidity shock" and (2) "the initial liquidity shock makes private lenders uncertain about the accuracy (appropriateness) of their traditional underwriting techniques and judgments." (Flannery, 1996, p. 806). He finds that discount window funds (i.e., funds obtained by banks from the Federal Reserve to meet temporary liquidity shortages) are largely unnecessary during normal times, but during financial crises, they become important because of the impairment of private lenders.

8. Several other studies use some or all of these financial crises to address various issues. Lee ▶ (2014) examines how the last three financial crises affected the economic value of US financial conglomerates. Temesvary (2015) also focuses on the last three crises and addresses how bank and foreign market characteristics affect US banks' foreign market entry and exit decisions in normal times and financial crises. Saheruddin (2014) examines how the specialness of bank loans varies between normal times and financial crises. Berger and Bouwman (2015) study the effects of monetary policy during normal times and financial crises (discussed in Chapter 13) and analyze whether high-detrended aggregate bank liquidity creation helps predict financial crises (discussed in Chapter 9).

Table 7.5 shows the timing of the five crises and Box 7.1 describes these crises in detail.

TABLE 7.5 Five Financial Crises Defined and Dated by Berger and Bouwman (2013)

Crisis	Dates
Banking crises	
Credit crunch	1990:Q1–1992:Q4
Subprime lending crisis	2007:Q3–2009:Q4
Market crises	
Stock market crash	1987:Q4
Russian debt crisis/LTCM bailout	1998:Q3–1998:Q4
Bursting of the dot.com bubble and Sept 11 terrorist attack	2000:Q2–2002:Q3

This table shows the two banking crises (crises that originate in the banking sector) and the three market crisis (crises that originate in the nonbank financial market).

7.6   FINANCIAL CRISES USED IN THE EMPIRICAL ANALYSES IN THIS BOOK

For the empirical analyses in this book, the choice of what is and is not a crisis period is important. All of the summary statistics and new empirical analyses in this book use quarterly data on US commercial banks over the 31-year-period 1984:Q1–2014:Q4. The period starts in 1984:Q1 because quarterly bank Call Report data provide sufficient detail on both on- and off-balance-sheet activities needed to calculate liquidity creation from that moment onward. It ends in 2014:Q4, the last quarter of Call Reports available at the time of this writing. The choice is then to determine which crises occurred in the United States over this time period.

While Demirguc-Kunt and Detragiache (1998), Reinhart and Rogoff (2009), and Laeven and Valencia (2013) focus on policy interventions to help define the crises, the definition of crises in this book follows Von Hagen and Ho's (2007) suggestion not to do so. Unlike Von Hagen and Ho (2007), however, the book does not limit itself to liquidity shocks because many important US crises do not involve liquidity problems for banks. For example, the US credit crunch of

◀ Berger and Sedunov (2015) examine the real effects of bank liquidity creation per capita on state GDP per capita during normal times and these financial crises (discussed in Chapter 15). Berger, El Ghoul, Guedhami, and Roman (2015) studies how internationalization of US banks affects bank risk during normal times and these financial crises. Roman (2015) studies the effects of shareholder activism on bank performance and risk during normal times and these financial crises.

BOX 7.1 Description of Five US Financial Crises From 1984:Q1 to 2010:Q4

This box describes the two banking and three market crises classified by Berger and Bouwman (2013) that occurred in the United States from 1984:Q1 to 2010:Q4, and is adapted from that paper.

Two banking crises

Credit crunch (1990:Q1–1992:Q4): During the first three years of the 1990s, bank commercial and industrial lending declined in real terms, particularly for small banks and for small loans. The ascribed causes of the credit crunch include a fall in bank capital from the loan loss experiences of the late 1980s,[a] increases in bank-leverage requirements, implementation of Basel I risk-based capital standards, and enforcement of Prompt Corrective Action rules of the FDIC Improvement Act (FDICIA) during this time period, an increase in supervisory toughness evidenced in worse examination ratings for given bank conditions, and reduced loan demand because of macroeconomic and regional recessions.[b] The existing research provides some support for each of these hypotheses (e.g., Bernanke and Lown, 1991; Bizer, 1993; Berger and Udell, 1994; Hancock, Laing, and Wilcox, 1995; Peek and Rosengren, 1995a, b; Thakor, 1996; and Berger, Kyle, and Scalise, 2001).

Subprime lending crisis (2007:Q3–2009:Q4): The subprime lending crisis took shape in 2007:Q3 when losses on securities backed by subprime mortgages started to spread to other markets, including the syndicated loan market, the interbank lending market, and the commercial paper market. Many banks experienced substantial losses in capital. Massive loan losses at Countrywide resulted in a takeover by Bank of America. Bear Stearns suffered a fatal loss of confidence among its financiers and was sold at a fire-sale price to JPMorgan Chase, with the Federal Reserve Bank of New York guaranteeing $29 billion in potential losses. Washington Mutual became the biggest financial institution failure in US history. JPMorgan Chase purchased the banking business while the rest of the organization filed for bankruptcy. IndyMac Bank was seized by the FDIC after it suffered substantial losses and depositors had started to run on the bank. The FDIC sold all deposits and most of the assets to OneWest Bank, FSB, and incurred an estimated loss of about $4 billion – $8 billion. These large bank failures plus the failure of many small banks resulted in the FDIC Deposit Insurance Fund falling into a deficit position. The Federal Reserve also intervened in some unprecedented ways in the market, including quantitative easing.[c] It increased the maturities of and lowered the rates charged on discount window loans, and instituted the Term Auction Facility (TAF) to encourage banks to borrow more from the Federal Reserve.[d] It also extended its safety-net privileges to investment banks and one insurance company (AIG), and intervened in the commercial paper market. Under the TARP bailout program begun in October 2008, the Treasury initially set aside $250 billion out of its $700 billion bailout package (TARP program) to enhance capital ratios of selected banks. This included a total of $125 billion essentially forced on eight large banking organizations and Merrill Lynch on October 28, 2008. Other banks completed formal applications and voluntarily received TARP funds over the rest of 2008 and 2009. By the end of 2009, the US Treasury via TARP had infused capital of $204.9 billion into 709 banking organizations. The subprime lending crisis was considered to be over by 2009:Q4 since by this time, much of the TARP funds invested in financial institutions had been repaid, order had been restored to most of the financial markets, and the Federal Reserve shortly thereafter began rolling back expansions to the discount window and concluded the TAF auctions. For additional details on the subprime lending crisis, see review papers by Lo (2012) and Thakor (2015).

Three market crises

Stock market crash (1987:Q4): On Monday, October 19, 1987, the stock market crashed, with the S&P500 index falling about 20%. During the years before the crash, the level of the stock market had increased dramatically, causing some concern that the market had become overvalued.[e] A few days before the crash, two events occurred that may have helped precipitate the crash: (1) legislation was enacted to eliminate certain tax benefits associated with financing mergers; and (2) information was released that the trade deficit was above expectations. Both events seemed to have added to the selling pressure and a record trading volume on Oct 19, in part caused by program trading, overwhelmed many systems.[f]

Russian debt crisis/LTCM bailout (1998:Q3–1998:Q4): Since its inception in March 1994, hedge fund Long Term Capital Management (LTCM) followed an arbitrage strategy that was avowedly "market neutral," designed to make money regardless of whether prices were rising or falling. When Russia defaulted on its sovereign debt on August 17, 1998, investors fled from other government paper to the safe haven of US treasuries. This flight to liquidity caused an unexpected widening of spreads on supposedly low-risk portfolios. By the end of August 1998, LTCM's capital had dropped to $2.3 billion, less than 50% of its December 1997 value, with assets standing at $126 billion. In the first three weeks of September, LTCM's capital dropped further to $600 million without shrinking the portfolio. Banks began to doubt its ability to meet margin calls.[g] To prevent a potential systemic meltdown triggered by the collapse of the world's largest hedge fund, the Federal Reserve Bank of New York helped organize a $3.5 billion bailout by LTCM's major creditors on September 23, 1998. In 1998:Q4, several large banks had to take substantial write-offs as a result of losses on their investments.

Bursting of the dot.com bubble and Sept 11 terrorist attack (2000:Q2–2002:Q3): The dot.com bubble was a speculative stock price bubble that was built up during the mid-1990s to early 2000s. During this period, many internet-based companies, commonly referred to as "dot.coms," were founded. Rapidly increasing stock prices and widely available venture capital (early stage equity financing provided to high-potential growth startups) created an environment in which many of these companies seemed to focus largely on increasing market share. At the height of the boom, many dot.coms were able to go public and raise substantial amounts of money even if they had never earned any profits, and in some cases had not even earned any revenues. On March 10, 2000, the Nasdaq composite index peaked at more than double its value just a year before, triggering the bursting of the bubble. Many dot.coms subsequently ran out of capital and were acquired or filed for bankruptcy (examples of the latter include WorldCom and Pets.com). The US economy started to slow down and business investments

(Continued)

began falling. The September 11, 2001 terrorist attacks may have exacerbated the stock market downturn by adversely affecting investor sentiment. By 2002:Q3, the Nasdaq index had fallen by 78%, wiping out $5 trillion in market value of mostly technology firms.

a. These loan losses were due in part due to the bursting of commercial real-estate bubbles in the late 1980s as well as undue competition from Savings & Loans who were gambling for resurrection during the S&L crisis (see footnote 2 on the S&L crisis in Section 7.1).

b. FDICIA was passed in 1991 to improve bank supervision and to reduce the cost of resolving failing institutions. Section 38 of FDICIA requires federal banking regulators to take "prompt corrective action" (PCA) in case of capital deficiencies at insured depository institutions. The PCA specifies a set of mandatory actions that regulators must take and a set of discretionary actions that regulators may take as banks fall into lower capital ranges. The mandatory actions include the filing of an acceptable capital restoration plan, dividend restrictions, and restrictions on accepting new deposits at a substantially higher yield than the yield paid on similar deposits. If capital is in the lower ranges, institutions may also not be allowed to pay bonuses, increase senior executive pay, or pay interest or principal on subordinated debt.

c. The term "quantitative easing" was first used by the Bank of Japan in 2001. Quantitative easing is a form of monetary policy used by central banks to stimulate the economy when ordinary monetary policy tools are ineffective. For example, central banks typically first try to stimulate the economy by buying short-term government bonds in an attempt to reduce short-term interest rates. When those rates are (close to) zero, this does not work. Central banks can then use quantitative easing: they can buy financial assets with longer maturities from commercial banks and other institutions, thereby raising the prices of these assets and lowering their yield (i.e., lowering longer-term interest rates).

d. Since its inception in 1913, the Federal Reserve has served as a lender of last resort (LOLR) to US banks by providing banks that face temporary liquidity shortages with short-term funds through the discount window. During the subprime lending crisis of 2007:Q3–2009:Q4, it increased the maturity of discount window funds initially to 30 and later to 90 days. To address a concern that discount window usage may be associated with "stigma" (usage can be perceived as a sign of weakness), the Federal Reserve created the Term Auction Facilities (TAF), a series of auctions for (28- or 84-day) funds available to eligible depository institutions in generally sound financial condition.

e. For example, "Raging bull, stock market's surge is puzzling investors: When will it end?" on page 1 of the *Wall Street Journal*, January 19, 1987.

f. Program trading is a computerized trading strategy used by large institutional investors in which large-volume trades of at least 15 stocks are entered directly into the market's computer system and executed automatically.

g. An investor who buys securities with a mix of own funds and funds borrowed from the broker, is buying on margin. Buying on margin magnifies gains if the security price increases, but also magnifies losses if the security price falls. For example, if the investor buys $100 in securities financed half with own funds and half with borrowed funds, and the securities' value increases to $125, the investor makes a 50% profit; if the value drops to $75, the investor makes a 50% loss. In addition, when the security price falls, the broker may send a margin call requiring the investor to contribute funds to restore the original equity (ownership) balance or close out the position. If the margin call cannot be met, the broker can close out the open position. Margin calls got their name because the broker would call the investor by phone.

1990:Q1–1992:Q4 was caused by capital shocks and increases in regulatory toughness, not a liquidity shock. Like Demirguc-Kunt and Detragiache (1998) and Laeven and Valencia (2013), the book includes banking crises, but also includes market crises, which often involve significant financial dislocations and can result in recessions (as occurred in the early 2000s after the bursting of the dot.com bubble and September 11 terrorist attack). Like Laeven and Valencia (2013), the book includes the financial crisis that started in 2007 in the United States, but does not include sovereign and currency crises, because none of these occurred in the United States during the sample period. Finally, it is important to include a sufficient number of crises, more than the one or two crises in the United States that most of the studies find over this period, to draw more general conclusions about financial crises.

For these reasons, the book uses the five banking and market crises classified in Berger and Bouwman (2013). While their data set ends in 2010:Q4, the book's data goes through 2014:Q4, but does not add additional financial crises since none occurred in the United States in the last four years of the sample period.[9]

7.7 SUMMARY

This chapter first outlines a number of approaches used in the literature to define and date financial crises. Some of them rely on the use of policy interventions and some focus on liquidity shocks. It then picks one that best suits the empirical analyses shown in this book, which focuses on the United States over the period 1984:Q1–2014:Q4. The chosen approach allows for the examination of crises that do not have significant policy interventions, and are generated by banking and market shocks that do not necessarily involve liquidity problems. The key takeaway is that there is no single formula or set of rules for defining and dating financial crises that is best for every situation – some judgment is needed.

---

9. There was a financial crisis after 2010:Q4 in Europe that affected some US banking organizations with overseas operations, but this crisis did not have widespread effects in the United States.

Chapter 8

How Much Liquidity Do Banks Create During Normal Times and Financial Crises?

This chapter shows how aggregate US bank liquidity creation has changed from 1984:Q1 to 2014:Q4, and how it behaves during normal times and financial crises over this time period. It examines "cat fat" liquidity creation and its components, on- and off-balance sheet liquidity creation, for the entire commercial banking sector and also separately by bank size class. It analyzes the dollar amount of aggregate bank liquidity creation and the dollar amount normalized by gross total assets (GTA). The evolution of two alternative liquidity creation measures, takedown probability-adjusted and securitization-adjusted "cat fat" liquidity creation (introduced in Sections 4.4 and 4.5, respectively) are also shown. Finally, the evolution of "cat fat" liquidity creation is compared to that of alternative measures of bank output (GTA, TA, and gross lending).

8.1 SAMPLE DESCRIPTION AND NUMBERS OF BANKS OVER TIME

For every bank in the United States, quarterly Call Report data are obtained over the 31-year period from 1984:Q1 to 2014:Q4. As discussed in Chapter 7, the start of the period is when the Call Report began to have sufficiently detailed information on both on- and off-balance sheet items to compute bank liquidity creation, and the end of the period is the most recent quarter available as of this writing. To take out the effect of inflation, all financial values are put into real 2014:Q4 dollars using the implicit GDP price deflator.[1] A bank is kept in the

---

1. The implicit price deflator is from the FRED database hosted by the Federal Reserve Bank of St. Louis (http://research.stlouisfed.org/fred2/data/GDPDEF.txt) as of early May 2015. At that point, the price deflator was 55.257 in 1984:Q1 and 108.618 in 2014:Q4. If a bank's assets in nominal terms were $2.5 billion in 1984:Q1 and $6 billion in 2014:Q4, that bank's assets in real terms would be $2.5 billion × (108.618/55.257) = $4.9 billion in 1984:Q1 and $6 billion × (108.618/108.618) = $6 billion in 2014:Q4. All amounts, including bank size cutoffs, are based on real dollars.

sample if it: (1) has a commercial bank charter;[2] (2) has commercial real estate or commercial and industrial loans outstanding; (3) has deposits; and (4) has GTA exceeding $25 million. The first three requirements ensure that the sample only includes commercial banks. The fourth requirement drops institutions that are so small that they are unlikely to be viable. The sample thus includes almost all commercial banks in the United States over the 31-year period.

Following standard practice in banking and liquidity creation analyses, the banks are divided into size classes because banks of different sizes differ significantly in portfolio composition and performance (e.g., Kashyap, Rajan, and Stein, 2002; and Berger, Miller, Petersen, Rajan, and Stein, 2005), and in liquidity creation (e.g., Berger and Bouwman, 2009).[3] Three size classes are used. Small banks have GTA up to $1 billion, medium banks have GTA exceeding $1 billion and up to $3 billion, and large banks have GTA exceeding $3 billion. As explained in Section 3.2, the definition of small banks conforms to the usual notion of "community banks." The $3 billion cutoff for GTA divides the remaining observations close to in half.[4] These splits are performed each quarter, meaning that banks can switch size classes over time.

Figure 8.1 shows the total numbers of US commercial banks and these numbers split into small, medium, and large banks from 1984:Q1 to 2014:Q4. The figure also shows vertical dashed lines to demarcate the five financial crises discussed in Section 7.5 – the 1987 stock market crash, the credit crunch of the early 1990s, the Russian debt crisis plus LTCM bailout in 1998, the bursting of the dot.com bubble plus September 11, and the subprime lending crisis of the late 2000s.

The numbers of banks for the beginning and end of the sample period can also be seen in Table 8.1, which is discussed in further detail in Section 8.2. There are several striking observations. First, the total number of banks has dropped dramatically by about 55% from 11,940 in 1984:Q1 to 5,402 in 2014:Q4. The decline in the number of banks is steepest from the late 1980s through the 1990s, when the effects of intrastate and interstate banking deregulation mostly took place.[5] Second, the consolidation of the banking industry generally occurred during both normal times and financial crises. Third, throughout the time period, the vast majority of commercial banks are small, although the percentage

---

2. A bank has a commercial bank charter if RSSD9048 = 200. This requirement is used to avoid an artificial increase in both the number of banks and liquidity creation in 2012:Q1. As of that date, thrifts have been required by the Dodd-Frank Act to file quarterly Call Reports instead of Thrift Financial Reports.

3. The Call Report examples of JPMorgan Chase and Community Bank of El Dorado Springs in Chapter 3 also make it clear that large and small banks have very different portfolios.

4. Berger and Bouwman (2009, 2013) also use these cutoffs. Their summary statistics differ slightly from the ones shown here because the financial data are deflated using different base years and because they did not impose the commercial bank charter restriction. Another reason for the differences is that both the Call Report data and the GDP deflator are revised over time and the data for these papers were drawn at different times from each other and from the data used here.

5. Both types of deregulation are discussed further in Section 15.5.

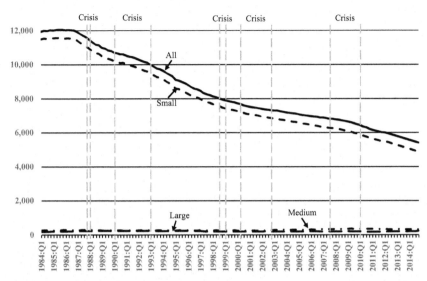

FIGURE 8.1 Numbers of US commercial banks over time. This figure shows the total numbers of US commercial banks and these numbers split into small/medium/large banks, i.e., banks with gross total assets or GTA up to $1 billion/$1 billion – $3 billion/exceeding $3 billion, from 1984:Q1 to 2014:Q4. GTA equals total assets plus the allowance for loan and lease losses and the allocated transfer risk reserve (a reserve for certain foreign loans). Five financial crises are demarcated with vertical dashed lines – the 1987 stock market crash, the credit crunch of the early 1990s, the Russian debt crisis plus LTCM bailout in 1998, the bursting of the dot.com bubble plus September 11, and the subprime lending crisis of the late 2000s.

of small banks has dropped from 96.3% to 90.0%. Clearly, the consolidation of the banking industry has greatly reduced the number of small banks, while medium and large banks actually increased in numbers.

8.2 "CAT FAT" LIQUIDITY CREATION AND ITS COMPONENTS OVER TIME

As shown in Table 8.1, banks created "cat fat" liquidity of $1.492 trillion in 1984:Q1, and this quadrupled in real terms to $5.929 trillion in 2014:Q4. At both times, most of the liquidity was created by large banks, 76.3% and 89.0%, respectively, despite making up only 1.5% and 4.1%, respectively, of the numbers of banks.

Interestingly, "cat fat" liquidity creation normalized by GTA went up considerably over time for small and medium banks. This suggests that these banks have become more illiquid over time.

It is also notable that large and medium banks are less liquid than small banks. At the end of the sample period, medium and large banks create "cat fat" liquidity per dollar of GTA of $0.46 and $0.41, respectively, compared to $0.37 for small banks. As shown in the following columns, this appears to be due to

TABLE 8.1 Summary Statistics

Panel A: Summary statistics as of 1984:Q1

	N	"Cat fat" liquidity creation		On-balance sheet liquidity creation		Off-balance sheet liquidity creation		Takedown probability-adjusted "cat fat" liquidity creation		Securitization-adjusted "cat fat" liquidity creation		GTA	TA	Gross loans
		$B	Normalized	$B	Normalized	$B	Normalized	$B	Normalized	$B	Normalized	$B	$B	$B
All	11,940	1,492	0.32	877	0.19	615	0.13	1,065	0.23	1,832	0.40	4,614	4,583	2,683
Large	183	1,138	0.41	581	0.21	558	0.20	752	0.27	1,293	0.47	2,748	2,728	1,675
Medium	260	119	0.28	92	0.21	28	0.06	100	0.23	161	0.37	432	429	246
Small	11,497	234	0.16	204	0.14	30	0.02	213	0.15	378	0.26	1,435	1,426	761

Panel B: Summary statistics as of 2014:Q4

	N	"Cat fat" liquidity creation		On-balance sheet liquidity creation		Off-balance sheet liquidity creation		Takedown probability-adjusted "cat fat" liquidity creation		Securitization-adjusted "cat fat" liquidity creation		GTA	TA	Gross loans
		$B	Normalized	$B	Normalized	$B	Normalized	$B	Normalized	$B	Normalized	$B	$B	$B
All	5,402	5,929	0.41	2,899	0.20	3,030	0.21	3,771	0.26	7,120	0.50	14,378	14,267	7,490
Large	223	5,274	0.41	2,354	0.18	2,920	0.23	3,193	0.25	6,396	0.50	12,744	12,649	6,444
Medium	315	234	0.46	192	0.38	42	0.08	205	0.40	252	0.50	508	504	333
Small	4,864	421	0.37	353	0.31	68	0.06	373	0.33	472	0.42	1,125	1,114	714

This table shows summary statistics for "cat fat" liquidity creation, its components (on- and off-balance sheet liquidity creation), two alternative liquidity creation measures (takedown probability-adjusted and securitization-adjusted "cat fat" liquidity creation), and alternative output measures (gross total assets or GTA, total assets or TA, and gross loans). GTA equals total assets plus the allowance for loan and lease losses and the allocated transfer risk reserve (a reserve for certain foreign loans). It gives the number of observations (N), the amounts in $ billion, and for the liquidity creation measures it also gives the amounts normalized by GTA.

greater normalized off-balance liquidity creation for large banks and greater normalized on-balance sheet liquidity creation for medium banks.

The table also shows that about half of all liquidity in the banking sector is created off of the balance sheet, with off-balance liquidity creation slightly exceeding on-balance liquidity creation at the end of the period. Although not shown, most of the off-balance sheet liquidity creation is due to loan commitments.

Figure 8.2 Panels A–C show "cat fat" liquidity creation and its on- and off-balance sheet components for all 104 quarters of the time period for all banks and for each of the size classes, as well as the crisis demarcation lines. Interestingly, overall liquidity creation in Figure 8.2 Panel A goes up almost the entire time period, often quite steeply, driven primarily by the large banks. Exceptions are that liquidity creation goes down during the two banking crises, particularly during the subprime lending crisis of 2007:Q3–2009:Q4. In both cases, liquidity creation was on an upward trend beforehand, and continued to grow somewhat into the crisis before falling later in the crisis.

Although it is difficult to discern here, "cat fat" liquidity creation tends to increase more before financial crises. This will become clearer in Section 9.2, where it is discussed that after the trend is removed, liquidity creation tends to be high before such crises.

Figure 8.2 Panels B and C illustrate the main reasons for the liquidity creation pattern during the subprime lending crisis. Most of the drop in liquidity creation during this crisis was likely due to borrowers drawing down their loan commitments, which decreased off-balance sheet liquidity creation. Campello,

Panel A: "Cat fat" liquidity creation ($ billion) over time

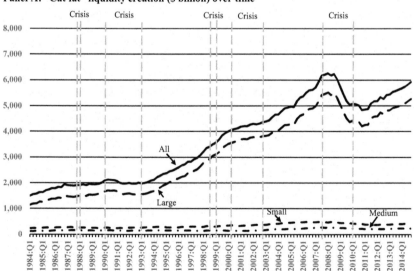

FIGURE 8.2 *(Continued)*

Panel B: On-balance sheet liquidity creation ($ billion) over time

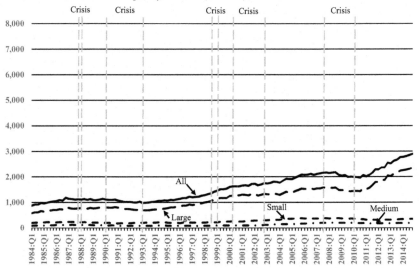

Panel C: Off-balance sheet liquidity creation ($ billion) over time

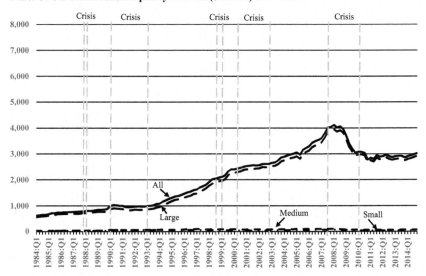

FIGURE 8.2 "Cat fat" liquidity creation and its components over time. Panels A–C show "cat fat" liquidity creation and its on- and off-balance sheet components from 1984:Q1 – 2014:Q4. Results are shown for all banks and for small/medium/large banks, i.e., banks with gross total assets or GTA up to $1 billion/$1 billion–$3 billion/exceeding $3 billion. GTA equals total assets plus the allowance for loan and lease losses and the allocated transfer risk reserve (a reserve for certain foreign loans). Five financial crises are demarcated with vertical dashed lines–the 1987 stock market crash, the credit crunch of the early 1990s, the Russian debt crisis plus LTCM bailout in 1998, the bursting of the dot.com bubble plus September 11, and the subprime lending crisis of the late 2000s.

Giambona, Graham, and Harvey (2011) confirm that firms significantly drew down their loan commitments during this crisis. This helped keep up lending (e.g., Ivashina and Scharfstein, 2010) so that on-balance sheet liquidity creation did not decline as much as it otherwise would have. As well, there was a surge in deposits during the crisis, in part because of a flight to safety, preventing the liquidity creation decline from being more severe.

Figure 8.3 Panels A–C show "cat fat" liquidity creation and its on- and off-balance sheet components normalized by GTA over the time period. As shown in Figure 8.3 Panel A, normalized liquidity creation generally goes down during financial crises for large banks, which drives the same result for the entire banking sector. This pattern is most pronounced during the subprime lending crisis, when normalized liquidity creation also went down for small and medium banks. As may be seen from Figure 8.3 Panels B and C, these changes occurred both on- and off-balance sheet, but the changes in the latter are more pronounced.

8.3 ALTERNATIVE LIQUIDITY CREATION MEASURES OVER TIME

Figure 8.4 Panels A and B show two alternative liquidity creation measures, the takedown probability-adjusted "cat fat" liquidity creation measure (see Section 4.4) and the securitization-adjusted "cat fat" liquidity creation measure (see Section 4.5).

Recall that the takedown probability-adjusted measure in Figure 8.4 Panel A is identical to the "cat fat" measure, except that the dollar amount of illiquid off-balance sheet guarantees is multiplied by 0.30, the observed frequency of

Panel A: "Cat fat" liquidity creation normalized by GTA over time

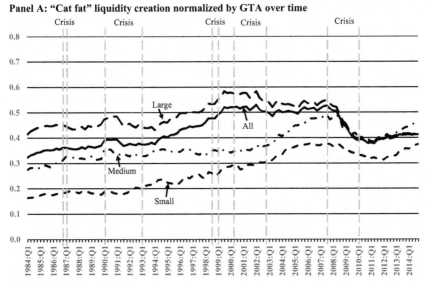

FIGURE 8.3 *(Continued)*

Panel B: On-balance sheet liquidity creation normalized by GTA over time

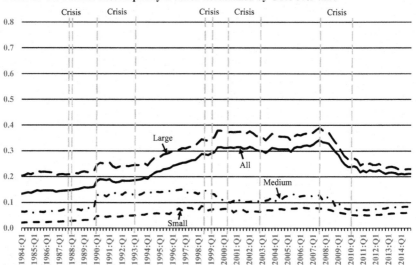

Panel C: Off-balance sheet liquidity creation normalized by GTA over time

FIGURE 8.3   "Cat fat" liquidity creation and its components normalized by gross total assets over time. Panels A–C show "cat fat" liquidity creation and its on- and off-balance sheet components, all normalized by gross total assets or GTA, from 1984:Q1 to 2014:Q4. GTA equals total assets plus the allowance for loan and lease losses and the allocated transfer risk reserve (a reserve for certain foreign loans). Results are shown for all banks and for small/medium/large banks, i.e., banks with GTA up to $1 billion/$1 billion–$3 billion/exceeding $3 billion. Five financial crises are demarcated with vertical dashed lines–the 1987 stock market crash, the credit crunch of the early 1990s, the Russian debt crisis plus LTCM bailout in 1998, the bursting of the dot.com bubble plus September 11, and the subprime lending crisis of the late 2000s.

Panel A: Takedown probability-adjusted "cat fat" liquidity creation ($ billion) over time

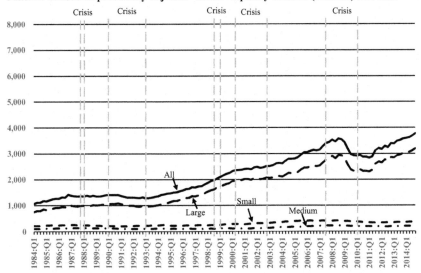

Panel B: Securitization-adjusted "cat fat" liquidity creation ($ billion) over time

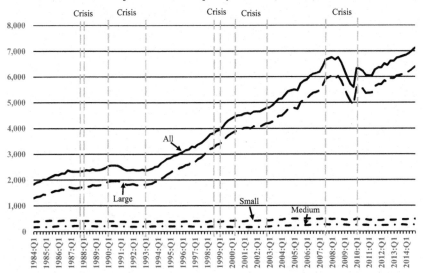

FIGURE 8.4   Alternative liquidity creation measures over time. Panels A–B show takedown probability-adjusted "cat fat" liquidity creation (see Section 4.4) and securitization-adjusted "cat fat" liquidity creation (see Section 4.5) from 1984:Q1 to 2014:Q4. Results are shown for all banks and for small/medium/large banks, i.e., banks with GTA up to $1 billion/$1 billion–$3 billion/ exceeding $3 billion. GTA equals total assets plus the allowance for loan and lease losses and the allocated transfer risk reserve (a reserve for certain foreign loans). Five financial crises are demarcated with vertical dashed lines–the 1987 stock market crash, the credit crunch of the early 1990s, the Russian debt crisis plus LTCM bailout in 1998, the bursting of the dot.com bubble plus September 11, and the subprime lending crisis of the late 2000s.

drawdowns, rather than using the full amount (acknowledging that the option of drawdown matters for liquidity creation) as in the "cat fat" measure. As shown in Figure 8.4 Panel A, liquidity creation is much smaller using this measure than using the "cat fat" measure and it changes less over time because of the reduced importance of off-balance guarantees. Not surprisingly, this affects in particular the liquidity created by large banks, since off-balance sheet activities are by far the biggest for these banks.

Recall that the securitization-adjusted measure is identical to the "cat fat" measure, except that for each loan category, the proportion of loans that are securitized nationally in a particular quarter is assumed to be the proportion that could be securitized by each bank in the same quarter. As shown in Figure 8.4 Panel B, liquidity creation using this measure has almost the same pattern over time as that based on the "cat fat" measure, but it is about 20% higher. The reason for this is likely that the "cat fat" measure assumes that all of the residential mortgages can be securitized (and hence get a weight of 0), whereas the securitization-adjusted measure assumes that only the percentage that was securitized nationally can be securitized, leaving a substantial portion of these loans as not securitizeable (with a weight of ½).

8.4   ALTERNATIVE MEASURES OF OUTPUT OVER TIME

Figure 8.5 Panels A–C show three alternative bank output measures – GTA, TA, and gross loans – over time. Chapter 5 gives arguments why "cat fat" liquidity creation is superior to these alternative bank output measures, and here we show their different patterns at the industry level.

Panel A: Gross total assets ($ billion) over time

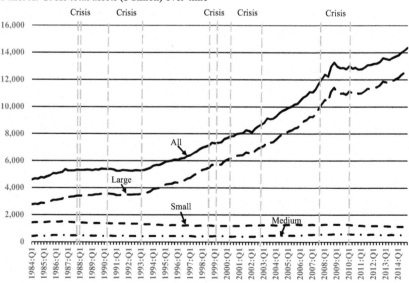

FIGURE 8.5   *(Continued)*

Panel B: Total assets ($ billion) over time

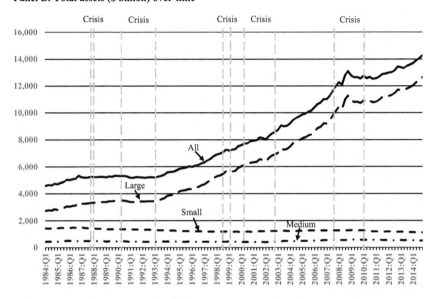

Panel C: Gross loans ($ billion) over time

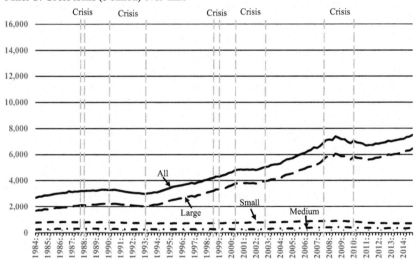

FIGURE 8.5   Alternative measures of bank output over time. Panels A–C show three alternative bank output measures – gross total assets or GTA, total assets, and gross loans – from 1984:Q1 to 2014:Q4. GTA equals total assets plus the allowance for loan and lease losses and the allocated transfer risk reserve (a reserve for certain foreign loans). Results are shown for all banks and for small/medium/large banks, i.e., banks with GTA up to $1 billion/$1 billion–$3 billion/exceeding $3 billion. Five financial crises are demarcated with vertical dashed lines–the 1987 stock market crash, the credit crunch of the early 1990s, the Russian debt crisis plus LTCM bailout in 1998, the bursting of the dot.com bubble plus September 11, and the subprime lending crisis of the late 2000s.

As shown in Figure 8.5 Panel A, GTA is much larger than "cat fat" liquidity creation, but its growth over time is less steep because it excludes off-balance sheet activities, which have grown at a faster rate than on-balance sheet assets. GTA is also less volatile during financial crises because it does not account for the large swings in off-balance sheet activities during these times. It can also be seen that large banks dominate the dollar values (accounting for 59.5% of industry GTA in 1984:Q1 and for 88.6% of industry GTA in 2014:Q4).

As shown in Figure 8.5 Panel B, TA is slightly smaller than GTA, and has a very similar pattern over time. This is not surprising since (as explained in Section 3.1), the difference between GTA and TA are the allowance for loan and lease losses (ALLL), an accounting item for expected losses, and the allocated transfer risk reserve (ATRR), which is zero for most banks.

Figure 8.5 Panel C shows that gross loans are slightly greater than half of assets, and have grown more slowly over time as banks put more of their assets into securities. It is also the least volatile of these output measures during financial crises, likely because loan commitments get drawn down during crises, helping to sustain lending.

8.5 SUMMARY

This chapter shows graphically how liquidity creation has changed over time and how it behaves during normal times and financial crises using US data from 1984:Q1–2014:Q4. It examines total "cat fat" liquidity creation, its on- and off-balance sheet components, and two alternative liquidity creation measures (takedown probability-adjusted and securitization-adjusted "cat fat" liquidity creation). It also analyzes three other measures of bank output (gross total assets, total assets, and gross loans). For all measures, results are shown for the entire commercial banking sector and also by bank size class (small, medium, and large banks) separately. The key takeaways are that US bank liquidity creation has grown tremendously over time, that about half is created off the balance sheet, that large banks create the vast majority of it while constituting only a small percentage of the banking sector in numbers, and that liquidity creation tends to be high before financial crises, and then falls during the crises.

Chapter 9

The Links Between Bank Liquidity Creation and Future Financial Crises

This chapter discusses the links between bank liquidity creation and future financial crises. It is shown both theoretically and empirically that abnormally high aggregate bank liquidity creation may be related to a high probability of future financial crises.

9.1 THEORETICAL LINK BETWEEN AGGREGATE LIQUIDITY CREATION AND FUTURE FINANCIAL CRISES

According to the theory, there may be a causal link through which unusually high bank liquidity creation may help propagate future financial crises. This can happen through both on- and off-balance sheet liquidity creation.

Rajan (1994) and Acharya and Naqvi (2012) argue that banks that create substantial liquidity may also pursue lending policies that generate asset price bubbles and thereby increase the fragility of the banking sector.[1] Put another way, high on-balance sheet liquidity creation can help create bubbles that burst and result in financial crises. An example of this may be the high quantities of subprime mortgage lending prior to the subprime lending crisis of 2007:Q3 – 2009:Q4 that helped fuel the run-up of real estate values that subsequently fell significantly and helped cause the crisis. This is consistent with Thakor (2015), who argues that an extended period of profitable growth creates a false sense of security among bankers and regulators that banks can withstand shocks. This leads politicians to advocate legislation such as the Community Reinvestment Act of 1977 that encourages universal home ownership that may have stimulated banks to extend risky loans to over-levered consumers

---

1. Asset price bubbles exist when the market prices of assets exceed their prices determined by fundamental factors by a substantial amount for a prolonged period. According to the efficient market hypothesis, bubbles cannot exist unless they are driven by irrational behavior or market rigidities, such as constraints on the short selling of assets (e.g., Evanoff, Kaufman, and Malliaris, 2012). Short-selling constraints are restrictions on the sale of assets that are not currently owned by the seller or that the seller has borrowed.

(Agarwal, Benmelech, Bergman, and Seru, 2012). Another channel through which this may have occurred is Fannie Mae and Freddie Mac lowering their credit standards by buying subprime mortgages in the mid-2000s, which encouraged banks to make such loans.

The argument extends in a somewhat different way to off-balance sheet liquidity creation. Thakor (2005) shows that excessive risk-taking and greater bank liquidity creation may occur off the balance sheet during economic booms, as banks shy away from exercising material adverse change clauses on loan commitments due to reputational concerns during such booms. Brunnermeier, Gorton, and Krishnamurthy (2011) argue that models that assess systemic risk should include liquidity build-ups in the financial sector.

Further enhancing this relation between high aggregate liquidity creation and financial crises, other research suggests that banks may make correlated asset portfolio choices when they are creating large quantities of liquidity and are fragile (Acharya, Mehran, and Thakor, 2010; and Farhi and Tirole, 2012). These correlated asset choices can be rationalized based on two grounds. First, institutions rationally anticipate that they will all be bailed out in case things go wrong at many institutions. This is the "too-many-to-fail" argument (e.g., Acharya and Yorulmazer, 2007; and Brown and Dinc, 2011). Second, managers may engage in herding behavior because of career concerns. Correlated portfolio choices can induce systemic risk and increase the probability of a system-wide crisis.

9.2 EMPIRICAL EVIDENCE ON THE LINK BETWEEN AGGREGATE BANK LIQUIDITY CREATION AND FUTURE FINANCIAL CRISES

Reinhart and Rogoff's (2009) examination of eight centuries of financial crises also points at empirical links among bank lending, bubbles, and financial crises. They show that high leverage in financial institutions facilitates growth in lending, which fuels asset price bubbles, which burst and cause financial crises.

Berger and Bouwman (2015) empirically test the hypothesis that excessive liquidity creation by the US banking sector is associated with an increased probability of a future financial crisis. Doing this is challenging for at least two reasons. First, as shown in Chapter 8, bank liquidity creation grows substantially over time in the US. So to distinguish what might be excessive liquidity creation from natural growth as well as seasonal factors, Berger and Bouwman (2015) use deseasonalized, detrended measures (henceforth "detrended measures" for short) of aggregate "cat fat" liquidity creation and its on- and off-balance sheet components.[2] Second, there have not been many crises over the time period for which US banking data are reliably available. They use the crisis data described

---

2. To deseasonalize the data, they use the XII procedure developed by the US Census Bureau, which identifies and adjusts for outliers. For detrending, they use the Hodrick-Prescott (1997) (HP) filter.

in Section 7.5, and essentially use the empirical relation between the level of detrended liquidity creation and the first four crises to predict when the fifth crisis would occur. They run a number of regressions, each of which uses only historical data because future data are not available for estimating prediction models. In each regression, they include not only lagged detrended aggregate liquidity creation, but also lagged detrended GDP to control for the state of the economy, the lagged federal funds rate to control for monetary policy, and the lagged average quarterly return on the value-weighted CRSP index to control for the behavior of the stock market.

They find that lagged detrended aggregate liquidity creation has a significantly positive effect on the probability of a future crisis, supporting the theories discussed in Section 9.1. The predicted probability of a future financial occurring was high right before the actual subprime lending crisis hit, and this seemed to be driven primarily by off-balance sheet liquidity creation.

9.3 NEW EMPIRICAL EVIDENCE ON THE LINK BETWEEN AGGREGATE BANK LIQUIDITY CREATION NORMALIZED BY GDP AND FUTURE FINANCIAL CRISES

One alternative theoretical possibility is that high liquidity creation relative to real activity is the driving force behind the results in Section 9.2. That is, it may not be a high detrended level of liquidity creation that matters most, but rather high liquidity creation relative to GDP that is the better predictor of future financial crises.

Figure 9.1 investigates this possibility graphically. Panel A shows aggregate US "cat fat" liquidity creation and its on- and off-balance sheet components normalized by GDP. Panel B shows the ratios based on deseasonalized and detrended data (labeled for convenience as "detrended") for both the numerator and the denominator. The deseasonalization and detrending procedures are the same as in Berger and Bouwman (2015) described in Section 9.2. Panel B begins in 1986:Q4 since the first 11 quarters from 1984:Q1 – 1986:Q3 are dropped as part of the detrending procedure.

The ratios in Panel A suggest that "cat fat" liquidity creation over GDP went up almost every quarter since 1993 (right after the credit crunch of 1990:Q1 – 1992:Q4) except for the precipitous decline during and slightly after the subprime lending crisis of 2007:Q3 – 2009:Q4. The only other times that "cat fat" liquidity creation relative to GDP declined were in the late 1980s and during the credit crunch, and the drops were small in both periods. In contrast, on-balance sheet liquidity creation normalized by GDP did not change much over time, except for a gradual increase after the subprime lending crisis of 2007:Q3 – 2009:Q4. As shown, the variation in the "cat fat" to GDP ratio is almost entirely due to changes in off-balance sheet liquidity creation. The ratios of the detrended data in Panel B show much the same pattern, except that they are smoothed out considerably.

Panel A: Liquidity creation normalized by GDP

Panel B: Detrended liquidity creation normalized by detrended GDP

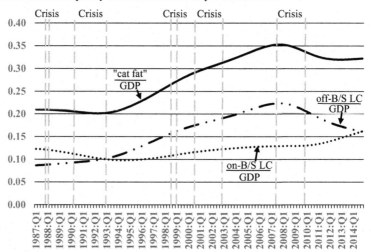

FIGURE 9.1   Aggregate US "cat fat" liquidity creation and its on- and off-balance sheet components normalized by GDP over time. Panel A shows aggregate "cat fat" liquidity creation and its on- and off-balance sheet components normalized by GDP from 1984:Q1 – 2014:Q4. "Cat fat" liquidity creation classifies bank activities other than loans based on maturity and product category combined, but classifies loans by category due to data limitations, and includes off-balance sheet activities. Panel B shows the ratios in which the numerators and denominators are deseasonalized and detrended (labeled for brevity as "detrended"). Panel B begins in 1986:Q4 – the first 11 quarters from 1984:Q1 to 1986:Q3 are dropped as part of the detrending procedure.

Overall, the data do not seem to support the alternative explanation that aggregate liquidity creation relative to output, with or without deseasonalization, better predicts financial crises than aggregate liquidity creation itself. These ratios primarily follow long-term trends that seem to be only broken by the onset of banking crises. A formal comparison or "horse race" between these alternatives would be needed to draw definitive conclusions about these different explanations.

9.4 ARE FINANCIAL CRISES ALWAYS SUBOPTIMAL?

While examining the links between bank liquidity creation and financial crises, it is important to note that the literature often assumes that financial crises are to be avoided. As discussed in Thakor (2014), however, it is not clear whether financial crises are always suboptimal – the boom that precedes financial crises may have positive economic value that offsets the social costs of the crises. An empirical analysis that weighs the costs and benefits of the booms and busts associated with financial crises would be interesting and policy-relevant.

9.5 SUMMARY

There are both theoretical and empirical connections between aggregate bank liquidity creation and future financial crises found in the literature. The theory suggests that high liquidity creation may cause future financial crises through several channels. The empirical evidence is consistent with the theories – high aggregate, detrended liquidity creation, especially off the balance sheet, is associated with future financial crises. An alternative explanation that liquidity creation relative to real activity is a good predictor of financial crises does not seem to be strongly supported by the data. The key takeaways are that the theories suggest that a future financial crisis is more likely when on- or off-balance sheet liquidity creation is abnormally high, and the empirical evidence is consistent with the theory, particularly for off-balance sheet liquidity creation.

Part IV

Causes and Consequences of Liquidity Creation

Chapter 10

Do Better Capitalized Banks Create More or Less Liquidity?

Bank capital ratios (defined as equity to assets or as regulatory capital ratios) are determined by a combination of market, regulatory, and management forces. The capital ratio that a bank chooses to keep is an important decision that is a component of its overall capital structure decisions that include its mix of deposits, subordinated debt, preferred stock and common equity, and maturities of its various liabilities. Higher capital generally make the bank safer (e.g., Bhattacharya and Thakor, 1993), unless this safety is offset by significantly higher portfolio risk.[1] Higher capital also strengthens the bank's incentives to monitor its borrowers (e.g., Holmstrom and Tirole, 1997; Allen, Carletti, and Marquez, 2011; and Mehran and Thakor, 2011), and reduces the contingent liability of the deposit insurer (e.g., Boot and Greenbaum, 1993). However, when equity replaces debt in the bank's capital structure, the bank also loses some debt tax shield and experiences a reduction in the put option value of government guarantees (Merton, 1977).

However, while considering this prudential role of bank capital, it is also useful to consider how bank capital ratios impact liquidity creation, since bank liquidity creation is an important channel through which banks perform their basic intermediation function and may be an important driver of economic growth. In this chapter, we examine the theoretical arguments on the role of bank capital in bank liquidity creation and also discuss the empirical evidence.

10.1 WHY DO WE CARE?

Over the past few decades, and in particular, following the subprime lending crisis of 2007:Q3 – 2009:Q4, there have been many discussions on the need for banks to operate with higher capital ratios. While the regulations that will impose higher capital requirements are discussed in Chapter 13, it is important

---

1. Some theories argue that more capital can hurt bank safety. Koehn and Santomero (1980) and Calem and Rob (1999) suggest that banks may increase their portfolio risk when capital is sufficiently high, such that their overall risk of failure is increased. Besanko and Kanatas (1996) argue that higher capital can hurt bank safety since the benefit of reduced asset-substitution moral hazard could be more than offset by the cost of lower effort exerted by insiders whose ownership could be diluted at higher capital.

to first understand how capital affects liquidity creation regardless of whether there are any changes in capital requirements.

Capital ratios may affect the incentives of banks to create liquidity. For example, if bank capital adversely affects liquidity creation by banks, then higher capital requirements may promote greater safety and soundness, but at the expense of economic growth, suggesting an important regulatory tradeoff. But if higher bank capital means greater bank liquidity creation, then there would be little concern with bank capital requirements being too high from the standpoint of economic growth.

Another consideration is whether banks may create too much liquidity and how capital impacts this. As discussed in Chapters 9 and 15, there may be an optimal level of liquidity creation for the industry and for individual banks, in part because when there is "excessive" bank liquidity creation, the risks of a financial crisis and individual bank failure seem to go up. Thus, there is a lot at stake in understanding how bank capital affects bank liquidity creation.

10.2   WHAT DO THE THEORIES SAY?

The theories are split on the effects of capital ratios on bank liquidity creation. Some suggest that bank capital may impede liquidity creation by making banks' capital structure less fragile (e.g., Diamond and Rajan, 2000, 2001). Fragile capital structures encourage banks to commit to monitoring their borrowers because depositors can run on the bank if the bank threatens to withhold effort. Equity capital makes it harder for less-fragile banks to commit to monitoring because shareholders cannot run on the bank, which in turn hampers banks' abilities to create liquidity.[2] Capital may also reduce liquidity creation because it "crowds out" or replaces deposits, which are an important source of liquidity creation (e.g., Gorton and Winton, 2000). Berger and Bouwman (2009) refer to these theories jointly as the "financial fragility-crowding out" hypothesis.

An alternative view is that higher capital improves banks' ability to absorb risk and hence their ability to create liquidity. This insight is based on two strands of the literature. One strand consists of papers that argue that liquidity creation exposes banks to liquidity risk and raises the likelihood and severity of losses associated with having to dispose of illiquid assets or miss out on lending opportunities to meet customers' liquidity demands and (Allen and Santomero, 1998; and Allen and Gale, 2004). The second strand consists of papers that posit that bank capital absorbs risk and expands banks' risk-bearing capacity (e.g., Bhattacharya and Thakor, 1993; Repullo, 2004; Von Thadden, 2004; and Coval and Thakor, 2005), so higher capital ratios may allow banks to create more liquidity. Berger and Bouwman (2009) collectively refer to this second set of theories as the "risk absorption" hypothesis. A recent theory paper by Donaldson, Piacentino, and Thakor (2015), which does not fall in either of these

---

2. Diamond and Rajan build on Calomiris and Kahn (1991), who argue that uninsured depositors' ability to run on the bank in the event of expected wealth expropriation by bank managers is an important disciplining mechanism. Related to this, Flannery (1994) focuses on the disciplining effect of depositors' ability to withdraw funds on demand, which prevents the bank from expropriating depositor wealth through excessively risky investments.

two strands, formally shows that higher capital leads to more liquidity creation. Their paper shows that when a bank has more capital, it works harder to provide the intermediation service that justifies its existence. This increases the value of the bank's intermediation service, making it more valuable for borrowers, and hence more costly for borrowers to default and lose access to it. This, in turn, makes it incentive compatible for the bank to make more loans, which results in more liquidity being created.

10.3   EMPIRICAL EVIDENCE ON THE RELATION BETWEEN CAPITAL RATIOS AND LIQUIDITY CREATION

Berger and Bouwman (2009) test these opposing theoretical predictions by regressing the dollar amount of liquidity creation normalized by GTA on the lagged equity capital ratio and a number of control variables. The main analysis uses the preferred "cat fat" measure while additional tests use the other measures discussed in Sections 4.2, 4.4, and 4.5 above. The analyses use US annual data from 1993 to 2003. Using these data, they find empirical support for both hypotheses: the "risk absorption" effect empirically dominates for large banks (positive relation), which constitute most of the banking sector assets, and the "financial fragility-crowding out" effect dominates for small banks (negative relation), which constitute most of the banks.[3]

These results are consistent with expectations. The "risk absorption" effect is likely stronger for large banks because they are generally subject to greater regulatory scrutiny and market discipline than small banks, which may affect their capacity to absorb risk. In contrast, the "financial fragility-crowding out" effect is likely relatively strong for small banks because these banks deal more with entrepreneurial-type small businesses, where the close monitoring highlighted in Diamond and Rajan (2000, 2001) is important. In addition, small banks tend to raise funds locally, so that capital may "crowd out" deposits (as in Gorton and Winton, 2000), whereas large banks can more easily access funding from national or international capital markets.

Another at least partial explanation of the difference between large and small banks lies in the difference in off-balance sheet activities. When Berger and Bouwman (2009) use the "cat nonfat" or "mat nonfat" measures that exclude off-balance sheet activities, the positive relation between capital and liquidity creation for large banks becomes statistically insignificant.

Limited evidence exists from other countries. Only a handful of studies examine the effect of capital on liquidity creation and their findings are broadly consistent with Berger and Bouwman (2009). These papers typically find a significantly negative effect for small banks and an insignificant effect for large banks. The latter effect may be explained by off-balance sheet activities being

---

3. The theories suggest a causal relationship from capital to liquidity creation, but in practice both may be jointly determined. Berger and Bouwman (2009) address the endogeneity problem in their main regressions by using lagged capital ratios, and then more directly confront the problem using instrumental variable regressions and obtain consistent results. They do not claim to establish causation, but rather find interesting correlations between capital and liquidity creation that are consistent with the theories.

less prevalent for large banks outside the US. Lei and Song (2013) use data on banks in China from 1988 to 2008. They find that the effect of capital depends on bank ownership: the effect is negative and significant for domestic and state-owned banks, but not significant for foreign banks. Horvath, Seidler, and Weill (2014) use data on banks in the Czech Republic from 2000 to 2010, which tend to be small. They find a negative effect of capital on liquidity creation for these small banks. Fungacova, Weill, and Zhou (2010) use data on banks in Russia from 1999 to 2007. They find that the effect of capital is negative and significant for small banks, but not significant for large banks.[4]

There is additional evidence on the effects of capital on lending, a key component of liquidity creation. For example, studies of the US credit crunch of 1990:Q1 – 1992:Q4 generally find that more capital is associated with higher lending and that higher capital requirements are associated with reduced lending, suggesting that buffers over the regulatory minimums are needed for increased lending (e.g., Berger and Udell, 1994; Hancock, Laing, and Wilcox, 1995; Peek and Rosengren, 1995a, b; Shrieves and Dahl, 1995; and Thakor, 1996).[5] Studies of other time periods and/or other nations seem to confirm these results, although the effects are often smaller (Calomiris and Wilson, 2004; Francis and Osborne, 2009; Berrospide and Edge, 2010; Aiyar, Calomiris, and Wieladek, 2012; and Jimenez, Ongena, Peydro, and Saurina, 2012).

10.4 SUMMARY

It is important to understand how bank capital affects bank liquidity creation. The theories are split: some suggest that bank capital impedes liquidity creation, while others argue it improves liquidity creation. This chapter first reviews these theories and then summarizes the evidence to date. The US evidence shows that the results differ by bank size: based on the preferred "cat fat" measure, the effect is positive for large banks (most of the banking sector assets), while it is negative for small banks (most of the banks). Limited evidence from Europe and the rest of the world is broadly consistent with the US evidence, although the effect on liquidity creation by large bank seems to be weaker, perhaps because large banks in other nations have few off-balance sheet activities. The key takeaway is that bank capital may have either a positive or negative effect on liquidity creation, with different theories dominating for banks in different size classes and countries.

---

4. Distinguin, Roulet, and Tarazi (2013) examine causation both ways between regulatory capital and on-balance sheet liquidity creation using a sample of publicly-traded commercial banks in the United States and 20 European countries using data from 2000 – 2006. They find that banks decrease their regulatory capital ratios when they face higher illiquidity. The effect of capital on on-balance sheet liquidity creation is not significant in their subsample of US listed banks, consistent with Berger and Bouwman's (2009) large-bank finding of insignificant effects when off-balance sheet liquidity creation is excluded.

5. The unusual combination of several major changes in capital regulation and a recession makes it challenging to separate the effects of higher capital and higher capital requirements.

Chapter 11

Which Banks Create the Most and Least Liquidity?

Given the importance of bank liquidity creation to the economy, it is vital to understand which banks create the most and least liquidity and the relations of bank liquidity creation to other bank characteristics. This chapter shows new analyses using US data from 1984:Q1 to 2014:Q4 to investigate these issues. It first shows which banks create the most and least "cat fat," on-balance sheet, and off-balance sheet liquidity (in $ terms and normalized by gross total assets (GTA)) at the beginning and end of the sample period. It then examines the relations of normalized liquidity creation with key bank characteristics. The characteristics include bank size, capital ratio, portfolio risk, regulator identity, and bank holding company status.

11.1 TOP AND BOTTOM LIQUIDITY-CREATING BANKS IN EACH SIZE CLASS

11.1.1 Large Banks' Liquidity Creation in Dollar Terms

Tables 11.1–11.6 present the top and bottom liquidity creators among large banks (GTA exceeding $3 billion), medium banks (GTA exceeding $1 billion and up to $3 billion), and small banks (GTA up to $1 billion) for the start and end of the sample period, 1984:Q1 and 2014:Q4. Specifically, Table 11.1 shows the top 10 liquidity creators in dollar terms in 1984:Q1 and 2014:Q4 in Panels A and B, respectively, and the bottom liquidity creators in Panels C and D for the same two time periods. In each panel, Subpanels 1, 2, and 3 display the ranks based on the dollar amounts of "cat fat," on-balance sheet, and off-balance sheet liquidity creation, respectively. Table 11.2 shows the same ranks for "cat fat," on-balance sheet, and off-balance sheet liquidity creation normalized by GTA. Tables 11.3 and 11.4 show the same information for medium banks, and Tables 11.5 and 11.6 give the data for small banks.

In all cases, bank names are as reported on the Call Report (RSSD9010), many of which contain abbreviations and some of which are truncated. City and state location information for the banks' headquarters are from the Federal Reserve Bank of Chicago website. The locations are shown primarily because there are many repeated names among the small and medium banks, such as First National Bank,

Bank Liquidity Creation and Financial Crises

TABLE 11.1 Large Bank Top and Bottom Liquidity Creators (in $ Terms) in 1984:Q1 and 2014:Q4

Panel A1: The top large bank "cat fat" liquidity creators (in $ terms) in 1984:Q1

Rank	Name	City	State	"Cat fat" LC ($ billion)
1	Bank of Amer NT&SA	San Francisco	CA	117.14
2	Citibank NA	New York	NY	86.00
3	Manufacturers Han TC	New York	NY	68.77
4	Chase Manhattan BK NA	New York	NY	68.53
5	Chemical BK	New York	NY	55.60
6	Continental IL NB&TC Chicago	Chicago	IL	47.69
7	Security Pacific NB	Los Angeles	CA	38.55
8	Morgan Guaranty TC	New York	NY	36.31
9	First NB of Chicago	Chicago	IL	35.99
10	Bankers TC	New York	NY	29.33

Panel A2: The top large bank on-balance sheet liquidity creators (in $ terms) in 1984:Q1

Rank	Name	City	State	On-balance sheet LC ($ billion)
1	Bank of Amer NT&SA	San Francisco	CA	50.13
2	Citibank NA	New York	NY	40.01
3	Chase Manhattan BK NA	New York	NY	35.88
4	Manufacturers Han TC	New York	NY	33.82
5	Chemical BK	New York	NY	26.55
6	Continental IL NB&TC Chicago	Chicago	IL	25.96
7	Security Pacific NB	Los Angeles	CA	19.94
8	Wells Fargo BK NA	San Francisco	CA	16.84
9	First Intrst BK of CA	Los Angeles	CA	10.07
10	Crocker NB	San Francisco	CA	9.87

Panel A3: The top large bank off-balance sheet liquidity creators (in $ terms) in 1984:Q1

Rank	Name	City	State	Off-balance sheet LC ($ billion)
1	Bank of Amer NT&SA	San Francisco	CA	67.01
2	Citibank NA	New York	NY	45.99

TABLE 11.1 Large Bank Top and Bottom Liquidity Creators (in $ Terms) in 1984:Q1 and 2014:Q4 *(cont.)*

Panel A3: The top large bank off-balance sheet liquidity creators (in $ terms) in 1984:Q1 *(cont.)*

Rank	Name	City	State	Off-balance sheet LC ($ billion)
3	Manufacturers Han TC	New York	NY	34.94
4	Chase Manhattan BK NA	New York	NY	32.65
5	Chemical BK	New York	NY	29.04
6	Morgan Guaranty TC	New York	NY	27.18
7	First NB of Chicago	Chicago	IL	26.64
8	Bankers TC	New York	NY	22.87
9	Continental IL NB&TC Chicago	Chicago	IL	21.73
10	Security Pacific NB	Los Angeles	CA	18.61

Panel B1: The top large bank "cat fat" liquidity creators (in $ terms) in 2014:Q4

Rank	Name	City	State	"Cat fat" LC ($ billion)
1	Bank of Amer NA	Charlotte	NC	808.68
2	Wells Fargo BK NA	Sioux Falls	SD	619.08
3	Citibank NA	Sioux Falls	SD	430.36
4	JPMorgan Chase BK NA	Columbus	OH	398.13
5	US BK NA	Cincinnati	OH	254.14
6	Chase BK USA NA	Wilmington	DE	233.13
7	PNC BK NA	Wilmington	DE	186.57
8	Capital One NA	Mc Lean	VA	130.94
9	SunTrust BK	Atlanta	GA	118.02
10	TD BK NA	Wilmington	DE	98.62

Panel B2: The top large bank on-balance sheet liquidity creators (in $ terms) in 2014:Q4

Rank	Name	City	State	On-balance sheet LC ($ billion)
1	Bank of Amer NA	Charlotte	NC	419.88
2	Wells Fargo BK NA	Sioux Falls	SD	341.60
3	US BK NA	Cincinnati	OH	114.54
4	PNC BK NA	Wilmington	DE	108.41

(Continued)

TABLE 11.1 Large Bank Top and Bottom Liquidity Creators (in $ Terms) in 1984:Q1 and 2014:Q4 *(cont.)*

Panel B2: The top large bank on-balance sheet liquidity creators (in $ terms) in 2014:Q4 *(cont.)*

Rank	Name	City	State	On-balance sheet LC ($ billion)
5	JPMorgan Chase BK NA	Columbus	OH	79.80
6	SunTrust BK	Atlanta	GA	76.49
7	Capital One NA	Mc Lean	VA	67.13
8	TD BK NA	Wilmington	DE	67.11
9	Branch BKG&TC	Winston Salem	NC	62.61
10	Fifth Third BK	Cincinnati	OH	54.46

Panel B3: The top large bank off-balance sheet liquidity creators (in $ terms) in 2014:Q4

Rank	Name	City	State	Off-balance sheet LC ($ billion)
1	Citibank NA	Sioux Falls	SD	468.63
2	Bank of Amer NA	Charlotte	NC	388.80
3	JPMorgan Chase BK NA	Columbus	OH	318.33
4	Wells Fargo BK NA	Sioux Falls	SD	277.48
5	Chase BK USA NA	Wilmington	DE	248.48
6	US BK NA	Cincinnati	OH	139.60
7	Capital One BK USA NA	Glen Allen	VA	95.26
8	Discover BK	Greenwood	DE	84.55
9	PNC BK NA	Wilmington	DE	78.16
10	Capital One NA	Mc Lean	VA	63.81

Panel C1: The bottom large bank "cat fat" liquidity creators (in $ terms) in 1984:Q1

Rank	Name	City	State	"Cat fat" LC ($ billion)
1	Republic NB of NY	New York	NY	−4.13
2	Israel Discount BK of New York	New York	NY	−1.72
3	Fuji B&TC	New York	NY	−0.66
4	Boston Safe Deposit & TC	Boston	MA	−0.31

TABLE 11.1 Large Bank Top and Bottom Liquidity Creators (in $ Terms) in 1984:Q1 and 2014:Q4 *(cont.)*

Panel C1: The bottom large bank "cat fat" liquidity creators (in $ terms) in 1984:Q1 *(cont.)*

Rank	Name	City	State	"Cat fat" LC ($ billion)
5	Industrial BK of Japan TC	New York	NY	−0.15
6	Dauphin Deposit B&TC	Harrisburg	PA	−0.02
7	Banco De Ponce	Ponce	PR	0.17
8	Old Kent B&TC	Grand Rapids	MI	0.19
9	Wilmington TC	Wilmington	DE	0.41
10	Banco Popular DE PR	Hato Rey	PR	0.56

Panel C2: The bottom large bank on-balance sheet liquidity creators (in $ terms) in 1984:Q1

Rank	Name	City	State	On-balance sheet LC ($ billion)
1	Republic NB of NY	New York	NY	−4.81
2	Israel Discount BK of New York	New York	NY	−1.89
3	Fuji B&TC	New York	NY	−0.76
4	Industrial BK of Japan TC	New York	NY	−0.35
5	Boston Safe Deposit & TC	Boston	MA	−0.31
6	Old Kent B&TC	Grand Rapids	MI	−0.18
7	Dauphin Deposit B&TC	Harrisburg	PA	−0.06
8	Banco De Ponce	Ponce	PR	0.03
9	Banco Popular De PR	Hato Rey	PR	0.05
10	Bank of Tokyo TC	New York	NY	0.06

Panel C3: The bottom large bank off-balance sheet liquidity creators (in $ terms) in 1984:Q1

Rank	Name	City	State	Off-balance sheet LC ($ billion)
1	Fidelity Union Bank	Newark	NJ	0.00
2	Boston Safe Deposit & TC	Boston	MA	0.00
3	Citibank South Dakota NA	Sioux Falls	SD	0.01

(Continued)

TABLE 11.1 Large Bank Top and Bottom Liquidity Creators (in $ Terms) in 1984:Q1 and 2014:Q4 *(cont.)*

Panel C3: The bottom large bank off-balance sheet liquidity creators (in $ terms) in 1984:Q1 *(cont.)*

Rank	Name	City	State	Off-balance sheet LC ($ billion)
4	Wilmington TC	Wilmington	DE	0.03
5	Atlantic NB of Florida	Jacksonville	FL	0.03
6	Dauphin Deposit B&TC	Harrisburg	PA	0.04
7	First Intrst BK of AZ NA	Phoenix	AZ	0.05
8	First NB of Commerce	New Orleans	LA	0.07
9	Florida NB	Jacksonville	FL	0.07
10	Bank of HI	Honolulu	HI	0.08

Panel D1: The bottom large bank "cat fat" liquidity creators (in $ terms) in 2014:Q4

Rank	Name	City	State	"Cat fat" LC ($ billion)
1	State Street B&TC	Boston	MA	−50.26
2	Bank of NY Mellon	New York	NY	−36.87
3	Safra NB of NY	New York	NY	0.23
4	Century B&TC	Somerville	MA	0.37
5	RBC BK GA NA	Atlanta	GA	0.45
6	First Amer BK	Elk Grove Village	IL	0.47
7	First Security BK	Searcy	AR	0.59
8	Carter BK & TR	Martinsville	VA	0.64
9	First NB Alaska	Anchorage	AK	0.77
10	Southside BK	Tyler	TX	0.84

Panel D2: The bottom large bank on-balance sheet liquidity creators (in $ terms) in 2014:Q4

Rank	Name	City	State	On-balance sheet LC ($ billion)
1	State Street B&TC	Boston	MA	−67.07
2	Bank of NY Mellon	New York	NY	−55.86
3	Citibank NA	Sioux Falls	SD	−38.26
4	Chase BK USA NA	Wilmington	DE	−15.35

TABLE 11.1 Large Bank Top and Bottom Liquidity Creators (in $ Terms) in 1984:Q1 and 2014:Q4 *(cont.)*

Panel D2: The bottom large bank on-balance sheet liquidity creators (in $ terms) in 2014:Q4 *(cont.)*

Rank	Name	City	State	On-balance sheet LC ($ billion)
5	Northern TC	Chicago	IL	−7.64
6	Goldman Sachs BK USA	New York	NY	−1.68
7	Discover BK	Greenwood	DE	−0.68
8	Capital One BK USA NA	Glen Allen	VA	0.04
9	RBC BK GA NA	Atlanta	GA	0.08
10	First Amer BK	Elk Grove Village	IL	0.12

Panel D3: The bottom large bank off-balance sheet liquidity creators (in $ terms) in 2014:Q4

Rank	Name	City	State	Off-balance sheet LC ($ billion)
1	Bank of Amer CA NA	San Francisco	CA	0.00
2	Wells Fargo BK S CENT NA	Houston	TX	0.01
3	Carter BK & TR	Martinsville	VA	0.04
4	Safra NB of NY	New York	NY	0.05
5	Centerstate BK of FL NA	Winter Haven	FL	0.13
6	Scotiabank DE PR	Hato Rey	PR	0.15
7	Hanmi BK	Los Angeles	CA	0.16
8	Century B&TC	Somerville	MA	0.16
9	Hudson Valley BK NA	Yonkers	NY	0.17
10	Westamerica BK	San Rafael	CA	0.17

This table shows large bank top liquidity creators (in $ terms) in 1984:Q1 and 2014:Q4 in Panels A and B, respectively, and the bottom liquidity creators in Panels C and D for the same two-time periods. In each panel, Subpanels 1, 2, and 3 display the ranks based on the dollar amounts of "cat fat," on-balance sheet, and off-balance sheet liquidity creation, respectively. Large banks have GTA exceeding $3 billion. GTA equals total assets plus the allowance for loan and lease losses and the allocated transfer risk reserve (a reserve for certain foreign loans). "Cat fat" liquidity creation (LC) classifies bank activities other than loans based on maturity and product category combined, but classifies loans by category due to data limitations, and includes off-balance sheet activities. Bank names are as reported on the Call Report. Location information is from the Federal Reserve Bank of Chicago website.

which would be indistinguishable without the locations. However, as discussed subsequently, some of the locations of the large banks are counterintuitive.

The top large bank "cat fat" liquidity creators in 1984:Q1 shown in Table 11.1 Panel A1 are much as expected. They are all headquartered in large US cities in large US states: New York (NY), San Francisco (CA), Los Angeles (CA), and Chicago (IL). One reason for the concentration of top large banks in large states is that, as discussed in Box 1.1, interstate branching was prohibited in 1984:Q1, although interstate banking through BHCs was starting to be permitted. In some cases, states had unit-banking laws that required banks to have only one office. This was the case in Illinois, where two of the top 10, Continental Illinois and First Chicago, were located. Most of these large banks no longer exist, having been merged out of existence. Interestingly, five of the top 10, Manufacturers Hanover, Chase Manhattan, Chemical, Morgan Guaranty, and First National Bank of Chicago (as well as several others not in the top 10) are all today merged into JPMorgan Chase. Security Pacific is part of today's Bank of America, and one of the top 10, Continental Illinois, failed later in 1984.

Table 11.1 Panels A2 and A3 show that seven and 10 of the top 10 "cat fat" banks are also among the top 10 on- and off-balance sheet liquidity creators for the same time period, respectively. This consistency is notable because as will be shown, it does not always hold. For most of these large banks, even in 1984:Q1, off-balance sheet liquidity creation was greater than on-balance sheet liquidity creation.

Table 11.1 Panel B1 shows that in 2014:Q4, again the largest banks are represented among the top "cat fat" liquidity creators. The top four liquidity creators are also the largest four banks in terms of GTA. While a few of the names are the same as in 1984:Q1, most of these banks have been significantly transformed by mergers and acquisitions (M&As). The "cat fat" liquidity creation of these banks is generally many times higher in 2014:Q4, partly due to organic growth, but mostly due to M&As.

It is also notable that none of the headquarters of the top 10 "cat fat" liquidity-creating banks are in the largest cities and states in 2014:Q4 – they are mostly located in smaller cities and states. These headquarters locations, some of which are counterintuitive, are verified in several sources, including the Call Report, Summary of Deposits, and FDIC website. The counterintuitive locations are partly due to the fact that interstate banking was permitted in 2014:Q4, and multistate banks have a choice of where they locate their headquarters. This decision is driven in part by differences in state regulations and taxes.[1]

---

1. In contrast, the bank holding companies that own these banks are typically located in "expected" locations. While Bank of America Corp. is located in Charlotte (NC) like its main bank, Wells Fargo & Co. is located in San Francisco (CA), Citigroup Inc. is in New York (NY), and JPMorgan Chase & Co is also in New York (NY). It is also interesting to note that many BHCs are incorporated in Delaware because it has low taxes and an exceptionally corporate-friendly chancery court.

Turning to the top dollar on-balance sheet and off-balance sheet liquidity creators in Table 11.1 Panels B2 and B3, respectively, eight of each of the 10 are also in the top 10 "cat fat" liquidity creator list in Panel A. An exception is Citibank, which is the number three "cat fat" liquidity creator: it does not appear as a top on-balance sheet liquidity creator, but is the top off-balance sheet liquidity producer. This will be explained further when the bottom liquidity creators are examined. As in 1984:Q1, most of the top liquidity creators produced most of their liquidity off the balance sheet.

Table 11.1 Panel C shows the bottom large bank liquidity creators in dollar terms in 1984:Q1. In Panel C1, six of the large banks created negative "cat fat" liquidity, and all 10 of the bottom 10 are relatively small. In Panel C2, there are seven negative on-balance sheet liquidity creators, and the bottom 10 list is similar to the list of bottom 10 "cat fat" liquidity creators. Panel C3 shows a mostly different list of the bottom off-balance sheet liquidity creators – only four banks appear on the bottom 10 "cat fat" liquidity creator list. It is notable that none of the large banks have negative off-balance sheet liquidity creation,

Table 11.1 Panel D shows the bottom liquidity creators in 2014:Q4. Unlike in 1984:Q1, there are some very large banks with very large negative figures in this panel. For example, State Street Bank and Trust has −$50.26 billion in "cat fat" liquidity creation, and even larger in magnitude −$67.07 billion in on-balance sheet liquidity creation. Perhaps the biggest surprise is that Citibank has −$38.26 billion in on-balance sheet liquidity creation in 2014:Q4. Some further investigation reveals why this is the case. Although Citibank creates liquidity on the liability side, it destroys a bigger amount of liquidity on the asset side. Focusing on the asset side, it has more in liquid assets (securities, trading assets, cash and due from other financial institutions, and federal funds sold totaling $675.91 billion) which contribute negatively to liquidity creation, than in illiquid assets (largely commercial and industrial loans, commercial real estate loans, other loans, and other assets totaling $329.19 billion) which contribute positively. Again, there are no negative off-balance sheet liquidity creators among large banks in 2014:Q4.[2]

11.1.2   Large Banks' Normalized Liquidity Creation

Table 11.2 Panel A shows the top large bank normalized liquidity creators in 1984:Q1. As shown in Panel A1, "cat fat" liquidity creation normalized by GTA was well under 1.00 for all large banks, meaning that their liquidity creation was always less than assets. Only a few of the top large banks in terms of normalized "cat fat" liquidity creation in 1984:Q1 also appear in the top dollar value of "cat fat"

---

2. Although the names Bank of America and Wells Fargo appear in the bottom off-balance sheet liquidity creators, these are not the main banks with these names. Those appear in the top off-balance sheet liquidity creators.

TABLE 11.2 Large Bank Top and Bottom Normalized Liquidity Creators in 1984:Q1 and 2014:Q4

Panel A1: The top large bank normalized "cat fat" liquidity creators in 1984:Q1

Rank	Name	City	State	"Cat fat" LC/GTA
1	Mercantile TC NA	Saint Louis	MO	0.72
2	Texas American BK Fort Wrth NA	Fort Worth	TX	0.67
3	Texas Commerce BK NA	Houston	TX	0.63
4	Michigan NB of Detroit	Detroit	MI	0.61
5	Continental IL NB&TC Chicago	Chicago	IL	0.60
6	Manufacturers Han TC	New York	NY	0.60
7	Wells Fargo BK NA	San Francisco	CA	0.60
8	Seattle-First NB	Seattle	WA	0.59
9	Morgan BK DE	Wilmington	DE	0.58
10	First Wisconsin NB	Milwaukee	WI	0.58

Panel A2: The top large bank normalized on-balance sheet liquidity creators in 1984:Q1

Rank	Name	City	State	On-balance sheet LC/GTA
1	Lloyds BK California	Los Angeles	CA	0.41
2	Seattle-First NB	Seattle	WA	0.40
3	Baybank Middlesex	Burlington	MA	0.39
4	Chemical BK DE	Wilmington	DE	0.37
5	Wells Fargo BK NA	San Francisco	CA	0.37
6	Old Stone BK	Providence	RI	0.36
7	Rhode Island Hosp TR NB	Providence	RI	0.36
8	Michigan NB of Detroit	Detroit	MI	0.35
9	Continental BK	Norristown	PA	0.35
10	Branch BKG&TC	Wilson	NC	0.35

Panel A3: The top large bank normalized off-balance sheet liquidity creators in 1984:Q1

Rank	Name	City	State	Off-balance sheet LC/GTA
1	Mercantile TC NA	Saint Louis	MO	0.50
2	Provident NB	Bryn Mawr	PA	0.43
3	Morgan BK DE	Wilmington	DE	0.43
4	First NB of Chicago	Chicago	IL	0.39

TABLE 11.2 Large Bank Top and Bottom Normalized Liquidity Creators in 1984:Q1 and 2014:Q4 *(cont.)*

Panel A3: The top large bank normalized off-balance sheet liquidity creators in 1984:Q1 *(cont.)*

Rank	Name	City	State	Off-balance sheet LC/GTA
5	Texas Commerce BK NA	Houston	TX	0.34
6	Texas American BK Fort Wrth NA	Fort Worth	TX	0.32
7	Interfirst BK Dallas NA	Dallas	TX	0.31
8	Bank of Amer NT&SA	San Francisco	CA	0.31
9	Manufacturers Han TC	New York	NY	0.30
10	Northern TC	Chicago	IL	0.30

Panel B1: The top large bank normalized "cat fat" liquidity creators in 2014:Q4

Rank	Name	City	State	On-balance sheet LC/GTA
1	Wells Fargo FNCL NB	Las Vegas	NV	1.91
2	Chase BK USA NA	Wilmington	DE	1.75
3	Barclays BK DE	Wilmington	DE	1.46
4	First NB of Omaha	Omaha	NE	1.13
5	Capital One BK USA NA	Glen Allen	VA	1.02
6	Discover BK	Greenwood	DE	1.01
7	Texas Cap BK NA	Dallas	TX	0.90
8	Servisfirst BK	Birmingham	AL	0.81
9	Mizuho BK USA	New York	NY	0.80
10	Cardinal BK	Mc Lean	VA	0.78

Panel B2: The top large bank normalized on-balance sheet liquidity creators in 2014:Q4

Rank	Name	City	State	On-balance sheet LC/GTA
1	Texas Cap BK NA	Dallas	TX	0.73
2	Servisfirst BK	Birmingham	AL	0.66
3	Raymond James BK NA	Saint Petersburg	FL	0.62
4	Bell ST B&TC	Fargo	ND	0.61
5	Eaglebank	Bethesda	MD	0.61
6	Opus BK	Irvine	CA	0.61

(Continued)

TABLE 11.2 Large Bank Top and Bottom Normalized Liquidity Creators in 1984:Q1 and 2014:Q4 *(cont.)*

Panel B2: The top large bank normalized on-balance sheet liquidity creators in 2014:Q4 *(cont.)*

Rank	Name	City	State	On-balance sheet LC/GTA
7	Wintrust BK	Chicago	IL	0.57
8	Western Alli BK	Phoenix	AZ	0.57
9	National BK of AZ	Tucson	AZ	0.57
10	Community TR BK	Choudrant	LA	0.57

Panel B3: The top large bank normalized off-balance sheet liquidity creators in 2014:Q4

Rank	Name	City	State	Off-balance sheet LC/GTA
1	Chase BK USA NA	Wilmington	DE	1.86
2	Wells Fargo FNCL NB	Las Vegas	NV	1.61
3	Barclays BK DE	Wilmington	DE	1.37
4	Capital One BK USA NA	Glen Allen	VA	1.02
5	Discover BK	Greenwood	DE	1.01
6	First NB of Omaha	Omaha	NE	0.73
7	TD BK USA NA	Wilmington	DE	0.55
8	Mizuho BK USA	New York	NY	0.47
9	US BK NA	Cincinnati	OH	0.35
10	Citibank NA	Sioux Falls	SD	0.34

Panel C1: The bottom large bank normalized "cat fat" liquidity creators in 1984:Q1

Rank	Name	City	State	"Cat fat" LC/GTA
1	Israel Discount BK of New York	New York	NY	−0.25
2	Republic NB of NY	New York	NY	−0.21
3	Fuji B&TC	New York	NY	−0.17
4	Boston Safe Deposit & TC	Boston	MA	−0.10
5	Industrial BK of Japan TC	New York	NY	−0.04
6	Dauphin Deposit B&TC	Harrisburg	PA	−0.01
7	Old Kent B&TC	Grand Rapids	MI	0.05
8	Banco De Ponce	Ponce	PR	0.05

TABLE 11.2 Large Bank Top and Bottom Normalized Liquidity Creators in 1984:Q1 and 2014:Q4 *(cont.)*

Panel C1: The bottom large bank normalized "cat fat" liquidity creators in 1984:Q1 *(cont.)*

Rank	Name	City	State	"Cat fat" LC/GTA
9	Banco Popular de PR	Hato Rey	PR	0.09
10	Wilmington TC	Wilmington	DE	0.12

Panel C2: The bottom large bank normalized on-balance sheet liquidity creators in 1984:Q1

Rank	Name	City	State	On-balance sheet LC/GTA
1	Israel Discount BK of New York	New York	NY	−0.28
2	Republic NB of NY	New York	NY	−0.25
3	Fuji B&TC	New York	NY	−0.19
4	Industrial BK of Japan TC	New York	NY	−0.10
5	Boston Safe Deposit & TC	Boston	MA	−0.10
6	Old Kent B&TC	Grand Rapids	MI	−0.04
7	Dauphin Deposit B&TC	Harrisburg	PA	−0.02
8	Bank of Tokyo TC	New York	NY	0.01
9	Banco de Ponce	Ponce	PR	0.01
10	Banco Popular de PR	Hato Rey	PR	0.01

Panel C3: The bottom large bank normalized off-balance sheet liquidity creators in 1984:Q1

Rank	Name	City	State	Off-balance sheet LC/GTA
1	Fidelity Union Bank	Newark	NJ	0.00
2	Citibank South Dakota NA	Sioux Falls	SD	0.00
3	Boston Safe Deposit & TC	Boston	MA	0.00
4	Atlantic NB of Florida	Jacksonville	FL	0.00
5	First Intrst BK of AZ NA	Phoenix	AZ	0.00
6	Florida NB	Jacksonville	FL	0.01
7	Wilmington TC	Wilmington	DE	0.01
8	Bank of HI	Honolulu	HI	0.01
9	Connecticut B&TC NA	Hartford	CT	0.01
10	Dauphin Deposit B&TC	Harrisburg	PA	0.01

(Continued)

TABLE 11.2 Large Bank Top and Bottom Normalized Liquidity Creators in 1984:Q1 and 2014:Q4 *(cont.)*

Panel D1: The bottom large bank normalized "cat fat" liquidity creators in 2014:Q4

Rank	Name	City	State	"Cat fat" LC/GTA
1	State Street B&TC	Boston	MA	−0.19
2	Bank of NY Mellon	New York	NY	−0.12
3	Safra NB of NY	New York	NY	0.04
4	BNY Mellon NA	Pittsburgh	PA	0.09
5	Washington FED NA	Seattle	WA	0.10
6	Century B&TC	Somerville	MA	0.10
7	Northern TC	Chicago	IL	0.11
8	First Security BK	Searcy	AR	0.13
9	First Amer BK	Elk Grove Village	IL	0.14
10	Carter BK & TR	Martinsville	VA	0.14

Panel D2: The bottom large bank normalized on-balance sheet liquidity creators in 2014:Q4

Rank	Name	City	State	On-balance sheet LC/GTA
1	State Street B&TC	Boston	MA	−0.25
2	Bank of NY Mellon	New York	NY	−0.18
3	Chase BK USA NA	Wilmington	DE	−0.12
4	Northern TC	Chicago	IL	−0.07
5	Citibank NA	Sioux Falls	SD	−0.03
6	Goldman Sachs BK USA	New York	NY	−0.01
7	Discover BK	Greenwood	DE	−0.01
8	Capital One BK USA NA	Glen Allen	VA	0.00
9	RBC BK GA NA	Atlanta	GA	0.03
10	Safra NB of NY	New York	NY	0.03

Panel D3: The bottom large bank normalized off-balance sheet liquidity creators in 2014:Q4

Rank	Name	City	State	Off-balance sheet LC/GTA
1	Bank of Amer CA NA	San Francisco	CA	0.00
2	Wells Fargo BK S Cent NA	Houston	TX	0.00

TABLE 11.2 Large Bank Top and Bottom Normalized Liquidity Creators in 1984:Q1 and 2014:Q4 *(cont.)*

Panel D3: The bottom large bank normalized off-balance sheet liquidity creators in 2014:Q4 *(cont.)*

Rank	Name	City	State	Off-balance sheet LC/GTA
3	Safra NB of NY	New York	NY	0.01
4	Carter BK & TR	Martinsville	VA	0.01
5	Signature BK	New York	NY	0.02
6	Washington Fed NA	Seattle	WA	0.02
7	Scotiabank de PR	Hato Rey	PR	0.03
8	Morgan Stanley PRIV BK NA	Purchase	NY	0.03
9	Centerstate BK of FL NA	Winter Haven	FL	0.03
10	Westamerica BK	San Rafael	CA	0.03

This table shows large bank top normalized liquidity creators in 1984:Q1 and 2014:Q4 in Panels A and B, respectively, and the bottom liquidity creators in Panels C and D for the same two-time periods. In each panel, Subpanels 1, 2, and 3 display the ranks based on "cat fat," on-balance sheet, and off-balance sheet liquidity creation, respectively, all three normalized by GTA. GTA equals total assets plus the allowance for loan and lease losses and the allocated transfer risk reserve (a reserve for certain foreign loans). Large banks have GTA exceeding $3 billion. "Cat fat" liquidity creation (LC) classifies bank activities other than loans based on maturity and product category combined, but classifies loans by category due to data limitations, and includes off-balance sheet activities. Bank names are as reported on the Call Report. Location information is from the Federal Reserve Bank of Chicago website.

liquidity creation in Table 11.1 Panel A. Similarly, only some of the large bank top normalized on- and off-balance sheet liquidity creators appear among the top large bank on- or off-balance sheet liquidity creators in dollar terms. As well, there is little correspondence among the three lists shown in Table 11.2 Panel A – only three of the top 10 normalized "cat fat" liquidity creators are also in the top 10 normalized on- and off-balance sheet liquidity creators. Table 11.2 Panel B shows that normalized "cat fat" liquidity creation and normalized off-balance sheet liquidity creation exceeded 1.00 for six and five banks, respectively in 2014:Q4. Most of the top normalized "cat fat" liquidity creators are also among the top normalized off-balance sheet liquidity creators, but there is little correspondence with the list of top normalized on-balance sheet liquidity creators. Finally, it is notable that only one very large bank is among the top normalized liquidity creator banks, and that is Citibank in 10th place among the top off-balance sheet liquidity creators.[3]

Turning to the 1984:Q1 bottom large bank normalized liquidity creators in Table 11.2 Panel C1, the bottom six normalized liquidity creators are the same

3. Although the names Wells Fargo Financial, Chase Bank USA, and Barclays Bank DE appear in Panels B1 and B3, these are not the main banks with these names.

as the bottom six dollar value liquidity creators in Table 11.1 Panel C1 because there are only six banks with negative liquidity creation. Panels C1, C2, and C3 show no very large banks among the bottom normalized liquidity creators. Panel C3 also shows that off-balance sheet normalized liquidity creation is very low for all 10 at the bottom. Table 11.2 Panel D shows the bottom normalized liquidity creators for 2014:Q4. Again, the signs are predictable from Table 11.1 Panel D (which shows liquidity creation in levels), but it is notable that Citibank has only a small negative ratio for normalized on-balance sheet liquidity creation of –0.03, despite the large negative dollar value because its GTA is so large.

11.1.3 Medium Banks' Liquidity Creation in Dollar Terms

Table 11.3 Panel A shows that for medium banks, the dollar values of the top liquidity creators are unsurprisingly small relative to the large bank totals shown in Table 11.1 Panel A. Of course, most of the names of the banks are relatively unknown. For these banks, off-balance sheet liquidity creation is generally considerably smaller than on-balance sheet liquidity creation. The top dollar value "cat fat" liquidity creators appear six times in the top 10 on-balance sheet liquidity creators and six times in the top 10 off-balance sheet liquidity creators. There is overlap of only three banks between the top on- and off-balance sheet liquidity creators, suggesting that these two components are not that highly related. Table 11.3 Panel B shows that the top liquidity creators in 2014:Q4 are very different from those in 1984:Q1, because by the later time period, two of the largest medium banks were large banks, two failed and were acquired with government assistance, while the remaining six were acquired without assistance. Again, on-balance sheet liquidity creation seems to be much larger than off-balance sheet liquidity creation. This is also reflected in that nine of the top 10 on-balance sheet liquidity creators are also in the top 10 "cat fat" liquidity creators, while only three of the top off-balance sheet liquidity creators are among the top "cat fat" liquidity creators.

Table 11.3 Panel C shows the bottom dollar value liquidity creators among medium banks in 1984:Q1. Seven of these banks created negative "cat fat" liquidity, nine created negative on-balance sheet liquidity, and one created negative off-balance sheet liquidity, and many created exact zero or close to zero off-balance sheet liquidity. As shown in Table 11.3 Panel D, by 2014:Q4, only two medium banks created negative "cat fat" liquidity, only three created negative on-balance sheet liquidity, and only two created near-zero off-balance sheet liquidity.

11.1.4 Medium Banks' Normalized Liquidity Creation

Table 11.4 Panel A shows that in 1984:Q1, the top normalized liquidity creators among medium banks created slightly less normalized "cat fat" and off-balance sheet liquidity than the top large banks at that time, and slightly more normalized on-balance sheet liquidity (Table 11.2 Panel A). Over time, medium bank normalized liquidity creation relative to large banks went down: in 2014:Q4,

TABLE 11.3 Medium Bank Top and Bottom Liquidity Creators (in $ Terms) in 1984:Q1 and 2014:Q4

Panel A1: The top medium bank "cat fat" liquidity creators (in $ terms) in 1984:Q1

Rank	Name	City	State	"Cat fat" LC ($ billion)
1	First City BK of Dallas	Dallas	TX	1.50
2	Interfirst BK Houston NA	Houston	TX	1.42
3	First Jersey NB	Jersey City	NJ	1.42
4	Texas CMRC BK-Austin NA	Austin	TX	1.41
5	Bank of the West	San Francisco	CA	1.28
6	United BK of AZ	Phoenix	AZ	1.26
7	Commerce BK of Kansas City NA	Kansas City	MO	1.23
8	First NB&TC	Tulsa	OK	1.19
9	Colonial BK	Waterbury	CT	1.18
10	Interfirst BK Austin NA	Austin	TX	1.17

Panel A2: The top medium bank on-balance sheet liquidity creators (in $ terms) in 1984:Q1

Rank	Name	City	State	On-balance sheet LC ($ billion)
1	United BK of AZ	Phoenix	AZ	1.12
2	Interfirst BK Houston NA	Houston	TX	1.03
3	Citytrust	Bridgeport	CT	1.03
4	Interfirst BK Austin NA	Austin	TX	1.03
5	Texas CMRC BK-Austin NA	Austin	TX	1.01
6	Colonial BK	Waterbury	CT	0.94
7	Central BK	San Francisco	CA	0.94
8	Barclays BK of New York NA	New York	NY	0.93
9	First Jersey NB	Jersey City	NJ	0.93
10	Imperial BK	Los Angeles	CA	0.93

Panel A3: The top medium bank off-balance sheet liquidity creators (in $ terms) in 1984:Q1

Rank	Name	City	State	Off-balance sheet LC ($ billion)
1	First City BK of Dallas	Dallas	TX	0.76
2	Commerce BK of Kansas City NA	Kansas City	MO	0.65

(Continued)

TABLE 11.3 Medium Bank Top and Bottom Liquidity Creators (in $ Terms) in 1984:Q1 and 2014:Q4 *(cont.)*

Panel A3: The top medium bank off-balance sheet liquidity creators (in $ terms) in 1984:Q1 *(cont.)*

Rank	Name	City	State	Off-balance sheet LC ($ billion)
3	Manufacturers Han BK DE	Wilmington	DE	0.64
4	First Jersey NB	Jersey City	NJ	0.49
5	La Salle NB	Chicago	IL	0.45
6	National BK of CMRC of	San Antonio	TX	0.42
7	Texas CMRC BK-Austin NA	Austin	TX	0.40
8	Bank of the West	San Francisco	CA	0.40
9	United MO BK Kansas City NA	Kansas City	MO	0.40
10	Interfirst BK Houston NA	Houston	TX	0.39

Panel B1: The top medium bank "cat fat" liquidity creators (in $ terms) in 2014:Q4

Rank	Name	City	State	"Cat fat" LC ($ billion)
1	Tristate Cap BK	Pittsburgh	PA	1.86
2	Fremont BK	Fremont	CA	1.81
3	Interbank	Oklahoma City	OK	1.80
4	American Chartered BK	Schaumburg	IL	1.79
5	Happy ST BK	Happy	TX	1.74
6	California United BK	Los Angeles	CA	1.74
7	Communitybank TX NA	Beaumont	TX	1.73
8	Peapack Gladstone BK	Bedminster	NJ	1.69
9	Grandpoint BK	Los Angeles	CA	1.66
10	Lake Forest B&TC	Lake Forest	IL	1.65

Panel B2: The top medium bank on-balance sheet liquidity creators (in $ terms) in 2014:Q4

Rank	Name	City	State	On-balance sheet LC ($ billion)
1	Interbank	Oklahoma City	OK	1.60
2	Peapack Gladstone BK	Bedminster	NJ	1.58

TABLE 11.3 Medium Bank Top and Bottom Liquidity Creators (in $ Terms) in 1984:Q1 and 2014:Q4 *(cont.)*

Panel B2: The top medium bank on-balance sheet liquidity creators (in $ terms) in 2014:Q4 *(cont.)*

Rank	Name	City	State	On-balance sheet LC ($ billion)
3	Happy ST BK	Happy	TX	1.47
4	Grandpoint BK	Los Angeles	CA	1.44
5	American Chartered BK	Schaumburg	IL	1.44
6	Communitybank TX NA	Beaumont	TX	1.43
7	Lake Forest B&TC	Lake Forest	IL	1.42
8	Fremont BK	Fremont	CA	1.41
9	California United BK	Los Angeles	CA	1.38
10	Centier BK	Whiting	IN	1.38

Panel B3: The top medium bank off-balance sheet liquidity creators (in $ terms) in 2014:Q4

Rank	Name	City	State	Off-balance sheet LC ($ billion)
1	TIB The Indep BankersBank	Farmers Branch	TX	0.63
2	Tristate Cap BK	Pittsburgh	PA	0.49
3	Fremont BK	Fremont	CA	0.40
4	Mercantile BK MI	Grand Rapids	MI	0.39
5	California United BK	Los Angeles	CA	0.36
6	Farmers & MRCH BK Cent CA	Lodi	CA	0.36
7	American Chartered BK	Schaumburg	IL	0.35
8	Bank of KY	Crestview Hills	KY	0.34
9	Amboy BK	Old Bridge	NJ	0.32
10	Enterprise B&TC	Lowell	MA	0.31

Panel C1: The bottom medium bank "cat fat" liquidity creators (in $ terms) in 1984:Q1

Rank	Name	City	State	"Cat fat" LC ($ billion)
1	Daiwa BK TC	New York	NY	−0.46
2	Banco de Santander-Puerto Rico	Hato Rey	PR	−0.25

(Continued)

TABLE 11.3 Medium Bank Top and Bottom Liquidity Creators (in $ Terms) in 1984:Q1 and 2014:Q4 *(cont.)*

Panel C1: The bottom medium bank "cat fat" liquidity creators (in $ terms) in 1984:Q1 *(cont.)*

Rank	Name	City	State	"Cat fat" LC ($ billion)
3	Amalgamated BK	New York	NY	−0.24
4	Banco Central Corp	Hato Rey	PR	−0.21
5	Bank of Canton of CA	San Francisco	CA	−0.15
6	Laredo NB	Laredo	TX	−0.09
7	Davenport B&TC	Davenport	IA	−0.05
8	Farmers & MRCH BK	Long Beach	CA	0.02
9	Gallatin NB	Uniontown	PA	0.03
10	MID America B&TC of	Louisville	KY	0.04

Panel C2: The bottom medium bank on-balance sheet liquidity creators (in $ terms) in 1984:Q1

Rank	Name	City	State	On-balance sheet LC ($ billion)
1	Daiwa BK TC	New York	NY	−0.51
2	Banco de Santander-Puerto Rico	Hato Rey	PR	−0.32
3	Amalgamated BK	New York	NY	−0.24
4	Banco Central Corp	Hato Rey	PR	−0.23
5	Bank of Canton of CA	San Francisco	CA	−0.18
6	UBAF Arab Amer BK	New York	NY	−0.15
7	Laredo NB	Laredo	TX	−0.10
8	Davenport B&TC	Davenport	IA	−0.05
9	Bank of the Southwest NA	Brownsville	TX	−0.04
10	Farmers & MRCH BK	Long Beach	CA	0.01

Panel C3: The bottom medium bank off-balance sheet liquidity creators (in $ terms) in 1984:Q1

Rank	Name	City	State	Off-balance sheet LC ($ billion)
1	Barnett BK of Palm Beach Count	Delray Beach	FL	−0.00
4	Ohio Citizens BK	Toledo	OH	0.00
4	Jefferson Guaranty BK	Metairie	LA	0.00

TABLE 11.3 Medium Bank Top and Bottom Liquidity Creators (in $ Terms) in 1984:Q1 and 2014:Q4 *(cont.)*

Panel C3: The bottom medium bank off-balance sheet liquidity creators (in $ terms) in 1984:Q1 *(cont.)*

Rank	Name	City	State	Off-balance sheet LC ($ billion)
4	Central TC NE Ohio NA	Canton	OH	0.00
4	Bradford Trust Company	New York	NY	0.00
4	First NB of Toms River	Toms River	NJ	0.00
7	Commonwealth B&TC NA	Williamsport	PA	0.00
8	Calcasieu Marine NB	Lake Charles	LA	0.00
9	Northern Central BK	Williamsport	PA	0.00
10	Pontiac ST BK	Pontiac	MI	0.00

Panel D1: The bottom medium bank "cat fat" liquidity creators (in $ terms) in 2014:Q4

Rank	Name	City	State	"Cat fat" LC ($ billion)
1	First ST BK	Uvalde	TX	−0.09
2	Crescent B&TC	New Orleans	LA	−0.06
3	Banamex USA	Los Angeles	CA	0.06
4	Citizens First BK	The Villages	FL	0.07
5	International BK of CMRC	Brownsville	TX	0.10
6	Interaudi BK	New York	NY	0.11
7	American Heritage BK	Sapulpa	OK	0.11
8	Blackhawk B&T	Milan	IL	0.12
9	DBA First Convenience BK	Killeen	TX	0.13
10	Bessemer TC NA	New York	NY	0.14

Panel D2: The bottom medium bank on-balance sheet liquidity creators (in $ terms) in 2014:Q4

Rank	Name	City	State	On-balance sheet LC ($ billion)
1	First ST BK	Uvalde	TX	−0.11
2	Banamex USA	Los Angeles	CA	−0.07
3	Crescent B&TC	New Orleans	LA	−0.06

(Continued)

TABLE 11.3 Medium Bank Top and Bottom Liquidity Creators (in $ Terms) in 1984:Q1 and 2014:Q4 *(cont.)*

Panel D2: The bottom medium bank on-balance sheet liquidity creators (in $ terms) in 2014:Q4 *(cont.)*

Rank	Name	City	State	On-balance sheet LC ($ billion)
4	Citizens First BK	The Villages	FL	0.02
5	International BK of CMRC	Brownsville	TX	0.05
6	Interaudi BK	New York	NY	0.06
7	Blackhawk B&T	Milan	IL	0.07
8	American Heritage BK	Sapulpa	OK	0.07
9	DBA First Convenience BK	Killeen	TX	0.12
10	Armed Forces BK NA	Fort Leavenworth	KS	0.13

Panel D3: The bottom medium bank off-balance sheet liquidity creators (in $ terms) in 2014:Q4

Rank	Name	City	State	Off-balance sheet LC ($ billion)
1	Intervest NB	New York	NY	0.00
2	Crescent B&TC	New Orleans	LA	0.00
3	Bessemer TC NA	New York	NY	0.01
4	DBA First Convenience BK	Killeen	TX	0.01
5	First ST BK	Uvalde	TX	0.02
6	Woori Amer BK	New York	NY	0.02
7	BAC FL BK	Coral Gables	FL	0.02
8	Texas CMNTY BK	Laredo	TX	0.03
9	Liberty BK	Springfield	MO	0.03
10	American Heritage BK	Sapulpa	OK	0.03

This table shows medium bank top liquidity creators (in $ terms) in 1984:Q1 and 2014:Q4 in Panels A and B, respectively, and the bottom liquidity creators in Panels C and D for the same two-time periods. In each panel, Subpanels 1, 2, and 3 display the ranks based on the dollar amounts of "cat fat," on-balance sheet, and off-balance sheet liquidity creation, respectively. Medium banks have GTA exceeding $1 billion and up to $3 billion. GTA equals total assets plus the allowance for loan and lease losses and the allocated transfer risk reserve (a reserve for certain foreign loans). "Cat fat" liquidity creation (LC) classifies bank activities other than loans based on maturity and product category combined, but classifies loans by category due to data limitations, and includes off-balance sheet activities. Bank names are as reported on the Call Report. Location information is from the Federal Reserve Bank of Chicago website.

TABLE 11.4 Medium Bank Top and Bottom Normalized Liquidity Creators in 1984:Q1 and 2014:Q4

Panel A1: The top medium bank normalized "cat fat" liquidity creators in 1984:Q1

Rank	Name	City	State	"Cat fat" LC/GTA
1	First City BK of Dallas	Dallas	TX	0.71
2	Continental NB of Fort Worth	Fort Worth	TX	0.65
3	Texas CMRC BK-Austin NA	Austin	TX	0.60
4	First Jersey NB	Jersey City	NJ	0.59
5	Bank of the West	San Francisco	CA	0.55
6	Manufacturers Han BK DE	Wilmington	DE	0.53
7	United States TC	Boston	MA	0.52
8	Corpus Christi NB	Corpus Christi	TX	0.52
9	First TN BK Knoxville TN	Knoxville	TN	0.52
10	American NB	Bakersfield	CA	0.52

Panel A2: The top medium bank normalized on-balance sheet liquidity creators in 1984:Q1

Rank	Name	City	State	On-balance sheet LC/GTA
1	Bradford Trust Company	New York	NY	0.48
2	American NB	Bakersfield	CA	0.46
3	Citytrust	Bridgeport	CT	0.43
4	Texas CMRC BK-Austin NA	Austin	TX	0.43
5	United BK of AZ	Phoenix	AZ	0.42
6	Central BK	San Francisco	CA	0.41
7	First TN BK Knoxville TN	Knoxville	TN	0.41
8	Jefferson Guaranty BK	Metairie	LA	0.41
9	Great Western B&TC	Phoenix	AZ	0.41
10	BankTexas Dallas NA	Dallas	TX	0.40

Panel A3: The top medium bank normalized off-balance sheet liquidity creators in 1984:Q1

Rank	Name	City	State	Off-balance sheet LC/GTA
1	First City BK of Dallas	Dallas	TX	0.36
2	Manufacturers Han BK DE	Wilmington	DE	0.30

(Continued)

TABLE 11.4 Medium Bank Top and Bottom Normalized Liquidity Creators in 1984:Q1 and 2014:Q4 *(cont.)*

Panel A3: The top medium bank normalized off-balance sheet liquidity creators in 1984:Q1 *(cont.)*

Rank	Name	City	State	Off-balance sheet LC/GTA
3	Corpus Christi NB	Corpus Christi	TX	0.29
4	Cullen CTR B&TC	Houston	TX	0.28
5	Continental NB of Fort Worth	Fort Worth	TX	0.27
6	Alamo NB	San Antonio	TX	0.25
7	Commerce BK of Kansas City NA	Kansas City	MO	0.23
8	First AL BK of Birmingham	Birmingham	AL	0.22
9	Baybank Harvard TC	Cambridge	MA	0.20
10	National BK of CMRC of	San Antonio	TX	0.20

Panel B1: The top medium bank normalized "cat fat" liquidity creators in 2014:Q4

Rank	Name	City	State	"Cat fat" LC/GTA
1	Atlantic Cap BK	Atlanta	GA	0.83
2	California United BK	Los Angeles	CA	0.77
3	Bridge BK NA	San Jose	CA	0.76
4	Enterprise B&TC	Lowell	MA	0.73
5	First Dakota NB	Yankton	SD	0.72
6	Southwest BK	Fort Worth	TX	0.72
7	American T&SB	Dubuque	IA	0.70
8	Interbank	Oklahoma City	OK	0.69
9	Central BK of ST Louis	Clayton	MO	0.68
10	West BK	West Des Moines	IA	0.68

Panel B2: The top medium bank normalized on-balance sheet liquidity creators in 2014:Q4

Rank	Name	City	State	On-balance sheet LC/GTA
1	Atlantic CAP BK	Atlanta	GA	0.67
2	Interbank	Oklahoma City	OK	0.61
3	California United BK	Los Angeles	CA	0.61

TABLE 11.4 Medium Bank Top and Bottom Normalized Liquidity Creators in 1984:Q1 and 2014:Q4 *(cont.)*

Panel B2: The top medium bank normalized on-balance sheet liquidity creators in 2014:Q4 *(cont.)*

Rank	Name	City	State	On-balance sheet LC/GTA
4	First Dakota NB	Yankton	SD	0.61
5	Southwest BK	Fort Worth	TX	0.61
6	Bridge BK NA	San Jose	CA	0.60
7	Peapack Gladstone BK	Bedminster	NJ	0.58
8	Enterprise B&TC	Lowell	MA	0.58
9	Happy ST BK	Happy	TX	0.57
10	Minnwest BK	Redwood Falls	MN	0.57

Panel B3: The top medium bank normalized off-balance sheet liquidity creators in 2014:Q4

Rank	Name	City	State	Off-balance sheet LC/GTA
1	TIB The Indep BankersBank	Farmers Branch	TX	0.29
2	American T&SB	Dubuque	IA	0.19
3	Dubuque B&TC	Dubuque	IA	0.18
4	Northbrook B&TC	Northbrook	IL	0.18
5	Tristate Cap BK	Pittsburgh	PA	0.17
6	Bank of KY	Crestview Hills	KY	0.17
7	Sovereign BK	Dallas	TX	0.16
8	Bridge BK NA	San Jose	CA	0.16
9	California United BK	Los Angeles	CA	0.16
10	Capstar BK	Nashville	TN	0.16

Panel C1: The bottom medium bank normalized "cat fat" liquidity creators in 1984:Q1

Rank	Name	City	State	"Cat fat" LC/GTA
1	Daiwa BK TC	New York	NY	−0.23
2	Banco de Santander-Puerto Rico	Hato Rey	PR	−0.15
3	Bank of Canton of CA	San Francisco	CA	−0.15

(Continued)

TABLE 11.4 Medium Bank Top and Bottom Normalized Liquidity Creators in 1984:Q1 and 2014:Q4 *(cont.)*

Panel C1: The bottom medium bank normalized "cat fat" liquidity creators in 1984:Q1 *(cont.)*

Rank	Name	City	State	"Cat fat" LC/GTA
4	Amalgamated BK	New York	NY	−0.10
5	Banco Central Corp	Hato Rey	PR	−0.09
6	Laredo NB	Laredo	TX	−0.06
7	Davenport B&TC	Davenport	IA	−0.03
8	Farmers & MRCH BK	Long Beach	CA	0.01
9	Gallatin NB	Uniontown	PA	0.02
10	MID America B&TC OF	Louisville	KY	0.03

Panel C2: The bottom medium bank normalized on-balance sheet liquidity creators in 1984:Q1

Rank	Name	City	State	On-balance sheet LC/GTA
1	Daiwa BK TC	New York	NY	−0.26
2	Banco de Santander-Puerto Rico	Hato Rey	PR	−0.18
3	Bank of Canton of CA	San Francisco	CA	−0.17
4	Amalgamated BK	New York	NY	−0.11
5	Banco Central Corp	Hato Rey	PR	−0.10
6	UBAF Arab Amer BK	New York	NY	−0.07
7	Laredo NB	Laredo	TX	−0.06
8	Bank of the Southwest NA	Brownsville	TX	−0.04
9	Davenport B&TC	Davenport	IA	−0.03
10	Farmers & MRCH BK	Long Beach	CA	0.01

Panel C3: The bottom medium bank normalized off-balance sheet liquidity creators in 1984:Q1

Rank	Name	City	State	Off-balance sheet LC/GTA
1	Barnett BK of Palm Beach Count	Delray Beach	FL	−0.00
2	Central TC NE Ohio NA	Canton	OH	0.00
3	Ohio Citizens BK	Toledo	OH	0.00

TABLE 11.4 Medium Bank Top and Bottom Normalized Liquidity Creators in 1984:Q1 and 2014:Q4 *(cont.)*

Panel C3: The bottom medium bank normalized off-balance sheet liquidity creators in 1984:Q1 *(cont.)*

Rank	Name	City	State	Off-balance sheet LC/GTA
4	Jefferson Guaranty BK	Metairie	LA	0.00
5	Bradford Trust Company	New York	NY	0.00
6	First NB of Toms River	Toms River	NJ	0.00
7	Commonwealth B&TC NA	Williamsport	PA	0.00
8	Calcasieu Marine NB	Lake Charles	LA	0.00
9	Amalgamated BK	New York	NY	0.00
10	Northern Central BK	Williamsport	PA	0.00

Panel D1: The bottom medium bank normalized "cat fat" liquidity creators in 2014:Q4

Rank	Name	City	State	"Cat fat" LC/GTA
1	First ST BK	Uvalde	TX	−0.07
2	Crescent B&TC	New Orleans	LA	−0.06
3	Citizens First BK	The Villages	FL	0.04
4	Banamex USA	Los Angeles	CA	0.05
5	Bessemer TC NA	New York	NY	0.06
6	Interaudi BK	New York	NY	0.06
7	International BK of CMRC	Brownsville	TX	0.10
8	DBA First Convenience BK	Killeen	TX	0.10
9	American Heritage BK	Sapulpa	OK	0.10
10	Blackhawk B&T	Milan	IL	0.11

Panel D2: The bottom medium bank normalized on-balance sheet liquidity creators in 2014:Q4

Rank	Name	City	State	On-balance sheet LC/GTA
1	First ST BK	Uvalde	TX	−0.08
2	Crescent B&TC	New Orleans	LA	−0.06
3	Banamex USA	Los Angeles	CA	−0.06

(Continued)

TABLE 11.4 Medium Bank Top and Bottom Normalized Liquidity Creators in 1984:Q1 and 2014:Q4 *(cont.)*

Panel D2: The bottom medium bank normalized on-balance sheet liquidity creators in 2014:Q4 *(cont.)*

Rank	Name	City	State	On-balance sheet LC/GTA
4	Citizens First BK	The Villages	FL	0.01
5	Interaudi BK	New York	NY	0.04
6	International BK of CMRC	Brownsville	TX	0.04
7	Bessemer TC NA	New York	NY	0.06
8	Blackhawk B&T	Milan	IL	0.06
9	American Heritage BK	Sapulpa	OK	0.07
10	Armed Forces BK NA	Fort Leavenworth	KS	0.08

Panel D3: The bottom medium bank normalized off-balance sheet liquidity creators in 2014:Q4

Rank	Name	City	State	Off-balance sheet LC/GTA
1	Intervest NB	New York	NY	0.00
2	Bessemer TC NA	New York	NY	0.00
3	Crescent B&TC	New Orleans	LA	0.00
4	DBA First Convenience BK	Killeen	TX	0.01
5	First ST BK	Uvalde	TX	0.01
6	BAC FL BK	Coral Gables	FL	0.02
7	Woori Amer BK	New York	NY	0.02
8	North CMNTY BK	Chicago	IL	0.02
9	Texas CMNTY BK	Laredo	TX	0.02
10	Parkway B&TC	Harwood Heights	IL	0.03

This table shows medium bank top normalized liquidity creators in 1984:Q1 and 2014:Q4 in Panels A and B, respectively, and the bottom liquidity creators in Panels C and D for the same two time periods. In each panel, Subpanels 1, 2, and 3 display the ranks based on "cat fat," on-balance sheet, and off-balance sheet liquidity creation, respectively, all three normalized by GTA. GTA equals total assets plus the allowance for loan and lease losses and the allocated transfer risk reserve (a reserve for certain foreign loans). Medium banks have GTA exceeding $1 billion and up to $3 billion. "Cat fat" liquidity creation (LC) classifies bank activities other than loans based on maturity and product category combined, but classifies loans by category due to data limitations, and includes off-balance sheet activities. Bank names are as reported on the Call Report. Location information is from the Federal Reserve Bank of Chicago website.

the top normalized medium bank liquidity creators had much less "cat fat" and off-balance sheet liquidity creation than the top large banks at that time, although their on-balance sheet liquidity creation was comparable. As shown in Table 11.4 Panel C, the bottom medium bank normalized liquidity creators all had negative or very low ratios for normalized "cat fat" and on-balance sheet liquidity creation and effectively zero normalized off-balance sheet liquidity creation. By 2014:Q4, the normalized figures were mostly positively, but still low (Table 11.4 Panel D).

11.1.5   Small Banks' Liquidity Creation in Dollar Terms

Table 11.5 Panel A shows that for small banks in 1984:Q1, the dollar values of the top liquidity creators are all under $1 billion as expected, but what is not expected is that some small banks have relatively large off-balance sheet liquidity creation, up to $0.68 billion. Table 11.5 Panel B shows that the top liquidity creators in 2014:Q4 are entirely different from those in 1984:Q1, because one of the largest small banks in the earlier time period closed voluntarily, two were acquired with government assistance, and the remaining seven were acquired without assistance. One small bank in 2014:Q4 has "cat fat" liquidity creation exceeding $1 billion, and this is entirely due to a very heavy presence of off-balance sheet liquidity creation – in fact its off-balance sheet liquidity creation exceeds its "cat fat" liquidity creation, implying negative on-balance sheet liquidity creation.[4] As shown in Table 11.5 Panel C, all of the bottom 10 small bank liquidity creators had negative "cat fat," on-balance sheet, and off-balance sheet liquidity creation in 1984:Q1. As indicated in Table 11.5 Panel D, the same largely held in 2014:Q4, except that only three had negative off-balance sheet liquidity creation at that time. Another 23 banks were tied with exactly zero off-balance sheet liquidity creation.

11.1.6   Small Banks' Normalized Liquidity Creation

Table 11.6 Panel A shows that in 1984:Q1, the top two normalized liquidity creators among small banks created normalized "cat fat" above 1.00 (i.e., more liquidity creation than GTA), higher than all the large and medium banks at that time. The top liquidity creators had fairly high on- and off-balance sheet liquidity creation as well. The top two normalized small bank liquidity creators had "cat fat" and off-balance sheet ratios above 1.00 in 2014:Q4, as shown in Table 11.6 Panel B, but by that time, several large banks also had this feature. As expected from the figures for the dollar values in Table 11.5, the bottom small bank normalized liquidity creators in 1984:Q1 all had negative ratios for normalized "cat fat," on-balance sheet, and off-balance sheet liquidity creation (Table 11.5 Panel C), and in 2014:Q4, all of these ratios were negative except

---

4. Table 11.5 Panel D shows that this bank is in the bottom 10 on-balance sheet liquidity creation with a negative value.

TABLE 11.5 Small Bank Top and Bottom Liquidity Creators (in $ Terms) in 1984:Q1 and 2014:Q4

Panel A1: The top small bank "cat fat" liquidity creators (in $ terms) in 1984:Q1

Rank	Name	City	State	"Cat fat" LC ($ billion)
1	Canadian Imperial BK of COM TC	New York	NY	0.91
2	Bank of NY DE	Wilmington	DE	0.75
3	National Blvd BK of Chicago	Chicago	IL	0.49
4	Alaska Mutual BK	Anchorage	AK	0.47
5	Texas American BK Dallas	Dallas	TX	0.44
6	Allied Lakewood BK	Dallas	TX	0.44
7	Michigan NB-Oakland	Southfield	MI	0.43
8	Central TC	Rochester	NY	0.42
9	Pacific Valley BK	San Jose	CA	0.40
10	First NB Jefferson PRSH	Gretna	LA	0.40

Panel A2: The top small bank on-balance sheet liquidity creators (in $ terms) in 1984:Q1

Rank	Name	City	State	On-balance sheet LC ($ billion)
1	Bank of NY DF	Wilmington	DE	0.75
2	Michigan NB-Oakland	Southfield	MI	0.38
3	Alaska Mutual BK	Anchorage	AK	0.37
4	Central TC	Rochester	NY	0.35
5	First NB Jefferson PRSH	Gretna	LA	0.33
6	Norwest BK St Paul NA	Saint Paul	MN	0.32
7	Pacific Valley BK	San Jose	CA	0.31
8	Continental BK	Phoenix	AZ	0.31
9	Union NB of Little Rock	Little Rock	AR	0.30
10	First City NB of Midland	Midland	TX	0.30

Panel A3: The top small bank off-balance sheet liquidity creators (in $ terms) in 1984:Q1

Rank	Name	City	State	Off-balance sheet LC ($ billion)
1	Canadian Imperial BK of COM TC	New York	NY	0.68
2	National Blvd BK of Chicago	Chicago	IL	0.20

TABLE 11.5 Small Bank Top and Bottom Liquidity Creators (in $ Terms) in 1984:Q1 and 2014:Q4 *(cont.)*

Panel A3: The top small bank off-balance sheet liquidity creators (in $ terms) in 1984:Q1 *(cont.)*

Rank	Name	City	State	Off-balance sheet LC ($ billion)
3	Abilene NB	Abilene	TX	0.16
4	Texas American BK Dallas	Dallas	TX	0.15
5	Allied Lakewood BK	Dallas	TX	0.15
6	Park BK of Florida	Saint Petersburg	FL	0.15
7	National BK of CMRC TR&SA	Lincoln	NE	0.14
8	Chicago-Tokyo BK	Chicago	IL	0.14
9	Norwest BK Bloomington NA	Bloomington	MN	0.12
10	Sun BK Suncoast NA	Saint Petersburg	FL	0.12

Panel B1: The top small bank "cat fat" liquidity creators (in $ terms) in 2014:Q4

Rank	Name	City	State	"Cat fat" LC ($ billion)
1	1st FNCL BK USA	Dakota Dunes	SD	1.01
2	Peoples NB	Mount Vernon	IL	0.69
3	Commerce BK of WA NA	Seattle	WA	0.68
4	Integrity BK	Camp Hill	PA	0.67
5	Old FL BK	Orlando	FL	0.67
6	Choice FNCL GRP	Fargo	ND	0.64
7	National BK of CMRC	Birmingham	AL	0.63
8	1st Constitution BK	Cranbury	NJ	0.62
9	First B&T	Evanston	IL	0.62
10	Sunwest BK	Irvine	CA	0.61

Panel B2: The top small bank on-balance sheet liquidity creators (in $ terms) in 2014:Q4

Rank	Name	City	State	On-balance sheet LC ($ billion)
1	Old FL BK	Orlando	FL	0.57
2	Peoples NB	Mount Vernon	IL	0.57
3	Choice FNCL GRP	Fargo	ND	0.56

(Continued)

TABLE 11.5 Small Bank Top and Bottom Liquidity Creators (in $ Terms) in 1984:Q1 and 2014:Q4 *(cont.)*

Panel B2: The top small bank on-balance sheet liquidity creators (in $ terms) in 2014:Q4 *(cont.)*

Rank	Name	City	State	On-balance sheet LC ($ billion)
4	Sunwest BK	Irvine	CA	0.55
5	Commerce BK of WA NA	Seattle	WA	0.51
6	National BK of CMRC	Birmingham	AL	0.51
7	Integrity BK	Camp Hill	PA	0.50
8	Bank of Springfield	Springfield	IL	0.49
9	Alma BK	Astoria	NY	0.49
10	Evans BK NA	Angola	NY	0.48

Panel B3: The top small bank off-balance sheet liquidity creators (in $ terms) in 2014:Q4

Rank	Name	City	State	Off-balance sheet LC ($ billion)
1	1st FNCL BK USA	Dakota Dunes	SD	1.10
2	TCM BK NA	Tampa	FL	0.28
3	First Arkansas B&T	Jacksonville	AR	0.27
4	Fidelity BK	Edina	MN	0.17
5	Commerce BK of WA NA	Seattle	WA	0.16
6	Integrity BK	Camp Hill	PA	0.16
7	Park BK	Milwaukee	WI	0.16
8	1st Constitution BK	Cranbury	NJ	0.15
9	Signature BK NA	Toledo	OH	0.15
10	Amalgamated BK Chicago	Chicago	IL	0.14

Panel C1: The bottom small bank "cat fat" liquidity creators (in $ terms) in 1984:Q1

Rank	Name	City	State	"Cat fat" LC ($ billion)
1	Provident of Delaware BK NA	Wilmington	DE	−0.13
2	Safrabank	Miami	FL	−0.11
3	First American Bank of NY	Albany	NY	−0.11
4	Banco CMRL	Mayaguez	PR	−0.10
5	Banco Central	New York	NY	−0.09

TABLE 11.5 Small Bank Top and Bottom Liquidity Creators (in $ Terms) in 1984:Q1 and 2014:Q4 *(cont.)*

Panel C1: The bottom small bank "cat fat" liquidity creators (in $ terms) in 1984:Q1 *(cont.)*

Rank	Name	City	State	"Cat fat" LC ($ billion)
6	South Chicago SVG BK	Chicago	IL	−0.08
7	Peoples BK	Cleveland	GA	−0.08
8	Comerica BK-Warren NA	Warren	MI	−0.08
9	Scotiabank de Puerto Rico	Hato Rey	PR	−0.08
10	Bank Audi USA	New York	NY	−0.07

Panel C2: The bottom small bank on-balance sheet liquidity creators (in $ terms) in 1984:Q1

Rank	Name	City	State	On-balance sheet LC ($ billion)
1	Provident of Delaware BK NA	Wilmington	DE	−0.13
2	First American Bank of NY	Albany	NY	−0.12
3	Safrabank	Miami	FL	−0.12
4	Scotiabank de Puerto Rico	Hato Rey	PR	−0.11
5	Banco CMRL	Mayaguez	PR	−0.10
6	Banco Central	New York	NY	−0.10
7	Bank Audi USA	New York	NY	−0.10
8	South Chicago SVG BK	Chicago	IL	−0.08
9	Peoples BK	Cleveland	GA	−0.08
10	Comerica BK-Warren NA	Warren	MI	−0.08

Panel C3: The bottom small bank off-balance sheet liquidity creators (in $ terms) in 1984:Q1

Rank	Name	City	State	Off-balance sheet LC ($ billion)
1	Peoples TC	Linton	IN	−0.02
2	F & M NB in Benton Harbor	Benton Harbor	MI	−0.01
3	Gulf NB	Gulfport	MS	−0.01
4	Texas American BK Dncnvle NA	Duncanville	TX	−0.01

(Continued)

TABLE 11.5 Small Bank Top and Bottom Liquidity Creators (in $ Terms) in 1984:Q1 and 2014:Q4 *(cont.)*

Panel C3: The bottom small bank off-balance sheet liquidity creators (in $ terms) in 1984:Q1 *(cont.)*

Rank	Name	City	State	Off-balance sheet LC ($ billion)
5	First Capitol BK	West Columbia	TX	−0.01
6	First City NB	Rio Rancho	NM	−0.01
7	First Security ST BK	Charleston	MO	−0.01
8	Benton CMNTY BK	Benton	IL	−0.01
9	Bank of Sikeston	Sikeston	MO	−0.01
10	First NB	Cleburne	TX	−0.01

Panel D1: The bottom small bank "cat fat" liquidity creators (in $ terms) in 2014:Q4

Rank	Name	City	State	"Cat fat" LC ($ billion)
1	Bank of Utica	Utica	NY	−0.28
2	Citizens ST BK	Buffalo	TX	−0.13
3	Citizens 1st BK	Tyler	TX	−0.08
4	International BK CMRC	Zapata	TX	−0.07
5	Fayetteville BK	Fayetteville	TX	−0.07
6	Industry ST BK	Industry	TX	−0.06
7	Farmers SVG BK	Spencer	OH	−0.05
8	Citizens BK of Winfield	Winfield	AL	−0.05
9	First NB	Shiner	TX	−0.05
10	Citizens BK	Carthage	TN	−0.05

Panel D2: The bottom small bank on-balance sheet liquidity creators (in $ terms) in 2014:Q4

Rank	Name	City	State	On-balance sheet LC ($ billion)
1	Bank of Utica	Utica	NY	−0.30
2	Citizens ST BK	Buffalo	TX	−0.14
3	1st FNCL BK USA	Dakota Dunes	SD	−0.09
4	Citizens 1st BK	Tyler	TX	−0.09
5	Industry ST BK	Industry	TX	−0.09
6	International BK CMRC	Zapata	TX	−0.08

TABLE 11.5 Small Bank Top and Bottom Liquidity Creators (in $ Terms) in 1984:Q1 and 2014:Q4 *(cont.)*

Panel D2: The bottom small bank on-balance sheet liquidity creators (in $ terms) in 2014:Q4 *(cont.)*

Rank	Name	City	State	On-balance sheet LC ($ billion)
7	Fayetteville BK	Fayetteville	TX	−0.08
8	Citizens BK	Carthage	TN	−0.06
9	Farmers SVG BK	Spencer	OH	−0.06
10	First NB	Bellville	TX	−0.06

Panel D3: The bottom small bank off-balance sheet liquidity creators (in $ terms) in 2014:Q4

Rank	Name	City	State	Off-balance sheet LC ($ billion)
1	Pacific Coast BKR BK	Walnut Creek	CA	−0.00
2	Trust Co BK	Memphis	TN	−0.00
3	Bessemer TC	Woodbridge	NJ	−0.00
4[a]	American T&SB	Lowden	IA	0.00
4[a]	Peoples B&TC	North Carrollton	MS	0.00
4[a]	McGehee BK	McGehee	AR	0.00
4[a]	Citizens BK Valley Head	Valley Head	AL	0.00
4[a]	Gratiot ST BK	Gratiot	WI	0.00
4[a]	Citizens B&TC	Atwood	TN	0.00
4[a]	Peoples BK	Chatham	LA	0.00

This table shows small bank top liquidity creators (in $ terms) in 1984:Q1 and 2014:Q4 in Panels A and B, respectively, and the bottom liquidity creators in Panels C and D for the same two time periods. In each panel, Subpanels 1, 2, and 3 display the ranks based on the dollar amounts of "cat fat," on-balance sheet, and off-balance sheet liquidity creation, respectively. Small banks have GTA up to $1 billion. GTA equals total assets plus the allowance for loan and lease losses and the allocated transfer risk reserve (a reserve for certain foreign loans). "Cat fat" liquidity creation (LC) classifies bank activities other than loans based on maturity and product category combined, but classifies loans by category due to data limitations, and includes off-balance sheet activities. Bank names are as reported on the Call Report. Location information is from the Federal Reserve Bank of Chicago website.
[a]23 banks are all ranked #4 with exactly $0 off-balance sheet liquidity creation. Seven are listed in the table. The remaining 16 are: Bank of Keystone (Keystone, NE), Reynold ST BK (Reynolds, IL), Bank of Pine Hill (Pine Hill, AL), Community BK Easton (Easton, IL), Freeland ST BK (Freeland, MI), Boston TR & Investment MNGT CO (Boston, MA), Fort Hood NB (Fort Hood, TX), Bank of Glen Ullin (Glen Ullin, ND), First ST BK of Fertile (Fertile, MN), Citizens ST BK of Glenville (Glenville, MN), Headwaters ST BK (Land O'Lakes, WI), Tri-State B&TC (Haughton, LA), Farmers BK of Cook (Cook, NE), State BK Wapello (Wapello, IA), State BK of Oskaloosa (Oskaloosa, KS) and Republic BK (Bountiful, UT).

TABLE 11.6 Small Bank Top and Bottom Normalized Liquidity Creators in 1984:Q1 and 2014:Q4

Panel A1: The top small bank normalized "cat fat" liquidity creators in 1984:Q1

Rank	Name	City	State	"Cat fat" LC/GTA
1	Canadian Imperial BK of COM TC	New York	NY	1.11
2	Independent BKR BK of FL	Orlando	FL	1.02
3	Allied BK Mockingbird	Dallas	TX	0.86
4	Bank of NY DE	Wilmington	DE	0.79
5	Bank of Orange CTY	Fountain Valley	CA	0.71
6	First NB in Eads	Eads	CO	0.70
7	United BK of Skyline NA	Denver	CO	0.68
8	Century BK	Los Angeles	CA	0.66
9	Truckee River BK	Truckee	CA	0.66
10	Texas American BK Dallas	Dallas	TX	0.65

Panel A2: The top small bank normalized on-balance sheet liquidity creators in 1984:Q1

Rank	Name	City	State	On-balance sheet LC/GTA
1	Independent BKR BK of FL	Orlando	FL	1.00
2	Bank of NY De	Wilmington	DE	0.79
3	Kings River ST BK	Reedley	CA	0.61
4	Bank of Boston Middlesex	Burlington	MA	0.58
5	Truckee River BK	Truckee	CA	0.56
6	Bank of Boston Barnstable NA	Yarmouth	MA	0.55
7	Farmers ST BK of Yuma	Yuma	CO	0.55
8	Sacramento Valley BK NA	Sacramento	CA	0.55
9	First NB of Arapahoe CTY	Aurora	CO	0.55
10	Intrawest BK of Aurora NA	Aurora	CO	0.54

Panel A3: The top small bank normalized off-balance sheet liquidity creators in 1984:Q1

Rank	Name	City	State	Off-balance sheet LC/GTA
1	Canadian Imperial BK of COM TC	New York	NY	0.82
2	Allied BK Mockingbird	Dallas	TX	0.50

TABLE 11.6 Small Bank Top and Bottom Normalized Liquidity Creators in 1984:Q1 and 2014:Q4 *(cont.)*

Panel A3: The top small bank normalized off-balance sheet liquidity creators in 1984:Q1 *(cont.)*

Rank	Name	City	State	Off-balance sheet LC/GTA
3	Century BK	Los Angeles	CA	0.36
4	Gulf South B&TC	Gretna	LA	0.34
5	Indian Head NB of Keene	Keene	NH	0.33
6	Merchants & Planters NB	Sherman	TX	0.28
7	First NB of Wisner	Wisner	NE	0.28
8	First NB in Eads	Eads	CO	0.27
9	Fort Worth B&TC	Fort Worth	TX	0.27
10	Texas American BK/Galleria	Houston	TX	0.26

Panel B1: The top small bank normalized "cat fat" liquidity creators in 2014:Q4

Rank	Name	City	State	"Cat fat" LC/GTA
1	1st FNCL BK USA	Dakota Dunes	SD	1.40
2	TCM BK NA	Tampa	FL	1.28
3	Farmers ST BK	Marion	SD	0.88
4	Core BK	Omaha	NE	0.88
5	Fidelity BK	Edina	MN	0.87
6	First ST BK of ND	Arthur	ND	0.80
7	Puget Sound BK	Bellevue	WA	0.79
8	Waterford BK NA	Toledo	OH	0.79
9	Seacoast CMRC BK	San Diego	CA	0.78
10	Parkside FNCL B&TC	Clayton	MO	0.78

Panel B2: The top small bank normalized on-balance sheet liquidity creators in 2014:Q4

Rank	Name	City	State	On-balance sheet LC/GTA
1	Seacoast CMRC BK	San Diego	CA	0.76
2	Heritage ST BK	Lawrenceville	IL	0.71
3	Core BK	Omaha	NE	0.70
4	Farmers ST BK	Marion	SD	0.68
5	Summit BK	Eugene	OR	0.67
6	State BK of Lismore	Lismore	MN	0.67

(Continued)

TABLE 11.6 Small Bank Top and Bottom Normalized Liquidity Creators in 1984:Q1 and 2014:Q4 *(cont.)*

Panel B2: The top small bank normalized on-balance sheet liquidity creators in 2014:Q4 *(cont.)*

Rank	Name	City	State	On-balance sheet LC/GTA
7	First ST BK of ND	Arthur	ND	0.67
8	Security ST BK	Tyndall	SD	0.65
9	Rolling Hills B&T	Atlantic	IA	0.65
10	Clarkston ST BK	Clarkston	MI	0.65

Panel B3: The top small bank normalized off-balance sheet liquidity creators in 2014:Q4

Rank	Name	City	State	Off-balance sheet LC/GTA
1	1st FNCL BK USA	Dakota Dunes	SD	1.52
2	TCM BK NA	Tampa	FL	1.43
3	First Arkansas B&T	Jacksonville	AR	0.40
4	Fidelity BK	Edina	MN	0.38
5	Haverford TC	Radnor	PA	0.38
6	Bankers BK of KS	Wichita	KS	0.31
7	First NB of Scott City	Scott City	KS	0.27
8	Parkside FNCL B&TC	Clayton	MO	0.25
9	Farmers & MRCH ST BK Bloomfiel	Bloomfield	NE	0.22
10	Waterford BK NA	Toledo	OH	0.22

Panel C1: The bottom small bank normalized "cat fat" liquidity creators in 1984:Q1

Rank	Name	City	State	"Cat fat" LC/GTA
1	Massachusetts Co	Boston	MA	−0.45
2	Citibank DE	New Castle	DE	−0.38
3	Hamilton CTY ST BK	Lockland	OH	−0.38
4	West Houston NB	Houston	TX	−0.35
5	Hopeton ST BK	Hopeton	OK	−0.33
6	Steiner BK	Birmingham	AL	−0.33
7	Abingdon B&TC	Abingdon	IL	−0.33
8	Financial CTR BK NA	San Francisco	CA	−0.32
9	First Progressive BK	Brewton	AL	−0.30
10	Peoples BK	Cleveland	GA	−0.30

TABLE 11.6 Small Bank Top and Bottom Normalized Liquidity Creators in 1984:Q1 and 2014:Q4 *(cont.)*

Panel C2: The bottom small bank normalized on-balance sheet liquidity creators in 1984:Q1

Rank	Name	City	State	On-balance sheet LC/GTA
1	Bank Audi USA	New York	NY	−0.47
2	Massachusetts Co	Boston	MA	−0.45
3	Citibank DE	New Castle	DE	−0.38
4	Hamilton CTY ST BK	Lockland	OH	−0.38
5	West Houston NB	Houston	TX	−0.35
6	Hopeton ST BK	Hopeton	OK	−0.34
7	Steiner BK	Birmingham	AL	−0.33
8	Abingdon B&TC	Abingdon	IL	−0.33
9	Volunteer B&TC	Chattanooga	TN	−0.33
10	Financial CTR BK NA	San Francisco	CA	−0.32

Panel C3: The bottom small bank normalized off-balance sheet liquidity creators in 1984:Q1

Rank	Name	City	State	Off-balance sheet LC/GTA
1	First City NB	Rio Rancho	NM	−0.13
2	Stone City BK of Bedford	Bedford	IN	−0.09
3	First Security ST BK	Cranfills Gap	TX	−0.08
4	Peoples TC	Linton	IN	−0.08
5	First Capitol BK	West Columbia	TX	−0.08
6	First ST BK	Smithville	TX	−0.08
7	First NB in Ashdown	Ashdown	AR	−0.08
8	Riverway BK	Houston	TX	−0.08
9	West Side NB	Pearland	TX	−0.08
10	Gretna ST BK	Gretna	NE	−0.07

Panel D1: The bottom small bank normalized "cat fat" liquidity creators in 2014:Q4

Rank	Name	City	State	"Cat fat" LC/GTA
1	Reynolds ST BK	Reynolds	IL	−0.30
2	Bank of Utica	Utica	NY	−0.29
3	Citizens BK of Winfield	Winfield	AL	−0.25

(Continued)

TABLE 11.6 Small Bank Top and Bottom Normalized Liquidity Creators in 1984:Q1 and 2014:Q4 *(cont.)*

Panel D1: The bottom small bank normalized "cat fat" liquidity creators in 2014:Q4 *(cont.)*

Rank	Name	City	State	"Cat fat" LC/GTA
4	Bank of Oak Ridge	Oak Ridge	LA	−0.24
5	Hill B&TC	Weimar	TX	−0.24
6	Union BKG Co	West Mansfield	OH	−0.24
7	Peoples B&TC	North Carrollton	MS	−0.23
8	Farmers & MRCH BK	Waterloo	AL	−0.23
9	Jonesboro ST BK	Jonesboro	LA	−0.23
10	First ST BK	Hemphill	TX	−0.22

Panel D2: The bottom small bank normalized on-balance sheet liquidity creators in 2014:Q4

Rank	Name	City	State	On-balance sheet LC/GTA
1	Bank of Utica	Utica	NY	−0.30
2	Reynolds ST BK	Reynolds	IL	−0.30
3	Citizens BK of Winfield	Winfield	AL	−0.27
4	Hill B&TC	Weimar	TX	−0.25
5	Bank of Oak Ridge	Oak Ridge	LA	−0.25
6	Union BKG Co	West Mansfield	OH	−0.24
7	Farmers & MRCH BK	Waterloo	AL	−0.24
8	Jonesboro ST BK	Jonesboro	LA	−0.23
9	Peoples B&TC	North Carrollton	MS	−0.23
10	First ST BK	Hemphill	TX	−0.22

Panel D3: The bottom small bank normalized off-balance sheet liquidity creators in 2014:Q4

Rank	Name	City	State	Off-balance sheet LC/GTA
1	Pacific Coast BKR BK	Walnut Creek	CA	−0.01
2	Trust Co BK	Memphis	TN	−0.00
3	Bessemer TC	Woodbridge	NJ	−0.00
4[a]	American T&SB	Lowden	IA	0.00
4[a]	Peoples B&TC	North Carrollton	MS	0.00
4[a]	McGehee BK	McGehee	AR	0.00
4[a]	Citizens BK Valley Head	Valley Head	AL	0.00

TABLE 11.6 Small Bank Top and Bottom Normalized Liquidity Creators in 1984:Q1 and 2014:Q4 *(cont.)*

Panel D3: The bottom small bank normalized off-balance sheet liquidity creators in 2014:Q4 *(cont.)*

Rank	Name	City	State	Off-balance sheet LC/GTA
4[a]	Gratiot ST BK	Gratiot	WI	0.00
4[a]	Citizens B&TC	Atwood	TN	0.00
4[a]	Peoples BK	Chatham	LA	0.00

This table shows small bank top normalized liquidity creators in 1984:Q1 and 2014:Q4 in Panels A and B, respectively, and the bottom liquidity creators in Panels C and D for the same two time periods. In each panel, Subpanels 1, 2, and 3 display the ranks based on "cat fat," on-balance sheet, and off-balance sheet liquidity creation, respectively, all three normalized by GTA. GTA equals total assets plus the allowance for loan and lease losses and the allocated transfer risk reserve (a reserve for certain foreign loans). Small banks have GTA up to $1 billion. "Cat fat" liquidity creation (LC) classifies bank activities other than loans based on maturity and product category combined, but classifies loans by category due to data limitations, and includes off-balance sheet activities. Bank names are as reported on the Call Report. Location information is from the Federal Reserve Bank of Chicago website.
[a]23 banks are all ranked #4 with exactly 0 normalized off-balance sheet liquidity creation. Seven are listed in the table. The remaining 16 are: Bank of Keystone (Keystone, NE), Reynold ST BK (Reynolds, IL), Bank of Pine Hill (Pine Hill, AL), Community BK Easton (Easton, IL), Freeland ST BK (Freeland, MI), Boston TR & Investment Mngt Co (Boston, MA), Fort Hood NB (Fort Hood, TX), Bank of Glen Ullin (Glen Ullin, ND), First ST BK of Fertile (Fertile, MN), Citizens ST BK of Glenville (Glenville, MN), Headwaters ST BK (Land O'Lakes, WI), Tri-State B&TC (Haughton, LA), Farmers BK of Cook (Cook, NE), State BK Wapello (Wapello, IA), State BK of Oskaloosa (Oskaloosa, KS), and Republic BK (Bountiful, UT).

for the 23 small banks with exactly zero normalized off-balance sheet ratios (Table 11.5 Panel D).

11.2 NEW EVIDENCE ON THE RELATIONS BETWEEN BANK LIQUIDITY CREATION AND BANK CHARACTERISTICS

It is useful to examine the relations between bank liquidity creation and bank performance. Tables 11.7–11.9 show how bank liquidity creation is associated with various bank characteristics for large, medium, and small banks, respectively. As in the literature discussed in Chapter 10 on the effects of capital, the focus here is on normalized liquidity creation rather than dollar values because most of the characteristics are also normalized.

11.2.1 Large Banks' Relations

Table 11.7 Panel A shows summary statistics for normalized liquidity creation and selected bank characteristics for large banks at the beginning of the sample period (1984:Q1), the end of the sample period (2014:Q4), and the full sample period. As already shown in Figure 8.3, normalized "cat fat" liquidity creation

TABLE 11.7 Large Bank Normalized Liquidity Creation – Bank Characteristics Summary Statistics and Correlations

Panel A: Large bank summary statistics

	1984:Q1			2014:Q4			1984:Q1–2014:Q4		
	Mean	Median	Std. Dev.	Mean	Median	Std. Dev.	Mean	Median	Std. Dev.
"Cat fat" LC / GTA	0.345	0.346	0.156	0.499	0.497	0.231	0.490	0.414	0.880
On-B/S LC / GTA	0.210	0.221	0.107	0.353	0.375	0.155	0.251	0.265	0.140
Off-B/S LC / GTA	0.135	0.118	0.093	0.146	0.099	0.210	0.239	0.122	0.886
GTA ($ billion)	15.124	5.943	30.577	57.150	7.367	225.601	31.436	7.715	121.730
Capital ratio	0.056	0.054	0.013	0.116	0.113	0.028	0.086	0.077	0.036
Portfolio risk	0.805	0.801	0.138	0.721	0.727	0.134	0.755	0.753	0.164
FDIC dummy	0.166	0.000	0.373	0.426	0.000	0.496	0.267	0.000	0.443
FED dummy	0.177	0.000	0.383	0.215	0.000	0.412	0.205	0.000	0.403
OCC dummy	0.657	1.000	0.476	0.359	0.000	0.481	0.528	1.000	0.499
BHC dummy	0.972	1.000	0.164	0.960	1.000	0.197	0.982	1.000	0.135

Panel B: Large bank correlations between normalized liquidity creation and bank characteristics

	1984:Q1			2014:Q4			1984:Q1–2014:Q4		
	"Cat fat" LC / GTA	On-B/S LC / GTA	Off-B/S LC / GTA	"Cat fat" LC / GTA	On-B/S LC / GTA	Off-B/S LC / GTA	"Cat fat" LC / GTA	On-B/S LC / GTA	Off-B/S LC / GTA
GTA ($ billion)	0.222	0.004	0.367	-0.094	-0.277	0.100	-0.004	-0.133	0.017
Capital ratio	-0.237	-0.154	-0.219	0.153	0.047	0.133	0.169	0.023	0.165
Portfolio risk	0.487	0.136	0.660	0.662	0.617	0.271	0.255	0.336	0.200

Panel C: Large bank normalized liquidity creation – means by regulator identity and BHC status

	1984:Q1			2014:Q4			1984:Q1–2014:Q4		
	"Cat fat" LC / GTA	On-B/S LC / GTA	Off-B/S LC / GTA	"Cat fat" LC / GTA	On-B/S LC / GTA	Off-B/S LC / GTA	"Cat fat" LC / GTA	On-B/S LC / GTA	Off-B/S LC / GTA
FDIC dummy = 1	0.250	0.169	0.081	0.502	0.384	0.118	0.436	0.247	0.189
FED dummy = 1	0.342	0.185	0.157	0.468	0.338	0.129	0.410	0.251	0.159
OCC dummy = 1	0.370	0.227	0.142	0.516	0.326	0.190	0.548	0.253	0.295
BHC dummy = 1	0.352	0.215	0.138	0.503	0.353	0.150	0.484	0.253	0.232
BHC dummy = 0	0.082	0.040	0.041	0.423	0.355	0.068	0.784	0.158	0.625

This table shows large bank summary statistics (means, medians, and standard deviations) and correlations for normalized liquidity creation and key bank characteristics. Large banks have GTA exceeding $3 billion. GTA equals total assets plus the allowance for loan and lease losses and the allocated transfer risk reserve (a reserve for certain foreign loans). Each panel shows "cat fat," on-balance sheet, and off-balance sheet liquidity creation normalized by GTA. "Cat fat" liquidity creation (LC) classifies bank activities other than loans based on maturity and product category combined, but classifies loans by category due to data limitations, and includes off-balance sheet activities. Capital ratio is equity capital as a proportion of GTA. Portfolio risk is defined as the bank's Basel I risk-weighted assets divided by GTA. The FDIC / FED / OCC dummies equal 1 if the Federal Deposit Insurance Corporation, the Federal Reserve Board, and the Office of the Comptroller of the Currency, respectively, are the primary bank regulators. BHC dummy equals 1 if the bank is part of a bank holding company.

TABLE 11.8 Medium Bank Normalized Liquidity Creation – Bank Characteristics Summary Statistics and Correlations

Panel A: Medium bank summary statistics

	1984:Q1			2014:Q4			1984:Q1–2014:Q4		
	Mean	Median	Std. Dev.	Mean	Median	Std. Dev.	Mean	Median	Std. Dev.
"Cat fat" LC / GTA	0.270	0.255	0.144	0.455	0.469	0.149	0.373	0.363	0.235
On-B/S LC / GTA	0.208	0.208	0.117	0.373	0.386	0.127	0.272	0.278	0.141
Off-B/S LC / GTA	0.061	0.046	0.059	0.082	0.076	0.037	0.101	0.076	0.184
GTA ($ billion)	1.661	1.540	0.534	1.614	1.430	0.521	1.661	1.509	0.542
Capital ratio	0.066	0.063	0.019	0.107	0.103	0.026	0.088	0.083	0.036
Portfolio risk	0.671	0.672	0.109	0.709	0.713	0.118	0.709	0.713	0.145
FDIC dummy	0.315	0.000	0.465	0.533	1.000	0.500	0.458	0.000	0.498
FED dummy	0.128	0.000	0.335	0.238	0.000	0.427	0.157	0.000	0.364
OCC dummy	0.556	1.000	0.498	0.229	0.000	0.421	0.386	0.000	0.487
BHC dummy	0.911	1.000	0.286	0.949	1.000	0.220	0.949	1.000	0.221

Panel B: Medium bank correlations between normalized liquidity creation and bank characteristics

	1984:Q1			2014:Q4			1984:Q1–2014:Q4		
	"Cat fat" LC / GTA	On-B/S LC / GTA	Off-B/S LC / GTA	"Cat fat" LC / GTA	On-B/S LC / GTA	Off-B/S LC / GTA	"Cat fat" LC / GTA	On-B/S LC / GTA	Off-B/S LC / GTA
GTA ($ billion)	0.128	0.108	0.099	0.110	0.114	0.050	0.048	0.017	0.049
Capital ratio	-0.187	-0.201	-0.058	-0.083	-0.088	-0.032	0.058	-0.021	0.090
Portfolio risk	0.686	0.645	0.401	0.766	0.754	0.489	0.552	0.564	0.273

Panel C: Medium bank normalized liquidity creation – means by regulator identity and BHC status

	1984:Q1			2014:Q4			1984:Q1–2014:Q4		
	"Cat fat" LC / GTA	On-B/S LC / GTA	Off-B/S LC / GTA	"Cat fat" LC / GTA	On-B/S LC / GTA	Off-B/S LC / GTA	"Cat fat" LC / GTA	On-B/S LC / GTA	Off-B/S LC / GTA
FDIC dummy = 1	0.261	0.207	0.054	0.450	0.367	0.083	0.375	0.283	0.092
FED dummy = 1	0.234	0.177	0.056	0.489	0.402	0.088	0.385	0.292	0.093
OCC dummy = 1	0.283	0.217	0.067	0.431	0.357	0.075	0.366	0.251	0.115
BHC dummy = 1	0.276	0.213	0.064	0.460	0.378	0.082	0.380	0.277	0.103
BHC dummy = 0	0.201	0.164	0.037	0.367	0.289	0.078	0.239	0.176	0.063

This table shows medium bank summary statistics (means, medians, and standard deviations) and correlations for normalized liquidity creation and key bank characteristics. Medium banks have GTA of $1 billion – $3 billion. GTA equals total assets plus the allowance for loan and lease losses and the allocated transfer risk reserve (a reserve for certain foreign loans). Each panel shows "cat fat," on-balance sheet, and off-balance sheet liquidity creation normalized by GTA. "Cat fat" liquidity creation (LC) classifies bank activities other than loans based on maturity and product category combined, but classifies loans by category due to data limitations, and includes off-balance sheet activities. Capital ratio is equity capital as a proportion of GTA. Portfolio risk is defined as the bank's Basel I risk-weighted assets divided by GTA. The FDIC / FED / OCC dummies equal 1 if the Federal Deposit Insurance Corporation, the Federal Reserve Board, and the Office of the Comptroller of the Currency, are the primary bank regulator. BHC dummy equals 1 if the bank is part of a bank holding company.

TABLE 11.9 Small Bank Normalized Liquidity Creation – Bank Characteristics Summary Statistics and Correlations

Panel A: Small bank summary statistics

	1984:Q1			2014:Q4			1984:Q1–2014:Q4		
	Mean	Median	Std. Dev.	Mean	Median	Std. Dev.	Mean	Median	Std. Dev.
"Cat fat" LC / GTA	0.131	0.124	0.146	0.330	0.340	0.182	0.212	0.207	0.469
On-B/S LC / GTA	0.118	0.116	0.136	0.280	0.292	0.160	0.172	0.174	0.157
Off-B/S LC / GTA	0.012	0.003	0.026	0.050	0.043	0.044	0.040	0.029	0.437
GTA ($ billion)	0.128	0.080	0.139	0.231	0.158	0.204	0.165	0.103	0.169
Capital ratio	0.084	0.080	0.025	0.110	0.104	0.034	0.096	0.089	0.033
Portfolio risk	0.591	0.590	0.123	0.655	0.666	0.133	0.626	0.631	0.131
FDIC dummy	0.590	1.000	0.492	0.679	1.000	0.467	0.611	1.000	0.488
FED dummy	0.070	0.000	0.255	0.141	0.000	0.348	0.100	0.000	0.300
OCC dummy	0.340	0.000	0.474	0.180	0.000	0.384	0.289	0.000	0.453
BHC dummy	0.597	1.000	0.491	0.836	1.000	0.370	0.765	1.000	0.424

Panel B: Small bank correlations between normalized liquidity creation and bank characteristics

	1984:Q1			2014:Q4			1984:Q1–2014:Q4		
	"Cat fat" LC / GTA	On-B/S LC / GTA	Off-B/S LC / GTA	"Cat fat" LC / GTA	On-B/S LC / GTA	Off-B/S LC / GTA	"Cat fat" LC / GTA	On-B/S LC / GTA	Off-B/S LC / GTA
GTA ($ billion)	0.200	0.155	0.315	0.272	0.237	0.261	0.114	0.249	0.033
Capital ratio	−0.329	−0.336	−0.096	−0.245	−0.268	−0.037	−0.055	−0.257	0.033
Portfolio risk	0.844	0.848	0.315	0.800	0.794	0.412	0.316	0.814	0.047

Panel C: Small bank normalized liquidity creation – means by regulator identity and BHC status

	1984:Q1			2014:Q4			1984:Q1–2014:Q4		
	"Cat fat" LC / GTA	On-B/S LC / GTA	Off-B/S LC / GTA	"Cat fat" LC / GTA	On-B/S LC / GTA	Off-B/S LC / GTA	"Cat fat" LC / GTA	On-B/S LC / GTA	Off-B/S LC / GTA
FDIC dummy = 1	0.128	0.118	0.011	0.337	0.287	0.050	0.210	0.173	0.037
FED dummy = 1	0.118	0.106	0.013	0.342	0.288	0.053	0.245	0.200	0.045
OCC dummy = 1	0.137	0.123	0.014	0.296	0.249	0.047	0.205	0.160	0.045
BHC dummy = 1	0.161	0.145	0.015	0.335	0.285	0.050	0.228	0.186	0.042
BHC dummy = 0	0.086	0.079	0.007	0.304	0.256	0.047	0.161	0.127	0.034

This table shows small bank summary statistics (means, medians, and standard deviations) and correlations for normalized liquidity creation and key bank characteristics. Small banks have GTA up to $1 billion. GTA equals total assets plus the allowance for loan and lease losses and the allocated transfer risk reserve (a reserve for certain foreign loans). Each panel shows "cat fat," on-balance sheet, and off-balance sheet liquidity creation normalized by GTA. "Cat fat" liquidity creation (LC) classifies bank activities other than loans based on maturity and product category combined, but classifies loans by category due to data limitations, and includes off-balance sheet activities. Capital ratio is equity capital as a proportion of GTA. Portfolio risk is defined as the bank's Basel I risk-weighted assets divided by GTA. The FDIC / FED / OCC dummies equal 1 if the Federal Deposit Insurance Corporation, the Federal Reserve Board, and the Office of the Comptroller of the Currency, are the primary bank regulator. BHC dummy equals 1 if the bank is part of a bank holding company.

and its on-balance sheet component in particular, grew significantly over the sample period. As well, average bank size of large banks, as measured by GTA more than tripled over time. Capital ratios (equity capital/GTA) doubled over time, likely due to higher capital requirements, stress tests, and supervisory pressure that are discussed more in Chapter 12. Portfolio risk (Basel I risk-weighted assets/GTA) decreased slightly. In terms of regulator identity, most of the large banks had national charters and so were supervised by the Office of the Comptroller of the Currency (OCC) in 1984:Q1, but a much smaller fraction had such charters in 2014:Q4. Finally, the vast majority of large banks are in BHCs for the entire time period.

Table 11.7 Panel B shows correlations between normalized liquidity creation and the bank characteristics that are continuous variables. There are some clear changes over time. Normalized "cat fat" and off-balance sheet liquidity creation were strongly positively related to GTA, while normalized on-balance sheet liquidity creation had very little correlation with size in 1984:Q1, but the correlations of normalized "cat fat" and on-balance sheet liquidity creation with GTA turned negative in 2014:Q4, and the correlation of normalized off-balance sheet liquidity creation with GTA was reduced considerably. The correlations of the capital ratio with all three normalized liquidity creation ratios were negative in 1984:Q1, but all were positive in 2014:Q4. These dramatic shifts call for care in mixing data from very different points in time because economic relations can change. Portfolio risk remains strongly positively correlated with the three normalized liquidity creation ratios in all cases. This is not surprising, since many assets and off-balance sheet activities that contribute positively to risk-weighted assets also contribute positively to liquidity creation.

Table 11.7 Panel C shows the means of normalized liquidity creation for the regulator identity and BHC status dummy variables. The regulator identity variables do not seem to be very strongly related to the normalized liquidity creation ratios, except that FDIC-regulated banks have smaller normalized off-balance sheet means in 1984:Q1, which may be explained by the fact that the FDIC generally supervises smaller banks within the large size class. Banks in BHCs create much more liquidity per dollar of assets than unaffiliated banks, and this again may be related to the relatively small size of unaffiliated banks. However, there may be too few unaffiliated large banks to draw strong conclusions.

11.2.2 Medium Banks' Relations

Table 11.8 Panel A shows the same data items for medium banks. Notable differences between the medium-bank size class and the large-bank size class include much smaller normalized off-balance sheet ratios, obviously much smaller GTA, lower portfolio risk, and a lower frequency of national bank charters and BHC membership. The correlations for the medium banks in Table 11.8 Panel B differ from the large banks in that the correlations with

GTA remain positive at the end of the sample period and correlations with capital remain negative in 2014:Q4, although they are slightly positive for the sample as a whole. The means in Table 11.8 Panel C suggest that regulator identity makes little difference to normalized liquidity creation. The means for the BHC-affiliated versus unaffiliated banks are much closer to each other, perhaps because of a greater number of observations for the unaffiliated banks.

11.2.3 Small Banks' Relations

Table 11.9 Panel A shows that small banks have much lower mean normalized liquidity creation than the other size classes. Most of these banks are regulated by the FDIC and fewer of them are in BHCs. The correlations with GTA are positive for both the beginning and end of the sample period, and the correlations with capital ratios are all negative, consistent with the literature summarized in Chapter 10. The correlations with portfolio risk are also higher than for the other size classes. Again, the regulator identity does not matter much and BHC-affiliated small banks have higher normalized liquidity creation than unaffiliated small banks

The discussions here are focused on summary statistics and correlations. It would be interesting to do a full-fledged regression analysis, which controls for multiple factors simultaneously and deals with potential endogeneity problems. This is left as a future research exercise.

11.3   SUMMARY

To gain a deeper understanding into what drives bank liquidity creation, this chapter provides new empirical evidence on the banks that create the most and least liquidity, and the relations between bank liquidity creation and bank characteristics. The key takeaways are that the banks that create the most and least liquidity look very different in 1984:Q1 and 2014:Q4, that the top and bottom creators also differ substantially across size classes, and that the relations between normalized liquidity creation and bank characteristics differ considerably over time and across bank size classes.

Chapter 12

How Do Government Policies and Actions Affect Bank Liquidity Creation During Normal Times and Financial Crises?

This chapter discusses government policies and actions that may affect liquidity creation. These effects may differ during financial crises and normal times. The policies and actions cover bank capital requirements, stress tests, liquidity requirements, regulatory interventions, capital support or bailouts, central bank funding, and monetary policy.

12.1 THE EFFECTS OF CAPITAL REQUIREMENTS ON LIQUIDITY CREATION

One of the most important government interventions in banking is the setting of minimum capital requirements, which may have significant effects on bank liquidity creation. Historically, the main purpose of these requirements has been microprudential, seeking to improve the safety and soundness of individual institutions. Capital may achieve this by providing a cushion to absorb future losses and by reducing the moral hazard incentive to take on excessive risk caused by deposit insurance and other aspects of the government safety net for banks, such as too-big-to-fail protection for the largest institutions. In the aftermath of the subprime lending crisis of 2007:Q3–2009:Q4, macropruden-tial considerations were added: capital should be high enough to limit systemic risk. See Thakor (2014) for an extensive discussion of the role of bank capital in financial stability.

It seems clear that in the aftermath of the US subprime lending crisis (2007:Q3–2009:Q4) and the European debt crisis (end of 2009–?), capital requirements are going up around the world. It is therefore important to understand how higher capital requirements affect liquidity creation by banks.

The existing literature focuses on the effects of capital, rather than capital requirements, on liquidity creation. As discussed in Chapter 10, capital has a positive effect on "cat fat" liquidity creation at large US banks, and a negative effect on "cat fat" liquidity creation at small US banks. Based on the less-desired "cat nonfat" measure, which excludes off-balance sheet activities, the effect is not significant for large banks but remains significantly negative for small banks. The limited evidence on this topic from other countries seems broadly consistent, showing a negative effect for small banks, and an insignificant effect for large banks, which might occur because large banks in other nations may have fewer off-balance sheet activities.

Of course, the relation between bank capital and liquidity creation is not necessarily the same as the relation between bank capital requirements and liquidity creation because bank capital is determined only in part by capital requirements. Any increase in capital requirements may be met by increasing the numerator and/or decreasing the denominator of the capital ratio. In the short run, it may be difficult to quickly increase capital in the numerator. It may be easier or less costly to reduce the denominator: as shown in Section 12.1.1, the denominators in different capital requirements are total assets, total assets plus off-balance sheet exposures, and risk-weighted assets. All three can be reduced by cutting back on business loans, which reduce liquidity creation. The latter two can also be reduced by cutting back on business loans and off-balance sheet guarantees, which again reduce liquidity creation. The evidence from the credit crunch of 1990:Q1–1992:Q4 and similar events in other countries discussed in Chapter 7 is consistent with the reduction in lending, but the effect on off-balance sheet activities is not measured. In the long run, the effects of higher capital requirements are more likely to be consistent with the effects of capital on liquidity creation shown in Chapter 10, increased liquidity creation at large US banks (which create most of the liquidity of the banking sector), particularly through off-balance sheet activities, and reduced liquidity creation at small US banks.

The rest of this section discusses recent changes in the regulatory landscape regarding capital requirements in the United States and elsewhere. It is useful to be familiar with these changes since they raise interesting topics for research. For example, it would be very helpful to study how proposed increases in different types of regulatory capital requirements affect liquidity creation. Also, while the very largest banks typically benefit from the expectation of being too big to fail, the new regulatory regimes in the United States and elsewhere put these institutions under far greater scrutiny. It would be interesting to examine whether the effects are different for the largest banks that are under the most scrutiny.

12.1.1   Basel III Capital Requirements

Basel III, released in December 2010 and to be fully implemented by 2019, increases bank capital requirements and raises the quality of capital at banks in participating nations (which include most of the developed countries) around the world. In the United States, banks of all sizes and BHCs with over $500 million in assets are subject to Basel III. Box 12.1 provides background information on the origins of the Basel Accords and Box 12.2 provides important details about the Basel III capital requirements.

BOX 12.1 Origins of the Basel Accords

Prior to the 1990s, there were several problems with the capital requirements imposed by regulators in the United States and other nations. First, the requirements were mostly on the ratio of some measure of bank capital (especially equity) to assets, which ignored obvious differences in risk across assets (e.g., business loans are riskier than government securities). Second, many large banks were engaging in substantial off-balance sheet activities, which generated risk that was not accounted for in capital requirements. Third, different nations had substantially different capital requirements,[a] which gave competitive advantages to international banking organizations headquartered in nations with lax requirements.

In 1988, the Basel Committee on Banking Regulations and Supervisory Practices, under the auspices of the Bank for International Settlements (BIS) in Basel, Switzerland, addressed these three problems with what was called the Basel Accord at that time, now called Basel I. It introduced risk-based capital requirements: it specified four risk buckets (0% (least risky), 20%, 50%, and 100% (most risky)), assigned assets to these buckets based on their perceived credit risk, and required more capital for assets in the higher-risk buckets. For example, business loans in the 100% category had twice the capital required of residential mortgages in the 50% category. In addition, capital was required against credit risk associated with off-balance sheet activities, with the weights depending on the nature of the activities and the risk category of the counterparties. Finally, the capital requirements were largely harmonized for internationally active banks headquartered in the Group of Ten (G-10) countries[b] as of 1992. Basel I was not generally required for other banks in these nations, but the United States adopted it for all banks and the requirements were phased in between 1990 and 1992. Eventually, over 100 other countries also adopted, at least in name, the principles prescribed under Basel I.

By the 2000s, some deficiencies of Basel I were evident, particularly that all business loans were assigned to the 100% risk category even though some loans were made to highly rated corporations while others were extended to much riskier distressed firms, and Basel II was developed. Basel II introduced three pillars. Pillar 1 specifies revised risk-based capital requirements. Pillar 2 specifies the importance of regulatory review, and was designed to ensure sound internal processes to manage capital adequacy. Pillar 3 specifies detailed guidance on disclosure of capital structure, risk exposure, and capital adequacy of banks with the goal of improving market discipline. The key change to the risk-based capital requirements was assigning business loans to the various risk buckets, including a new 150% bucket, based on credit ratings and in the case of the very largest institutions, internal risk models. Basel II was implemented in the mid-2000s in Europe, but was never fully implemented in the United States. It was being phased in by having parallel runs with Basel I, with only Basel I being enforced when the subprime lending crisis of 2007:Q3–2009:Q4 occurred.

The Dodd-Frank Act of 2010 (discussed later) essentially invalidated Basel II for US banks because it forbade regulations based on credit ratings. Thus, US institutions were left on Basel I and being phased into Basel III.

Basel III, released in December 2010, imposes higher capital requirements and raises the quality of capital to address several seeming deficiencies of Basel I and II:

(Continued)

the prior Accords did not give proper incentives to hold sufficient capital, did not adequately reflect the risks posed by securitization, lacked liquidity standards, and failed to incorporate systemic risks associated with the buildup of leverage in the financial system. The European Union applies Basel III to all financial institutions. The United States applies it to all insured depository institutions, top-tier BHCs with at least $500 million in consolidated assets, and top-tier savings and loan holding companies.

a. Even within the United States, capital requirements were not uniform across the three regulators (Federal Reserve, the Office of the Comptroller of the Currency, and the Federal Deposit Insurance Corporation), but ranged from 5% to 6%.
b. The G-10 countries include 11 countries: Belgium, Canada, France, Germany, Italy, Japan, The Netherlands, Sweden, Switzerland, the United Kingdom, and the United States.

BOX 12.2 Basel III Capital Requirements

Basel III imposes minimum capital requirements and three additional buffers (of which one only applies to the very largest banks), which are outlined here.
- Basel III's minimum capital requirements are:
  - 4.5% Common Equity Tier 1 Risk-Based Ratio (new to Basel III)
  - 6% Tier 1 Risk-Based Ratio (2% higher than in Basel I and Basel II)
  - 8% Total Risk-Based Ratio (same as in Basel I and Basel II)
  - 3% Tier 1 Leverage Ratio (Tier 1 capital to on- and off-balance sheet exposures) (new to Basel III)[a]
- The United States imposes two additional leverage ratios:
  - Tier 1 Leverage Ratio (Tier 1 capital/total assets) ≥ 4% to be met by all banks
  - Tier 1 Supplementary Leverage Ratio (SLR) (defined as the Basel III ratio) ≥ 3% to be met by large and internationally active banks and bank holding companies (so the minimum Tier 1 Leverage Ratio as defined in Basel III is 6%)
- A countercyclical buffer of 0%–2.5% Common Equity Tier 1 capital may be imposed by a country's regulator when excess aggregate credit growth is deemed to be associated with a build-up of systemic risk, to ensure that the banking sector has a buffer to protect itself against future potential losses.
- A capital conservation buffer (to be fully phased in by 2019) of 2.5% Common Equity Tier 1 capital is established above the minimum capital requirements to ensure that banks have extra capital during periods of stress. If a bank's buffer is less than 2.5%, capital distribution constraints are imposed, including limits on dividend payments, share buy-backs, and bonus payments to executives. This effectively increases the three risk-based capital requirements to 7%, 8.5%, and 10.5%, respectively.
  - The capital conservation buffer for globally systemically important banks (G-SIBs) proposed by Basel III is 1.0%–3.5% higher ("G-SIB surcharge") than for other banks. G-SIBs are banks whose distress or disorderly failure would significantly disrupt the wider financial system and economic activity. They are identified every year in November based on five characteristics: size, complexity, interconnectedness, lack of substitutability, and cross-jurisdictional activity. The size of the capital conservation buffer is the highest value generated by two calculation methods, the first of which is

based on these same five characteristics, and the second of which replaces one characteristic, substitutability, with a measure of the firm's reliance on short-term wholesale funding. The 2014 G-SIBs (in alphabetical order within each bucket) and their buffer sizes are listed below (these buffer sizes are superseded for US institutions by higher requirements established in July 2015 described right after this overview):

G-SIB buffer: 1.0%	G-SIB buffer: 1.5%	G-SIB buffer: 2.0%	G-SIB buffer: 2.5%	G-SIB buffer: 3.5%
Agricultural Bank of China	Bank of America	Barclays	HSBC	(Empty)
Bank of China	Credit Suisse	BNP Paribas	JPMorgan Chase	
Bank of New York Mellon	Goldman Sachs	Citigroup		
BBVA	Mitsubishi UFJ FG	Deutsche Bank		
Groupe BPCE	Morgan Stanley			
Group Credit Agricole	Royal Bank of Scotland			
Industrial and Commercial Bank of China Limited				
ING Bank				
Mizuho FG				
Nordea				
Santander				
Societe Generale				
Standard Chartered				
State Street				
Sumitomo Mitsui FG				
UBS				
Unicredit Group				
Wells Fargo				

- In July 2015, the Federal Reserve established capital conservation buffers ranging from 1.0% to 4.5% for the eight US G-SIBs. For all but Bank of New York Mellon, these are higher than the minimums suggested by the Basel Committee, and are given below:

G-SIB buffer:	G-SIB buffer:	G-SIB buffer:	G-SIB buffer:	G-SIB buffer:	G-SIB buffer:
1.0%	1.5%	2.0%	3.0%	3.5%	4.5%
Bank of New York Mellon	State Street	Wells Fargo	Bank of America	Citigroup	JPMorgan Chase
			Goldman Sachs		
			Morgan Stanley		

a. The Basel III Leverage Ratio will be subject to further calibration until 2017, with final implementation expected by January 18, 2018.

12.1.2 The Dodd-Frank Act and Systemically Important Financial Institutions (SIFIs)

The Dodd-Frank Act, passed in the United States in 2010, requires domestic systemically important financial institutions (SIFIs), financial institutions whose failure may trigger a financial crisis, to be supervised by the Federal Reserve. The Federal Reserve may require SIFIs to hold capital in excess of the Basel III standards, and intends to do so as explained in Box 12.2 above. Box 12.3 summarizes the Dodd-Frank Act and Box 12.4 shows the list of domestic SIFIs, which includes all banking organizations with at least $50 billion in total assets (TA), as well as four other large nonbank financial institutions that are also designated as systemically important.

BOX 12.3 The Dodd-Frank Act

The Dodd-Frank Wall Street Reform and Consumer Protection Act (commonly referred to as Dodd-Frank) was named after the two legislators who created it: Senator Christopher Dodd and Congressman Barney Frank. It was passed as a response to the subprime lending crisis of 2007:Q3–2009:Q4 and was signed into law in July 2010. Its goal was to mitigate the risk to financial stability that could emerge from the distress or failure of large, interconnected financial institutions. Dodd-Frank has brought major changes to financial regulation in particular in the following eight areas:

1. It created a Financial Stability Oversight Council (FSOC) to identify risks that affect the entire financial sector, to oversee nonbank financial firms, and break up large, complex firms. The law specified that any domestic bank holding company with at least $50 billion in assets would be a systemically important financial institution (SIFI), as would any foreign bank with worldwide assets of $50 billion or more that operates in the United States. The FSOC is also in charge of designating nonbank financial companies as SIFIs;

2. It created a Consumer Financial Protection Bureau (CFPB) within the Federal Reserve to protect consumers and ensure fair and nondiscriminatory access to credit;

3. It imposed the Volcker Rule, which prohibits proprietary trading (i.e., it does not allow banks to trade and take positions in securities that are not at the request of clients) and limits aggregate investment and sponsorship of hedge funds and private equity funds to 3% of the Tier 1 capital of the banking institution;
4. It requires that hedge funds (which were unregulated prior to the crisis) register with the SEC and provide information on their trades and portfolios;
5. It requires that risky derivatives (such as credit default swaps) be regulated and that a clearinghouse for trading them be set up;[a]
6. It created an Office of Credit Ratings within the SEC to examine credit rating agencies and improve the accuracy of ratings;
7. It created the Federal Insurance Office to monitor risk in the insurance industry;
8. It limits the Federal Reserve's emergency lending authority and required it to make public the names of recipients of emergency loans during the subprime-lending crisis.

---

a. A credit default swap (CDS) is a financial instrument that effectively provides insurance against non-payment on debt. A lender who is concerned that a firm may default on a loan (or an investor who fears that a firm may default on a bond or other security) can purchase a CDS to transfer the credit exposure to the CDS seller, typically an insurance company or other CDS seller. Speculators who believe that a firm may default purchase CDS contracts as well. The CDS market was unregulated until 2009. ICE Clear Credit (formerly ICE Trust) became the first clearinghouse to process CDS transactions. A clearinghouse requires that collateral be pledged and then takes on the credit risk of the transaction. That is, if one party cannot meet its obligation, the clearinghouse still pays the counterparty using the collateral and other funds.

BOX 12.4 US Systemically Important Financial Institutions (SIFIs) as of 2015

Number	Banking entities
1	Ally Financial Inc.
2	American Express Company
3	Bank of America Corporation
4	The Bank of New York Mellon Corporation
5	BB&T Corporation
6	BBVA Compass Bancshares, Inc.
7	BMO Financial Corp.
8	Capital One Financial Corporation
9	Citigroup Inc.
10	Comerica Incorporated
11	Deutsche Bank Trust Corporation
12	Discover Financial Services
13	Fifth Third Bancorp
14	The Goldman Sachs Group, Inc.
15	HSBC North America Holdings Inc.
16	Huntington Bancshares Incorporated

(Continued)

Number	Banking entities
17	JPMorgan Chase & Co.
18	KeyCorp
19	M&T Bank Corporation
20	Morgan Stanley
21	MUFG Americas Holdings Corporation
22	Northern Trust Corporation
23	The PNC Financial Services Group, Inc.
24	RBS Citizens Financial Group, Inc.
25	Regions Financial Corporation
26	Santander Holdings USA, Inc.
27	State Street Corporation
28	SunTrust Banks, Inc.
29	US Bancorp
30	Wells Fargo & Co.
31	Zions Bancorporation
Number	**Non-Bank entities**
1	AIG
2	GE Capital
3	Metlife Insurance
4	Prudential Insurance

12.2   STRESS TESTS IN THE UNITED STATES AND EUROPE

The largest banking organizations in the United States and Europe are also subject to stress tests, which require these organizations to have adequate capital to weather adverse future scenarios.

The first stress test in the United States took place in 2009 and was called the Supervisory Capital Assessment Program (SCAP). Since 2011, the Comprehensive Capital Analysis and Review (CCAR), which is similar, has taken its place. Under the stress tests, a banking organization has to show that it would have enough capital to withstand three scenarios – a baseline, adverse, and severely adverse scenario.[1] Each bank has its capital plan reviewed and approved

---

1. The adverse and severely adverse supervisory scenarios differ every year. In 2015, they included trajectories for 28 variables. Specifically, the severely adverse scenario was characterized by a substantial global weakening in economic activity, including a severe recession in the United States, large drops in asset prices, significant widening of corporate bond spreads, and a sharp increase in equity market volatility. The adverse scenario featured a global weakening in economic activity and an increase in US inflationary pressures that overall result in rapid increases in both short- and long-term US Treasury rates. For full details, see Board of Governors of the Federal Reserve System (2015).

or rejected by the Federal Reserve on the basis of the results of the stress tests. Originally, the 19 largest banking organizations with over $100 billion in total assets were subject to the stress tests. Since 2012, they are applied to all banking institutions with at least $50 billion in consolidated assets – the same list as the domestic banking SIFIs in Box 12.4.[2]

Banks in Europe are also subject to stress tests. Some of these tests are by the European Banking Authority (EBA), an independent regulatory authority of the European Union (EU) that was established in 2011 and is headquartered in London. It conducts stress tests on European banks to increase transparency in the European financial system and identify weaknesses in banks' capital structures. The EBA conducted stress tests in 2011 and 2014.[3] In 2014, the EU-wide stress test was carried out on 123 banks at the highest level of consolidation from 22 countries with assets totaling approximately €28 trillion as of year-end 2013, covering more than 70% of banking assets in the EU. These institutions are shown in Table 12.1. Similar to the United States, the EBA stress tests include several scenarios (a baseline and adverse scenario) to assess whether the banks' balance sheets are healthy enough to withstand further economic shocks.[4] The results of the stress tests in 2014 revealed that 24 participating banks had capital shortfalls totaling €24.6 billion. The EBA tests are checked by the European Central Bank (ECB) for institutions in the euro zone, and by the national central banks in other nations.

In the United Kingdom, the Bank of England started to conduct its own stress tests in 2014, which will take place on an annual basis. The 2014 stress test was conducted as a "UK version" of the EBA's EU-wide stress test with additional emphasis on risks in Britain's housing market. Eight UK banks were subjected to the stress tests, including four banks that were part of the EBA tests (Barclays, HSBC, Lloyds Banking Group, and Royal Bank of Scotland) and four more banks (Standard Chartered, Co-operative Bank, the UK arm of Santander, and Nationwide Building Society). All banks passed the tests.

In the euro zone, the Single Supervisory Mechanism granted the ECB the task to directly supervise the largest Euro area banks from November 2014 onward. In preparation, the ECB conducted a comprehensive assessment, including an asset quality review (AQR) and stress tests, of 130 banks, listed in Table 12.2. Going forward, the ECB will directly supervise 120 so-called

---

2. In addition to the Federal Reserve-run stress tests, institutions with at least $50 billion in assets have to have two internal stress tests per year, and those with at least $10 billion but less than $50 billion are required to have one internal stress test per year.
3. The Committee of European Banking Supervisors (CEBS) conducted two other tests in 2009 and 2010, and the EBA then took over its responsibilities.
4. The 2014 adverse scenario reflects the systemic risks that were assessed to be the most pertinent threats to stability in the EU banking sector: an increase in global bond yields amplified by an abrupt reversal in risk assessment, especially toward emerging market economies; a further deterioration of credit quality in countries with feeble demand; stalling policy reforms jeopardizing confidence in the sustainability of public finances; and the lack of necessary bank balance sheet repair to maintain affordable market funding.

TABLE 12.1 European Union (EU) Institutions Subject to the European Banking Authority (EBA) 2014 Stress Tests

Number	Country	Bank name
1	Austria	BAWAG P.S.K. Bank für Arbeit und Wirtschaft und Österreichische Postsparkasse AG
2	Austria	Erste Group Bank AG
3	Austria	Raiffeisen Zentralbank Österreich AG
4	Austria	Raiffeisenlandesbank Niederösterreich-Wien AG
5	Austria	Raiffeisenlandesbank Oberösterreich AG
6	Austria	Österreichische Volksbanken-AG with credit institutions affiliated according to Article 10 of the CR
7	Belgium	AXA Bank Europe SA
8	Belgium	Belfius Banque SA
9	Belgium	Dexia NV
10	Belgium	Investar (Holding of Argenta Bank- en Verzekeringsgroep)
11	Belgium	KBC Group NV
12	Cyprus	Bank of Cyprus Public Company Ltd
13	Cyprus	Co-operative Central Bank Ltd
14	Cyprus	Hellenic Bank Public Company Ltd
15	Germany	Aareal Bank AG
16	Germany	Bayerische Landesbank
17	Germany	Commerzbank AG
18	Germany	DZ Bank AG Deutsche Zentral-Genossenschaftsbank
19	Germany	DekaBank Deutsche Girozentrale
20	Germany	Deutsche Apothekerund Ärztebank eG
21	Germany	Deutsche Bank AG
22	Germany	HASPA Finanzholding
23	Germany	HSH Nordbank AG
24	Germany	Hypo Real Estate Holding AG
25	Germany	IKB Deutsche Industriebank AG
26	Germany	KfW IPEX-Bank GmbH
27	Germany	Landesbank BadenWürttemberg
28	Germany	Landesbank Berlin Holding AG
29	Germany	Landesbank Hessen-Thüringen Girozentrale
30	Germany	Landeskreditbank Baden-Württemberg-Förderbank
31	Germany	Landwirtschaftliche Rentenbank
32	Germany	Münchener Hypothekenbank eG

TABLE 12.1 European Union (EU) Institutions Subject to the European Banking Authority (EBA) 2014 Stress Tests *(cont.)*

Number	Country	Bank name
33	Germany	NRW.Bank
34	Germany	Norddeutsche LandesbankGirozentrale
35	Germany	Volkswagen Financial Services AG
36	Germany	WGZ Bank AG Westdeutsche GenossenschaftsZentralbank
37	Germany	Wüstenrot Bank AG Pfandbriefbank
38	Germany	Wüstenrot Bausparkasse AG
39	Denmark	Danske Bank
40	Denmark	Jyske Bank
41	Denmark	Nykredit
42	Denmark	Sydbank
43	Spain	Banco Bilbao Vizcaya Argentaria
44	Spain	Banco Financiero y de Ahorros
45	Spain	Banco Mare Nostrum
46	Spain	Banco Popular Español
47	Spain	Banco Santander
48	Spain	Banco de Sabadell
49	Spain	Bankinter
50	Spain	Caja de Ahorros y M.P. de Zaragoza
51	Spain	Caja de Ahorros y Pensiones de Barcelona
52	Spain	Cajas Rurales Unidas
53	Spain	Catalunya Banc
54	Spain	Kutxabank
55	Spain	Liberbank
56	Spain	MPCA Ronda
57	Spain	NCG Banco
58	Finland	OP-Pohjola Group
59	France	BNP Paribas
60	France	BPI France (Banque Publique d'Investissement)
61	France	Banque PSA Finance
62	France	C.R.H. – Caisse de Refinancement de l'Habitat
63	France	Groupe BPCE
64	France	Groupe Crédit Agricole
65	France	Groupe Crédit Mutuel
66	France	La Banque Postale

(Continued)

TABLE 12.1 European Union (EU) Institutions Subject to the European Banking Authority (EBA) 2014 Stress Tests *(cont.)*

Number	Country	Bank name
67	France	RCI Banque
68	France	Société Générale
69	France	Société de Financement Local
70	Greece	Alpha Bank
71	Greece	Eurobank Ergasias
72	Greece	National Bank of Greece
73	Greece	Piraeus Bank
74	Hungary	OTP Bank Ltd
75	Ireland	Allied Irish Banks plc
76	Ireland	Permanent tsb plc.
77	Ireland	The Governor and Company of the Bank of Ireland
78	Italy	Banca Carige S.P.A. Cassa di Risparmio di Genova e Imperia
79	Italy	Banca Monte dei Paschi di Siena S.p.A.
80	Italy	Banca Piccolo Credito Valtellinese
81	Italy	Banca Popolare Dell'Emilia Romagna – Società Cooperativa
82	Italy	Banca Popolare Di Milano – Società Cooperativa A Responsabilità Limitata
83	Italy	Banca Popolare di Sondrio
84	Italy	Banca Popolare di Vicenza – Società Cooperativa per Azioni
85	Italy	Banco Popolare – Società Cooperativa
86	Italy	Credito Emiliano S.p.A.
87	Italy	Iccrea Holding S.p.A
88	Italy	Intesa Sanpaolo S.p.A.
89	Italy	Mediobanca – Banca di Credito Finanziario S.p.A.
90	Italy	UniCredit S.p.A.
91	Italy	Unione Di Banche Italiane Società Cooperativa Per Azioni
92	Italy	Veneto Banca S.C.P.A.
93	Luxembourg	Banque et Caisse d'Epargne de l'Etat
94	Luxembourg	Precision Capital S.A. (Holding of Banque Internationale à Luxembourg and KBL European Private Bankers S.A.)
95	Latvia	ABLV Bank

TABLE 12.1 European Union (EU) Institutions Subject to the European Banking Authority (EBA) 2014 Stress Tests *(cont.)*

Number	Country	Bank name
96	Malta	Bank of Valletta plc
97	Netherlands	ABN AMRO Bank N.V.
98	Netherlands	Bank Nederlandse Gemeenten N.V.
99	Netherlands	Coöperatieve Centrale Raiffeisen-Boerenleenbank B.A.
100	Netherlands	ING Bank N.V.
101	Netherlands	Nederlandse Waterschapsbank N.V.
102	Netherlands	SNS Bank N.V.
103	Norway	DNB Bank Group
104	Poland	Alior Bank SA
105	Poland	Bank BPH SA
106	Poland	Bank Handlowy W Warszawie SA
107	Poland	Bank Ochrony Srodowiska SA
108	Poland	Getin Noble Bank SA
109	Poland	Powszechna Kasa Oszczednosci Bank Polski S.A. (PKO Bank Polski)
110	Portugal	Banco BPI
111	Portugal	Banco Comercial Português
112	Portugal	Caixa Geral de Depósitos
113	Sweden	Nordea Bank AB (publ)
114	Sweden	Skandinaviska Enskilda Banken AB (publ) (SEB)
115	Sweden	Svenska Handelsbanken AB (publ)
116	Sweden	Swedbank AB (publ)
117	Slovenia	Nova Kreditna Banka Maribor d.d.
118	Slovenia	Nova Ljubljanska banka d. d.
119	Slovenia	SID – Slovenska izvozna in razvojna banka
120	United Kingdom	Barclays plc
121	United Kingdom	HSBC Holdings plc
122	United Kingdom	Lloyds Banking Group plc
123	United Kingdom	Royal Bank of Scotland Group plc

This table lists the 123 EU banks that were subject to stress tests by the European Banking Authority in 2014.

TABLE 12.2 Institutions Subject to the European Central Bank (ECB)
Comprehensive Assessment in 2014

Number	Country	Bank name
1	Austria	BAWAG P.S.K. Bank für Arbeit und Wirtschaft und Österreichische Postsparkasse AG
2	Austria	Erste Group Bank AG
3	Austria	Raiffeisenlandesbank Oberösterreich AG
4	Austria	Raiffeisenlandesbank Niederösterreich-Wien AG
5	Austria	Raiffeisen Zentralbank Österreich AG
6	Austria	Österreichische Volksbanken-AG with credit institutions affiliated according to Article 10 of the CRR
7	Belgium	AXA Bank Europe SA
8	Belgium	Belfius Banque SA
9	Belgium	Dexia NV
10	Belgium	Investar (Holding of Argenta Bank- en Verzekeringsgroep)
11	Belgium	KBC Group NV
12	Belgium	The Bank of New York Mellon SA
13	Cyprus	Bank of Cyprus Public Company Ltd
14	Cyprus	Cooperative Central Bank Ltd
15	Cyprus	Hellenic Bank Public Company Ltd
16	Cyprus	Russian Commercial Bank (Cyprus) Ltd (RCB Bank Ltd)
17	Germany	Aareal Bank AG
18	Germany	Bayerische Landesbank
19	Germany	Commerzbank AG
20	Germany	DekaBank Deutsche Girozentrale
21	Germany	Deutsche Apotheker – und Ärztebank eG
22	Germany	Deutsche Bank AG
23	Germany	DZ Bank AG Deutsche ZentralGenossenschaftsbank
24	Germany	HASPA Finanzholding
25	Germany	HSH Nordbank AG
26	Germany	Hypo Real Estate Holding AG
27	Germany	IKB Deutsche Industriebank AG
28	Germany	KfW IPEX-Bank GmbH
29	Germany	Landesbank Baden-Württemberg
30	Germany	Landesbank Berlin Holding AG
31	Germany	Landesbank Hessen-Thüringen Girozentrale
32	Germany	Landeskreditbank Baden-Württemberg-Förderbank
33	Germany	Landwirtschaftliche Rentenbank

TABLE 12.2 Institutions Subject to the European Central Bank (ECB) Comprehensive Assessment in 2014 *(cont.)*

Number	Country	Bank name
34	Germany	Münchener Hypothekenbank eG
35	Germany	Norddeutsche Landesbank-Girozentrale
36	Germany	NRW.Bank
37	Germany	SEB AG
38	Germany	Volkswagen Financial Services AG
39	Germany	WGZ Bank AG Westdeutsche GenossenschaftsZentralbank
40	Germany	Wüstenrot Bank AG Pfandbriefbank
41	Germany	Wüstenrot Bausparkasse AG
42	Estonia	AS DNB Bank
43	Estonia	AS SEB Pank
44	Estonia	Swedbank AS
45	Spain	Banco Bilbao Vizcaya Argentaria, SA (BBVA)
46	Spain	Banco de Sabadell, SA (Sabadell)
47	Spain	Banco Financiero y de Ahorros, SA (BFA/Bankia)
48	Spain	Banco Mare Nostrum, SA
49	Spain	Banco Popular Español, SA
50	Spain	Bankinter, SA
51	Spain	Banco Santander, SA (Santander)
52	Spain	Caja de Ahorros y M.P. de Zaragoza, Aragón y Rioja (Ibercaja)
53	Spain	Caja de Ahorros y Pensiones de Barcelona (La Caixa)
54	Spain	MPCA Ronda, Cádiz, Almería, Málaga, Antequera y Jaén (Unicaja-Ceiss)
55	Spain	Cajas Rurales Unidas, Sociedad Cooperativa de Crédito
56	Spain	Catalunya Banc, SA
57	Spain	Kutxabank, SA
58	Spain	Liberbank, SA
59	Spain	NCG Banco, SA
60	Finland	Danske Bank plc (Finland)
61	Finland	Nordea Bank Finland Abp
62	Finland	OP-Pohjola Group
63	France	Banque Centrale de Compensation (LCH Clearnet)
64	France	Banque PSA Finance
65	France	BNP Paribas
66	France	C.R.H. – Caisse de Refinancement de l'Habitat

(Continued)

TABLE 12.2 Institutions Subject to the European Central Bank (ECB) Comprehensive Assessment in 2014 *(cont.)*

Number	Country	Bank name
67	France	Groupe BPCE
68	France	Groupe Crédit Agricole
69	France	Groupe Crédit Mutuel
70	France	HSBC France
71	France	La Banque Postale
72	France	BPI France (Banque Publique d'Investissement)
73	France	RCI Banque
74	France	Société de Financement Local
75	France	Société Générale
76	Greece	Alpha Bank, SA
77	Greece	Eurobank Ergasias, SA
78	Greece	National Bank of Greece, SA
79	Greece	Piraeus Bank, SA
80	Ireland	Allied Irish Banks plc
81	Ireland	Merrill Lynch International Bank Limited
82	Ireland	Permanent tsb plc.
83	Ireland	The Governor and Company of the Bank of Ireland
84	Ireland	Ulster Bank Ireland Limited
85	Italy	Banca Carige S.P.A. – Cassa di Risparmio di Genova e Imperia
86	Italy	Banca Monte dei Paschi di Siena S.p.A.
87	Italy	Banca Piccolo Credito Valtellinese, Società Cooperativa
88	Italy	Banca Popolare Dell'Emilia Romagna – Società Cooperativa
89	Italy	Banca Popolare Di Milano – Società Cooperativa A Responsabilità Limitata
90	Italy	Banca Popolare di Sondrio, Società Cooperativa per Azioni
91	Italy	Banca Popolare di Vicenza – Società Cooperativa per Azioni
92	Italy	Banco Popolare – Società Cooperativa
93	Italy	Credito Emiliano S.p.A.
94	Italy	Iccrea Holding S.p.A
95	Italy	Intesa Sanpaolo S.p.A.
96	Italy	Mediobanca – Banca di Credito Finanziario S.p.A.
97	Italy	UniCredit S.p.A.
98	Italy	Unione Di Banche Italiane Società Cooperativa Per Azioni

TABLE 12.2 Institutions Subject to the European Central Bank (ECB) Comprehensive Assessment in 2014 *(cont.)*

Number	Country	Bank name
99	Italy	Veneto Banca S.C.P.A.
100	Luxembourg	Banque et Caisse d'Epargne de l'Etat, Luxembourg
101	Luxembourg	Clearstream Banking SA
102	Luxembourg	Precision Capital SA (Holding of Banque Internationale à Luxembourg and KBL European Private Bankers SA)
103	Luxembourg	RBC Investor Services Bank SA
104	Luxembourg	State Street Bank Luxembourg SA
105	Luxembourg	UBS (Luxembourg) SA
106	Latvia	ABLV Bank, AS
107	Latvia	AS SEB banka
108	Latvia	Swedbank AS
109	Lithuania	AB DNB bankas
110	Lithuania	AB SEB bankas
111	Lithuania	Swedbank AB
112	Malta	Bank of Valletta plc
113	Malta	HSBC Bank Malta plc
114	Malta	Deutsche Bank (Malta) Ltd
115	Netherlands	ABN AMRO Bank N.V.
116	Netherlands	Bank Nederlandse Gemeenten N.V.
117	Netherlands	Coöperatieve Centrale Raiffeisen-Boerenleenbank B.A.
118	Netherlands	ING Bank N.V.
119	Netherlands	Nederlandse Waterschapsbank N.V.
120	Netherlands	The Royal Bank of Scotland N.V.
121	Netherlands	SNS Bank N.V.
122	Portugal	Banco BPI, SA
123	Portugal	Banco Comercial Português, SA
124	Portugal	Caixa Geral de Depósitos, SA
125	Slovenia	Nova Kreditna Banka Maribor d.d.
126	Slovenia	Nova Ljubljanska banka d. d., Ljubljana
127	Slovenia	SID – Slovenska izvozna in razvojna banka, d.d., Ljubljana
128	Slovakia	Slovenská sporiteľňa, a.s.
129	Slovakia	Všeobecná úverová banka, a.s.
130	Slovakia	Tatra banka, a.s.

This table lists the 130 largest banks in the Euro area that were subject to the European Central Bank's 2014 comprehensive assessment, which comprised an asset quality review (AQR) and stress tests.

significant supervised institutions.[5] The significance of these institutions is based on: asset value, importance for the economy of the country in which they are located or the EU, the scale of their cross-border activities, and whether they requested or received financial assistance from the European Stability Mechanism or the European Financial Stability Facility.

12.3 LIQUIDITY REQUIREMENTS

As discussed in Chapter 6, Basel III also imposes liquidity requirements: the Liquidity Coverage Ratio (LCR), which promotes short-term resilience, and the Net Stable Funding Ratio (NSFR), which promotes long-run resilience. As shown there, the Basel III liquidity ratios are inversely related to the liquidity creation measures, suggesting that the enforcement of these minimum liquidity ratios may be expected to reduce bank liquidity creation.

It is important to realize that liquidity requirements and capital requirements address different problems and affect different sides of the balance sheet. Liquidity requirements focus on withdrawal risk on the liability side and off the balance sheet, and deal with it by requiring that a fraction of the bank's assets be held as cash or deposits with the central bank. Capital requirements focus on asset-substitution risk and deal with it by requiring that a fraction of the bank's liabilities be in the form of equity. Little is known about how liquidity requirements and capital requirements may interact and jointly affect liquidity creation. Two theory papers try to address this. Acharya, Mehran, and Thakor (2013) show that it is optimal to impose a regular minimum capital requirement and a liquidity requirement when a bank faces two moral hazard problems, too little monitoring by managers and risk shifting by shareholders. Calomiris, Heider, and Hoerova (2013) argue that capital requirements and liquidity requirements act as (imperfect) substitutes since the market will recognize that risk management decisions are more prudent at a bank with a higher cash balance. See Bouwman (2015) for a discussion.

12.4 REGULATORY INTERVENTIONS, CAPITAL SUPPORT OR BAILOUTS, AND CENTRAL BANK FUNDING

Liquidity creation may also be affected by other government policies. Bank-regulatory agencies often intrude into individual institutions in response to perceived problems. Examples include placing restrictions on lending or deposits, or in more extreme cases, issuing cease-and-desist orders.[6] As well, often during financial crises and occasionally at other times, authorities provide capital support or bailouts to banks, such as the TARP program in the United States. In addition, central banks often provide short-term funds to banks in their role of lender of last resort during normal times and especially during financial crises.

---

5. The complete 2015 list is contained in European Central Bank (2015).
6. A cease and desist order requires the bank to halt some activity ("cease") and not take it up again later ("desist").

Empirical evidence on the effects of these actions on bank liquidity creation is scarce. Berger, Bouwman, Kick, and Schaeck (2014) use data on both regulatory interventions and capital support in Germany from 1999 to 2009 to examine how these actions affect liquidity creation. They find that regulatory interventions, such as restrictions on lending activities, significantly reduce bank liquidity creation, while capital support or bailouts have no significant effect.

Several papers examine the effects of the TARP bank bailouts in the United States over 2008:Q4–2009:Q4. Most of those studies focus on one key component of liquidity creation, lending, and document an increase in lending, particularly by small banks (Black and Hazelwood, 2013; Li, 2013; Puddu and Walchli, 2014; and Duchin and Sosyura, 2014). One of the studies researches the effects on lending and off-balance sheet guarantees, another important component of liquidity creation, and finds increases in both (Berger and Roman, 2015).

Finally, one study on the effects of funds from the central bank during the subprime lending crisis (2007:Q3–2009:Q4) in the United States finds that Federal Reserve funds provided through the discount window and Term Auction Facilities (TAF) had a strong positive effect on lending (Berger, Black, Bouwman, and Dlugosz, 2015).

12.5   MONETARY POLICY

Bank liquidity creation may also be an important part of the transmission of monetary policy to the economy. To ameliorate liquidity concerns and to stimulate the economy, monetary policy is typically loosened during financial crises and economic downturns. According to the bank lending channel literature, monetary policy may affect the real economy through stimulating bank lending (for survey papers on this, see Bernanke and Gertler, 1995; and Kashyap and Stein, 1997).[7] However, this literature has paid less attention to the fact that monetary policy may also affect off-balance sheet activities like loan commitments (e.g., Woodford, 1996; and Morgan, 1998). This may be an important omission, given that these commitments may affect economic growth as well.

A recent paper extends this literature by measuring the effects of monetary policy on both on- and off-balance sheet liquidity creation in normal times and

---

7. The bank lending channel is one of several different potential ways in which monetary policy may be effective (others include the balance sheet channel and the money view), and works through policy-induced changes in the supply of bank credit. A loosening of monetary policy may result in an increase in bank deposits, which releases financial constraints, especially at banks that have difficulty obtaining non-deposit funding or face high marginal costs of such funds, and they may increase credit availability. A monetary expansion may also result in a higher supply of bank credit because it improves the balance sheets of the banks. For example, a decrease in market interest rates increases the present value of fixed-rate loans in a bank's portfolio. The resulting increase in bank net worth may result in an increase in credit supply. Another necessary condition for the bank lending channel to be an effective conduit of monetary policy is that the policy-induced increase in loan supply induces some borrowers to increase real spending.

financial crises (Berger and Bouwman, 2015). The authors use both single-equation models in the spirit of Romer and Romer (2004) and Vector Autoregression (VAR) models. They measure monetary policy using Romer and Romer (2004) monetary policy shocks, and study the period 1984:Q1–2008:Q4 for the United States, stopping the data there because of the introduction of unconventional monetary policy measures like quantitative easing.[8] They find that during normal times, monetary policy significantly affects liquidity creation only for small banks. This result is primarily driven by the response of on-balance sheet liquidity creation to monetary policy. They also find that the effects of monetary policy on both on- and off-balance sheet liquidity creation are weaker during financial crises than during normal times for all size classes.

12.6 SUMMARY

This chapter discusses the existing evidence from the United States and a few other countries on the effects of government policies and actions – such as Basel III's capital and liquidity requirements, regulatory interventions, capital support or bailouts, and funds from the central bank – on bank liquidity creation. These effects may differ during financial crises and normal times. The key takeaway is that government policies and actions can have important effects on bank liquidity creation that should be studied carefully before changing these policies or actions.

---

8. The change in the federal funds rate is the traditional measure of changes in monetary policy because the Federal Reserve explicitly targets the federal funds rate. A drawback of this measure is that it may contain anticipatory movements, responding to information about future developments in the economy. The monetary policy shock measure developed in Romer and Romer (2004) takes such endogeneity into account.

Chapter 13

Bank Liquidity Creation: Value, Performance, and Persistence

This chapter reviews the existing evidence on the effects of bank liquidity creation on individual bank value. A new empirical analysis examines the relations between normalized bank liquidity creation and key bank performance measures. Finally, there is a new analysis on the degree to which liquidity creation is persistent – that is, whether banks that are high or low liquidity creators tend to remain in those roles.

13.1 LITERATURE ON BANK LIQUIDITY CREATION AND BANK VALUE

Bank value should reflect the net present value of future cash flows. It is interesting to determine how market participants assess the value of liquidity creation. There are three studies that relate bank liquidity creation to bank value.

Berger and Bouwman (2009) show summary statistics, which suggest that liquidity creation itself and liquidity creation normalized by GTA are positively correlated with market-to-book ratios and price-earnings ratios for traded banks and banks in traded bank holding companies. This suggests that some surplus value is associated with liquidity creation, and that shareholders get part of this surplus.

Berger, Bouwman, Imbierowicz, and Rauch (2015) examine how liquidity creation is valued. They do so in a merger and acquisition (M&A) context because an acquirer presumably has superior information on the target bank from the due diligence performed, and hence has a well-informed estimate of the target's value. They find a significant positive relation between the target's liquidity creation and the deal premium, suggesting that acquirers are willing to pay more for higher liquidity creation. They also investigate the change in goodwill recorded on the acquirer's balance sheet in the quarter after the M&A transaction (following Mehran and Thakor, 2011).[1] They find a significant positive relation between the target's liquidity creation and the recorded goodwill, again suggesting positive value associated with liquidity creation.

Cowan and Salotti (2015) focus on premiums paid in FDIC failed bank auctions.[2] They use recent increases in aggregate bank liquidity creation as an

---

1. Goodwill is the purchase price minus the fair value of the assets.
2. When an insured bank fails, the FDIC may close the institution, but more often tries to sell the institution's deposits and assets by auction.

indicator of industry health, and find that such increases are positively related to the premiums paid.

13.2 NEW EVIDENCE ON THE RELATIONS BETWEEN BANK LIQUIDITY CREATION AND BANK PERFORMANCE

The relations between bank liquidity creation and performance are examined here.[3] The performance measures include two profitability measures: return on equity (ROE) is net income divided by equity; and return on assets (ROA) is net income divided by GTA. The performance measures also include three risk measures: the Z-score is the distance to default, measured using 12 quarters of data, and defined as the average ROA plus the average equity ratio, both divided by the standard deviation of ROA; Net charge-offs/GTA is the net amount of charge-offs divided by GTA; and Nonperforming/GTA is nonperforming assets divided by GTA. A bank is riskier when the Z-score is lower, Net charge-offs/GTA is higher, and Nonperforming/GTA is higher. As in the analysis of bank characteristics in Chapter 11, the focus here is on normalized liquidity creation rather than on dollar values, because the performance measures are also all normalized.

13.2.1 Large Banks' Performance

Tables 13.1–13.3 show summary statistics on the key bank performance measures and their relations with bank liquidity creation normalized by GTA over time for large, medium, and small banks, respectively.

Table 13.1 Panel A shows summary statistics for the performance measures for large banks in 1984:Q1, 2014:Q4, and the full sample period 1984:Q1 – 2014:Q4.[4] Bank performance has changed between 1984:Q1 and 2014:Q4, but no clear pattern emerges. ROE went down, while ROA went up. This difference may be due to the increase in the average capital ratio over time. Banks became safer over time as witnessed by the increase in the Z-score and drop in the nonperforming assets ratio, but risker as measured by the increase in the net charge-offs ratio. The increase in the Z-score is due in part to the higher average capital ratio over time. The mean Z-score for the full sample period is lower than for either endpoint, at least in part because many of the large banks became very risky and had very low Z-scores during the subprime lending crisis of 2007:Q3 – 2009:Q4.

Table 13.1 Panel B shows correlations between normalized liquidity creation and performance for large banks. In 1984:Q1, normalized liquidity creation was associated with worse earnings (ROE and ROA) and more risk (lower Z-score, higher net charge-offs ratio, and higher nonperforming assets ratio). By 2014:Q1, the earnings correlations became positive, but higher normalized liquidity creation ratios were still generally associated with more risk. For the full sample period and for

---

3. This investigation is based on summary statistics and correlations – a full-fledged econometric analysis is left for future research.
4. The summary statistics for normalized bank liquidity creation ("cat fat" and its on- and off-balance sheet components) for large banks in these time periods are presented in Table 11.7.

TABLE 13.1 Large Bank Normalized Liquidity Creation – Bank Performance Summary Statistics and Correlations

Panel A: Large bank performance summary statistics

	1984:Q1			2014:Q4			1984:Q1 – 2014:Q4		
	Mean	Median	Std Dev.	Mean	Median	Std Dev.	Mean	Median	Std Dev.
ROE	0.123	0.133	0.074	0.088	0.089	0.090	0.114	0.134	0.170
ROA	0.007	0.007	0.004	0.010	0.010	0.008	0.010	0.010	0.013
Z-score	47.318	39.046	32.415	69.021	54.162	57.707	38.282	27.545	36.976
Net charge-offs/GTA	0.001	0.000	0.001	0.002	0.001	0.004	0.003	0.001	0.007
Nonperforming/GTA	0.016	0.012	0.013	−0.004	−0.003	0.009	0.010	0.006	0.016

Panel B: Large bank normalized liquidity creation – bank performance correlations

	1984:Q1			2014:Q4			1984:Q1 – 2014:Q4		
	"Cat fat" LC/GTA	On-B/S LC/GTA	Off-B/S LC/GTA	"Cat fat" LC/GTA	On-B/S LC/GTA	Off-B/S LC/GTA	"Cat fat" LC/GTA	On-B/S LC/GTA	Off-B/S LC/GTA
ROE	−0.186	−0.076	−0.223	0.136	0.001	0.148	0.065	−0.086	0.078
ROA	−0.263	−0.140	−0.279	0.222	0.011	0.235	0.159	−0.084	0.171
Z-score	−0.044	−0.021	−0.050	−0.083	0.007	−0.096	−0.055	0.111	−0.073
Net charge-offs/GTA	0.264	0.215	0.195	0.415	−0.256	0.643	0.217	−0.077	0.227
Nonperforming/GTA	0.471	0.368	0.365	0.044	−0.122	0.138	0.032	0.020	0.029

This table shows large bank summary statistics (means, medians, and standard deviations) and correlations for normalized liquidity creation and key bank performance measures. Large banks have gross total assets (GTA) exceeding $3 billion. Each panel shows "cat fat," on-balance sheet, and off-balance sheet liquidity creation normalized by GTA. GTA equals total assets plus the allowance for loan and lease losses and the allocated transfer risk reserve (a reserve for certain foreign loans). "Cat fat" liquidity creation (LC) classifies bank activities other than loans based on maturity and product category combined, but classifies loans by category due to data limitations, and includes off-balance sheet activities. ROE is return on equity, measured as net income divided by equity. ROA is return on assets, measured as net income divided by GTA. Z-score is the distance to default, measured using 12 quarters of data, and defined as the average ROA plus the average equity ratio, both divided by the standard deviation of ROA. Net charge-offs/GTA is the net amount of charge-offs divided by GTA. Nonperforming/GTA is nonperforming assets divided by GTA.

TABLE 13.2 Medium Bank Normalized Liquidity Creation – Bank Performance Summary Statistics and Correlations

Panel A: Medium bank performance summary statistics

	1984:Q1			2014:Q4			1984:Q1 – 2014:Q4		
	Mean	Median	Std Dev.	Mean	Median	Std Dev.	Mean	Median	Std Dev.
ROE	0.126	0.130	0.102	0.097	0.090	0.131	0.101	0.125	0.171
ROA	0.008	0.008	0.006	0.010	0.009	0.016	0.009	0.010	0.014
Z-score	37.272	31.299	28.890	61.496	52.533	44.179	43.514	33.738	37.989
Net charge-offs/GTA	0.001	0.000	0.001	0.001	0.001	0.002	0.003	0.001	0.006
Nonperforming/GTA	0.014	0.009	0.017	−0.005	−0.004	0.007	0.008	0.005	0.019

Panel B: Medium bank normalized liquidity creation – bank characteristics correlations

	1984:Q1			2014:Q4			1984:Q1 – 2014:Q4		
	"Cat fat" LC/GTA	On-B/S LC/GTA	Off-B/S LC/GTA	"Cat fat" LC/GTA	On-B/S LC/GTA	Off-B/S LC/GTA	"Cat fat" LC/GTA	On-B/S LC/GTA	Off-B/S LC/GTA
ROE	−0.101	−0.058	−0.132	0.001	−0.003	0.013	−0.020	−0.073	0.030
ROA	−0.191	−0.160	−0.151	0.008	0.013	−0.013	−0.004	−0.075	0.053
Z-score	−0.101	−0.077	−0.095	0.012	−0.015	0.101	−0.023	0.041	−0.061
Net charge-offs/GTA	0.286	0.204	0.295	−0.183	−0.165	−0.166	0.092	−0.029	0.139
Nonperforming/GTA	0.292	0.278	0.163	0.023	0.018	0.032	0.015	0.015	0.008

This table shows medium bank summary statistics (means, medians, and standard deviations) and correlations for normalized liquidity creation and key bank performance measures. Medium banks have gross total assets (GTA) exceeding $1 billion and up to $3 billion. GTA equals total assets plus the allowance for loan and lease losses and the allocated transfer risk reserve (a reserve for certain foreign loans). Each panel shows "cat fat," on-balance sheet, and off-balance sheet liquidity creation normalized by GTA. "Cat fat" liquidity creation (LC) classifies bank activities other than loans based on maturity and product category combined, but classifies loans by category due to data limitations, and includes off-balance sheet activities. ROE is return on equity, measured as net income divided by equity. ROA is return on assets, measured as net income divided by GTA. Z-score is the distance to default, measured using 12 quarters of data, and defined as the average ROA plus the average equity ratio, both divided by the standard deviation of ROA. Net charge-offs/GTA is the net amount of charge-offs divided by GTA. Nonperforming/GTA is nonperforming assets divided by GTA.

TABLE 13.3 Small Bank Normalized Liquidity Creation – Bank Performance Summary Statistics and Correlations

Panel A: Small bank performance summary statistics

	1984:Q1			2014:Q4			1984:Q1 – 2014:Q4		
	Mean	Median	Std Dev.	Mean	Median	Std Dev.	Mean	Median	Std Dev.
ROE	0.118	0.131	0.139	0.078	0.080	0.147	0.094	0.111	1.533
ROA	0.010	0.011	0.010	0.009	0.009	0.014	0.009	0.010	0.020
Z-score	23.758	18.628	19.027	47.500	38.532	38.464	32.666	25.062	28.561
Net charge-offs/GTA	0.001	0.000	0.008	0.001	0.000	0.003	0.002	0.000	0.005
Nonperforming/GTA	0.014	0.009	0.017	-0.006	-0.003	0.012	0.008	0.005	0.016

Panel B: Small bank normalized liquidity creation – bank characteristics correlations

	1984:Q1			2014:Q4			1984:Q1 – 2014:Q4		
	"Cat fat" LC/GTA	On-B/S LC/GTA	Off-B/S LC/GTA	"Cat fat" LC/GTA	On-B/S LC/GTA	Off-B/S LC/GTA	"Cat fat" LC/GTA	On-B/S LC/GTA	Off-B/S LC/GTA
ROE	-0.087	-0.094	0.003	0.093	0.085	0.072	-0.001	-0.005	0.001
ROA	-0.183	-0.189	-0.043	0.060	0.052	0.056	-0.007	-0.057	0.013
Z-score	-0.016	-0.033	0.089	-0.122	-0.141	0.011	-0.013	-0.050	0.004
Net charge-offs/GTA	0.043	0.046	0.002	0.036	0.028	0.047	0.031	0.078	0.005
Nonperforming/GTA	0.252	0.268	0.013	-0.048	-0.072	0.064	0.009	0.048	-0.008

This table shows small bank summary statistics (means, medians, and standard deviations) and correlations for normalized liquidity creation and key bank performance measures. Small banks have gross total assets (GTA) up to $1 billion. GTA equals total assets plus the allowance for loan and lease losses and the allocated transfer risk reserve (a reserve for certain foreign loans). Each panel shows "cat fat," on-balance sheet, and off-balance sheet liquidity creation normalized by GTA. "Cat fat" liquidity creation (LC) classifies bank activities other than loans based on maturity and product category combined, but classifies loans by category due to data limitations, and includes off-balance sheet activities. ROE is return on equity, measured as net income divided by equity. ROA is return on assets, measured as net income divided by GTA. Z-score is the distance to default, measured using 12 quarters of data, and defined as the average ROA plus the average equity ratio, both divided by the standard deviation of ROA. Net charge-offs/GTA is the net amount of charge-offs divided by GTA. Nonperforming/GTA is nonperforming assets divided by GTA.

the end of the sample period, the correlations between on- and off-balance sheet liquidity creation and the performance measures tend to have opposing signs. For example, over the full sample period, on-balance sheet liquidity creation is generally associated with lower earnings, while off-balance sheet liquidity creation is associated with higher earnings.

13.2.2   Medium Banks' Performance

Table 13.2 Panel A gives the performance summary statistics for medium banks. The changes in the performance variables over time are similar to those for large banks, except that the net charge-offs ratio remained approximately constant. Unlike for the large banks, the full sample Z-score for the medium banks lies between their 1984:Q1 and 2014:Q4 values, in part because these banks were less impacted by the crisis. The correlations for the medium banks in Table 13.2 Panel B have many of the same signs as for the large banks, but are smaller in magnitude.

13.2.3   Small Banks' Performance

Table 13.3 Panel A for small banks shows that similar to large banks, ROE declined possibly because of the mechanical effect of higher capital ratios.[5] Small banks have also become safer over time by all three measures. However, the Z-scores are generally smaller for small banks than for the other two size classes, despite small banks typically having higher capital ratios. The correlations in Table 13.3 Panel B are again generally of the same sign as for the other banks, but smaller in magnitude.

13.3   IS THERE LIQUIDITY CREATION PERSISTENCE?

The findings in Chapter 11 that the banks in the top and bottom 10 are the same in some cases in 1984:Q1 and 2014:Q4, and in other cases are quite different raise the question of persistence. Are banks that have recently been consistently high- or low-liquidity creators (in $ terms or normalized) likely to continue these patterns?

This question may be formally addressed using a nonparametric approach used to study winning persistence and losing persistence performance in banking (e.g., Berger, Bonime, Covitz, and Hancock, 2000) and in the mutual fund industry (e.g., Brown, Goetzmann, Ibbotson, and Ross, 1992; Goetzmann and Ibbotson, 1994; and Brown and Goetzmann, 1995).

The winning and losing persistence analyzed here are in terms of remaining in the top or bottom 50% of the liquidity creation distribution in a particular quarter conditional on having been there at least three of the four prior quarters. Formally, the j-period winning persistence at time t is defined as:

$$\text{WP}_{t,j} = \frac{\text{Prob}(\text{winning in time } t \mid \text{majority of winning during } t-1, \ldots t-j)}{\text{Prob}(\text{winning in time } t \mid \text{majority of losing during } t-1, \ldots t-j)}$$

---

5. This does not mean that higher capital banks have lower earnings. Rather, whatever earnings they have are divided by more equity capital.

This is the probability of winning (i.e., being in the top 50% of the distribution) conditioned on winning the majority of the prior j periods, divided by the probability of winning given losing the majority of the prior j periods.

This ratio is equal to 1 if there is no winning persistence since in that case, winning is equally likely after winning most of the prior j periods and after losing most of the prior j periods. A ratio above 1 indicates that winning is persistent. A value below 1 indicates that winning shows a reactionary pattern and tends to follow a series of mostly losing. Note that winning persistence is defined for a given time period, so it may have a different value each quarter. Since the data are quarterly from 1984:Q1 to 2014:Q4, the 4-quarter winning persistence is calculated for every quarter from 1985:Q1 to 2014:Q4, so that there are at least 4 past observations in every case. The probabilities are empirically estimated by frequency distributions, so that the 4-period winning persistence in 1985:Q1 is the proportion of banks winning at least three times in 1984 that are winning again in 1985:Q1, divided by the proportion of those losing at least three times in 1984 that are winning in 1985:Q1.

The j-period losing persistence is defined in a similar way as:

$$LP_{t,j} = \frac{\text{Prob(losing in time } t \mid \text{majority of losing during } t-1,\ldots t-j)}{\text{Prob(losing in time } t \mid \text{majority of winning during } t-1,\ldots t-j)}$$

Again, this ratio is equal to 1 if there is no losing persistence, a ratio above 1 indicates that losing is persistent, and a value below 1 indicates that losing follows a reactionary pattern. Losing persistence is also estimated for each period based on the frequency distributions.

Figures 13.1–13.6 show the winning and losing persistence for "cat fat," on-balance sheet, and off-balance sheet liquidity creation in dollar terms and normalized by GTA for large, medium, and small banks.

13.3.1   Large Banks' Liquidity Creation Persistence

Figure 13.1 Panels A and B show winning and losing persistence, respectively, for the dollar values of "cat fat" liquidity creation and its on- and off-balance sheet components for large banks from 1985:Q1 to 2014:Q4. All of the series are well above one in every quarter, clearly suggesting strong winning and losing persistence. Being in the top half of the distribution for most of a year makes it many times more likely that a bank will be in the top half the next quarter than if it was in the bottom half most of the year. This finding is perhaps not surprising given the wide range of liquidity creation in the large size class. To illustrate, looking back at Table 11.1, "cat fat" liquidity creation ranges from −$50.26 billion to $808.96 billion for large banks in 2014:Q4, so moving to the other side of the median in that quarter would mean a major change in liquidity creation for most large banks. The occasional large spikes in winning persistence likely reflect a small-sample problem in which very few banks switch from losing to winning in some of the quarters. Finally, there do not seem to be substantial differences in persistence between normal times and crisis periods.

Panel A: Large banks: winning persistence based on liquidity creation (in $ terms)

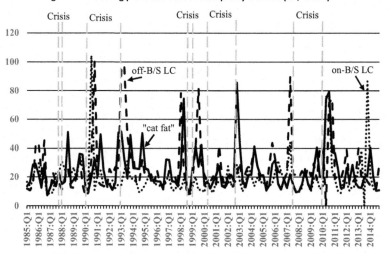

Panel B: Large banks: losing persistence based on liquidity creation (in $ terms)

FIGURE 13.1 **Large banks: winning and losing persistence based on liquidity creation (in $ terms).** This figure shows winning persistence (Panel A) and losing persistence (Panel B) based on liquidity creation (in $ terms) among large banks from 1985:Q1 to 2014:Q4. Winning persistence is estimated by the proportion of banks in the top 50% of the liquidity creation distribution (in $ terms) in their size class for a particular quarter given that the same banks were in the top 50% of the distribution in their size class in the majority of the last four quarters, divided by the proportion of banks in the top 50% of the distribution (in $ terms) in their size class in that quarter given that the same banks were in the bottom 50% of the distribution in their size class in the majority of the last four quarters. Losing persistence is estimated analogously. Large banks have gross total assets (GTA) exceeding $3 billion. GTA equals total assets plus the allowance for loan and lease losses and the allocated transfer risk reserve (a reserve for certain foreign loans). Each panel shows "cat fat," on-balance sheet, and off-balance sheet liquidity creation (in $ terms). "Cat fat" liquidity creation (LC) classifies bank activities other than loans based on maturity and product category combined, but classifies loans by category due to data limitations, and includes off-balance sheet activities.

Panel A: Large banks: winning persistence based on normalized liquidity creation

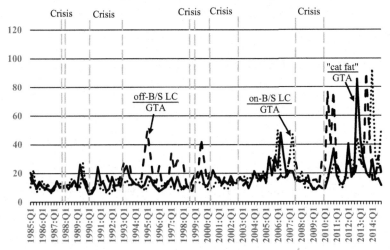

Panel B: Large banks: losing persistence based on normalized liquidity creation

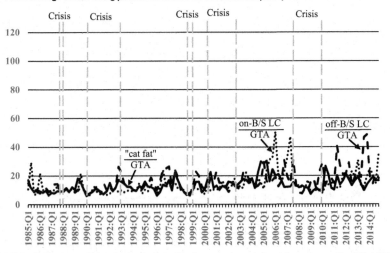

FIGURE 13.2   Large banks: winning and losing persistence based on normalized liquidity creation. This figure shows winning persistence (Panel A) and losing persistence (Panel B) based on normalized liquidity creation among large banks from 1985:Q1 to 2014:Q4. Winning persistence is estimated by the proportion of banks in the top 50% of the normalized liquidity creation distribution in their size class for a particular quarter given that the same banks were in the top 50% of the distribution in their size class in the majority of the last four quarters, divided by the proportion of banks in the top 50% of the normalized liquidity creation distribution in their size class in that quarter given that the same banks were in the bottom 50% in their size class in the majority of the last four quarters. Losing persistence is estimated analogously. Normalized liquidity creation is liquidity creation divided by gross total assets (GTA). GTA equals total assets plus the allowance for loan and lease losses and the allocated transfer risk reserve (a reserve for certain foreign loans). Large banks have GTA exceeding $3 billion. Each panel shows "cat fat," on-balance sheet, and off-balance sheet liquidity creation (in $ terms). "Cat fat" liquidity creation (LC) classifies bank activities other than loans based on maturity and product category combined, but classifies loans by category due to data limitations, and includes off-balance sheet activities.

Panel A: Medium banks: winning persistence based on liquidity creation (in $ terms)

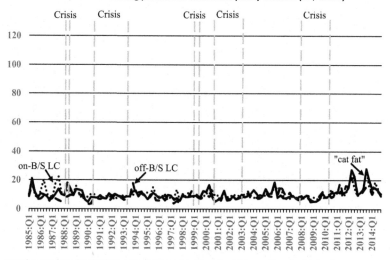

Panel B: Medium banks: losing persistence based on liquidity creation (in $ terms)

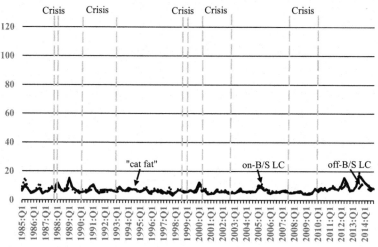

FIGURE 13.3 Medium banks: winning and losing persistence based on liquidity creation (in $ terms). This figure shows winning persistence (Panel A) and losing persistence (Panel B) based on liquidity creation (in $ terms) among medium banks from 1985:Q1 to 2014:Q4. Winning persistence is estimated by the proportion of banks in the top 50% of the liquidity creation distribution (in $ terms) in their size class for a particular quarter given that the same banks were in the top 50% of the distribution in their size class in the majority of the last four quarters, divided by the proportion of banks in the top 50% of the distribution (in $ terms) in their size class in that quarter given that the same banks were in the bottom 50% of the distribution in their size class in the majority of the last four quarters. Losing persistence is estimated analogously. Medium banks have gross total assets (GTA) of $1 billion – $3 billion. GTA equals total assets plus the allowance for loan and lease losses and the allocated transfer risk reserve (a reserve for certain foreign loans). Each panel shows "cat fat," on-balance sheet, and off-balance sheet liquidity creation (in $ terms). "Cat fat" liquidity creation (LC) classifies bank activities other than loans based on maturity and product category combined, but classifies loans by category due to data limitations, and includes off-balance sheet activities.

Panel A: Medium banks: winning persistence based on normalized liquidity creation

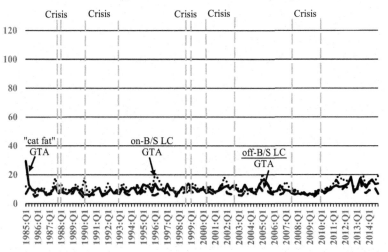

Panel B: Medium banks: losing persistence based on normalized liquidity creation

FIGURE 13.4   Medium banks: winning and losing persistence based on normalized liquidity creation. This figure shows winning persistence (Panel A) and losing persistence (Panel B) based on normalized liquidity creation among medium banks from 1985:Q1 to 2014:Q4. Winning persistence is estimated by the proportion of banks in the top 50% of the normalized liquidity creation distribution in their size class for a particular quarter given that the same banks were in the top 50% of the distribution in their size class in the majority of the last four quarters, divided by the proportion of banks in the top 50% of the normalized liquidity creation distribution in their size class in that quarter given that the same banks were in the bottom 50% in their size class in the majority of the last four quarters. Losing persistence is estimated analogously. Normalized liquidity creation is liquidity creation divided by gross total assets (GTA). GTA equals total assets plus the allowance for loan and lease losses and the allocated transfer risk reserve (a reserve for certain foreign loans). Medium banks have GTA of $1 billion – $3 billion. Each panel shows "cat fat," on-balance sheet, and off-balance sheet liquidity creation (in $ terms). "Cat fat" liquidity creation (LC) classifies bank activities other than loans based on maturity and product category combined, but classifies loans by category due to data limitations, and includes off-balance sheet activities.

Panel A: Small banks: winning persistence based on liquidity creation (in $ terms)

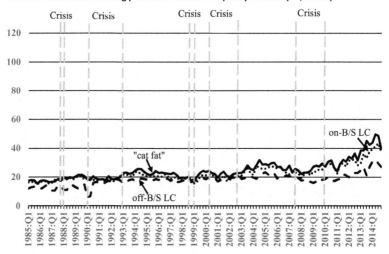

Panel B: Small banks: losing persistence based on liquidity creation (in $ terms)

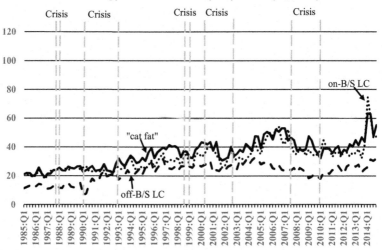

FIGURE 13.5   Small banks: winning and losing persistence based on liquidity creation (in $ terms). This figure shows winning persistence (Panel A) and losing persistence (Panel B) based on liquidity creation (in $ terms) among small banks from 1985:Q1 to 2014:Q4. Winning persistence is estimated by the proportion of banks in the top 50% of the liquidity creation distribution (in $ terms) in their size class for a particular quarter given that the same banks were in the top 50% of the distribution in their size class in the majority of the last four quarters, divided by the proportion of banks in the top 50% of the distribution (in $ terms) in their size class in that quarter given that the same banks were in the bottom 50% of the distribution in their size class in the majority of the last four quarters. Losing persistence is estimated analogously. Small banks have gross total assets (GTA) up to $1 billion. GTA equals total assets plus the allowance for loan and lease losses and the allocated transfer risk reserve (a reserve for certain foreign loans). Each panel shows "cat fat," on-balance sheet, and off-balance sheet liquidity creation (in $ terms). "Cat fat" liquidity creation (LC) classifies bank activities other than loans based on maturity and product category combined, but classifies loans by category due to data limitations, and includes off-balance sheet activities.

Panel A: Small banks: winning persistence based on normalized liquidity creation

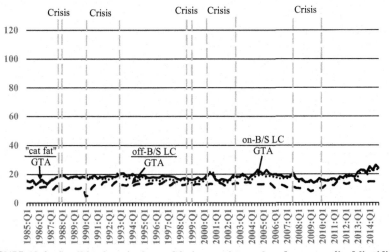

Panel B: Small banks: losing persistence based on normalized liquidity creation

FIGURE 13.6   Small banks: winning and losing persistence based on normalized liquidity creation. This figure shows winning persistence (Panel A) and losing persistence (Panel B) based on normalized liquidity creation among small banks from 1985:Q1 to 2014:Q4. Winning persistence is estimated by the proportion of banks in the top 50% of the normalized liquidity creation distribution in their size class for a particular quarter given that the same banks were in the top 50% of the distribution in their size class in the majority of the last four quarters, divided by the proportion of banks in the top 50% of the normalized liquidity creation distribution in their size class in that quarter given that the same banks were in the bottom 50% in their size class in the majority of the last four quarters. Losing persistence is estimated analogously. Normalized liquidity creation is liquidity creation divided by gross total assets (GTA). GTA equals total assets plus the allowance for loan and lease losses and the allocated transfer risk reserve (a reserve for certain foreign loans). Small banks have GTA up to $1 billion. Each panel shows "cat fat," on-balance sheet, and off-balance sheet liquidity creation (in $ terms). "Cat fat" liquidity creation (LC) classifies bank activities other than loans based on maturity and product category combined, but classifies loans by category due to data limitations, and includes off-balance sheet activities.

Figure 13.2 Panels A and B show winning and losing persistence, respectively, for normalized "cat fat" liquidity creation and its on- and off-balance sheet components for large banks from 1985:Q1-2014:Q4. Again, all of the series are well above one in every quarter, suggesting strong winning and losing persistence. The numbers are much smaller than for the dollar values of liquidity creation, suggesting that it is generally easier to change the size of different asset, liability, and off-balance sheet items relative to the bank's GTA than to make substantial changes in the total amount of liquidity creation itself. In most cases, normalized "cat fat," on-balance sheet, and off-balance sheet liquidity creation are comparably persistent. Again, there do not seem to be substantial differences between normal times and crisis periods.

13.3.2 Medium Banks' Liquidity Creation Persistence

Figures 13.3 and 13.4 show medium bank liquidity creation winning and losing persistence. Not surprisingly, there is less winning and losing persistence based on the dollar values of liquidity creation than for large banks because of the much smaller range of liquidity creation for this size class. For example, as shown in Table 11.1, "cat fat" liquidity creation ranges from −$0.09 billion to $1.86 billion for medium banks in 2014:Q4. In Figure 13.4 Panel A, there is one very large spike in normalized "cat fat" liquidity creation winning persistence in 2005:Q3, which may be due to a small-sample problem. Again, there do not seem to be substantial differences between normal times and crisis periods.

13.3.3 Small Banks' Liquidity Creation Persistence

Figures 13.5 and 13.6 show small bank liquidity creation winning and losing persistence. Perhaps surprisingly, the dollar values of liquidity creation are much more persistent than for medium banks, despite the smaller range of liquidity creation values. However, small bank normalized liquidity creation persistence is comparable to medium-bank persistence. As in the cases of large and medium banks, there are no clear differences in persistence between normal times and crisis periods.

13.4 SUMMARY

This chapter investigates whether banks that create more liquidity have greater or lesser value, perform better or worse, and whether liquidity creation is persistent over time. The limited existing research suggests that market participants place positive value on bank liquidity creation. The new empirical evidence suggests that the relations between normalized bank liquidity creation and bank performance are not uniform, but depend on time and size class. Liquidity creation is also highly persistent. The key takeaways are that high liquidity creation appears to be associated with higher market values and mixed performance; and that liquidity creation is both winning and losing persistent.

Part V

Looking Toward the Future

Chapter 14

How Can Bank Executives, Financial Analysts, Researchers (including Academics and Students), and Policy Makers (including Legislators, Regulators, and Central Bankers) Use Bank Liquidity Creation Data to Their Advantages?

This chapter discusses how bank liquidity creation data may be used by many parties to their advantages. They may help bank executives and financial analysts benchmark the positions of individual banks in the market, and help researchers (including academics and students) and policy makers (including legislators, regulators, and central bankers) predict financial crises, evaluate individual banks' risk-taking or likelihood of failure, and engage in future research and policy work. Chapter 15 discusses open research questions that researchers and policy makers may also address using liquidity creation data.

14.1 LIQUIDITY CREATION IS A NOVEL BENCHMARKING TOOL THAT CAN BE USED BY BANK EXECUTIVES AND FINANCIAL ANALYSTS TO EVALUATE A BANK'S PERFORMANCE AND COMPARE IT TO ITS PEER GROUP

At the time of publication, quarterly liquidity creation data for virtually all US commercial banks are available on the book's website (http://booksite.elsevier.com/9780128002339) for the 31-year-period from 1984:Q1 to 2014:Q4 (to be updated regularly). Using these data, bank executives and financial analysts can look up a bank's liquidity creation over a long period of time and perform at least two types of benchmarking.

14.1.1   Benchmark a Bank's Liquidity Creation against Those of its Peers

Chapter 12 shows that banks that create more liquidity (in dollar terms or normalized by assets) tend to have higher market values and may also perform better in other ways. This suggests a useful benchmarking exercise: compare the bank's liquidity creation to that of its peers, defined to be other banks in its size class, local market, or area of specialization.

If the bank's liquidity creation significantly lags behind that of its peers, it may be performance enhancing to create more liquidity. This can be done through, for example, extending additional business loans, taking in more transactions deposits, or providing more off-balance-sheet guarantees to customers. All of these actions may help to improve performance.

If, however, the bank's liquidity creation is far above that of its peers, it is useful to take a step back and consider whether creating so much liquidity is optimal. It may be optimal right after a financial crisis or when the economy is doing well because it signals excellent performance in those times. However, when there are signs that the economy is overheating, it may be better to cut back liquidity creation because the bank may be undertaking too much liquidity risk, which may unduly increase the probability of the bank's own financial distress or failure.

If the bank's liquidity creation is in line with that of its peers, it is useful to ask whether the bank should continue to stay in line with its peers, try to create more liquidity, or cut back. The answer again depends on the state of the economy.

14.1.2   Benchmark a Bank's Liquidity Creation Against its Own Past Liquidity Creation

It is also sensible to track an individual bank's liquidity creation (in dollar terms or normalized by assets) over time and compare it to its own past numbers.

If a bank is increasing its liquidity creation, it may be doing well, and a decline may indicate problems, given the general positive relation between liquidity creation and performance. Thus, a bank suffering a decrease may improve performance by reversing the decline through issuing more business loans, taking in more transactions deposits, or providing more off-balance-sheet guarantees.

However, a rapid increase in liquidity creation, particularly during a period in which the economy is overheating, may suggest that the bank should reduce or slow the growth of its liquidity creation. This will help to reduce exposure to liquidity risk and other potential problems associated with an impending financial crisis.

14.2   AGGREGATE BANK LIQUIDITY CREATION CAN BE USED BY RESEARCHERS AND POLICY MAKERS TO PREDICT FINANCIAL CRISES

Based on the results summarized in Chapter 9, excessive aggregate bank liquidity creation may increase the probability of a financial crisis occurring. This suggests that researchers and policy makers may wish to keep track of aggregate bank liquidity creation. When liquidity creation by the banking sector seems excessive, central bankers or regulators can try to reduce it through restrictive monetary policy or tightened prudential supervision and regulation. This may help to avoid or lessen the impact of future financial crises.

An important issue to resolve is, how much liquidity creation is "too much" (see also Section 15.8). The existing literature has focused on aggregate liquidity creation that is high relative to a trend (see Section 9.2). Alternative approaches could potentially focus on percentage increases in liquidity creation. For example, some papers that focus on lending indicate that increases in credit to the private sector may precede banking crises (e.g., Demirguc-Kunt and Detragiache, 1998; and Kaminsky and Reinhart, 1999).

14.3 LIQUIDITY CREATION CAN BE USED BY RESEARCHERS AND POLICY MAKERS TO ASSESS RISK TAKING AND TO PREDICT FAILURE OF INDIVIDUAL BANKS

Just like excessive aggregate liquidity creation helps to predict financial crises, too much liquidity created by an individual bank may help predict that bank's financial distress or failure. Only limited evidence currently exists on this important topic.

The existing literature on bank failure tends to focus on three possible reasons for bank failure: poor bank fundamentals, liquidity shortage, and poor governance. The first reason, poor bank fundamentals, implies that low capital ratios, high nonperforming loan (NPL) ratios, and poor earnings all increase the likelihood of bank failure (e.g., Cole and Gunther, 1995). The second reason for bank failure, liquidity shortage, focuses on the fact that banks finance their illiquid assets (such as business loans) with liquid liabilities (such as transactions deposits), and that this exposes them to external shocks. Given a sequential servicing constraint (depositors are dealt with on a first-come, first-served basis), when depositors fear the bank may be unable to meet its obligations, they will withdraw their money and a liquidity shortage arises (e.g., Diamond and Dybvig, 1983). The third reason for bank failure is corporate governance arrangements that encourage risk taking. This is discussed further in Section 15.7.

Fungacova, Turk Ariss, and Weill (2015) expand this literature by examining whether liquidity creation may affect bank failure. Specifically, they formulate the "High Liquidity Creation Hypothesis," which says that high bank liquidity creation increases its probability of failure. Their empirical tests focus on liquidity creation normalized by assets above certain thresholds (e.g., above the 90th percentile in a given quarter) using data on Russian banks from 2000 to 2007, and they find the data to be consistent with the hypothesis.

This evidence suggests that regulators may wish to track liquidity creation of individual institutions to see which is in danger of failure. In principle, liquidity creation could also be included as part of the formal stress tests discussed in Section 12.2. Depending on the severity of the situation, regulators can do a variety of things. If they are merely somewhat concerned about the level of liquidity creation or normalized liquidity creation, regulators can simply discuss the issue during the examination process with the institutions that create the most liquidity, alerting them to possible dangers of excessive liquidity creation. If the situation is more severe, regulators may want to intervene, for example, by imposing restrictions on business lending, loan commitments, and deposit taking, in order to reduce the risks. If a threat to the institution seems imminent, regulators can close the institution early to reduce the losses associated with bank failure.

14.4 USE OF LIQUIDITY CREATION IN FUTURE RESEARCH AND POLICY WORK

Researchers and policy makers are also encouraged to use the liquidity creation data. These may be used in further study of issues brought up in earlier chapters or in the relatively unexplored open questions identified in Chapter 15.

14.5 SUMMARY

This chapter shows how various parties can use the bank liquidity creation data on the book's website (http://booksite.elsevier.com/9780128002339) to their advantages. Liquidity creation may be used by bank executives and financial analysts to assess a bank against its peers and its own past behavior to pick an appropriate scale of liquidity creation (in dollar terms and/or normalized by assets). Policy makers (including legislators, regulators and central bankers) can use the data in designing legislation, prudential regulation and supervision, as well as monetary policy. Researchers (including academics and students) and policy makers can also use the data to investigate many existing and future issues in banking. The key takeaway is that the bank liquidity creation data are useful to a broad audience interested in benchmarking, research, and policy work.

Chapter 15

Where We Stand Now and the Open Research and Policy Questions

This chapter assesses the current status of the research on bank liquidity creation and financial crises and brings up major areas ripe for future research and policy work.

15.1 WHERE DO WE STAND NOW?

It is safe to say that research on bank liquidity creation and financial crises is just beginning and that there is a long way to go before the subjects mature. The literature scratches the surface on measuring bank liquidity creation in a few countries during normal times and during financial crises; assessing how capital affects bank liquidity creation in these countries during normal times; and examining the effects of government policies (such as monetary policy, regulatory interventions, and bank bailouts) on liquidity creation during normal times and during financial crises. The extant literature also links excess bank liquidity creation to future financial crises in the United States. Furthermore, it provides some evidence on the relations between liquidity creation and bank value using US data only.

In addition, the earlier chapters of this book expand on the extant empirical research by examining bank liquidity creation in the United States during normal times and financial crises, looking at characteristics of US banks that create more or less liquidity, and assessing the performance of US banks that create more liquidity.

In all of these cases – both the existing literature and the additional research in this book – more work remains to be done. The remainder of this chapter focuses more specifically on new important research questions to be addressed by future research using data from the US and many other nations during normal times and financial crises.

15.2 MEASURING BANK LIQUIDITY CREATION AND ITS CAUSES AND CONSEQUENCES AROUND THE WORLD

Most of the existing work on bank liquidity creation uses US data. Given the importance of bank liquidity creation to the economy, the causes and consequences of liquidity creation should be estimated in more countries. Some progress has already been made.

Box 15.1 lists the non-US countries in which liquidity creation has been measured and the topics examined in various studies.

BOX 15.1 Non-US Countries in which Bank Liquidity Creation has been Measured

Non-US country	Topics	Authors
China	• Effect of capital on bank liquidity creation	• Lei and Song (2013)
Czech Republic	• Effect of capital on bank liquidity creation • Effect of competition on bank liquidity creation	• Horvath, Seidler, and Weill (2014) • Horvath, Seidler, and Weill (2015)
Germany	• Determinants of bank liquidity creation • Effects of regulatory interventions and capital support on bank liquidity creation	• Hackethal, Rauch, Steffen, and Tyrell (2010) • Berger, Bouwman, Kick, and Schaeck (2015)
Japan	• Effect of macroeconomic factors and bank characteristics on bank liquidity creation	• Pana (2012)
Lithuania	• Calculate liquidity creation and examine its components • Liquidity creation and depositor panic	• Lakstutiene and Krusinskas (2010) • Lakstutiene, Krusinskas, and Rumsaite (2011)
Russia	• Effects of bank size and ownership on bank liquidity creation • How the introduction of explicit deposit insurance[a] affects the relation between bank capital and liquidity creation • Whether high liquidity creation increases the probability of bank failure	• Fungacova and Weill (2012) • Fungacova, Weill, and Zhou (2010) • Fungacova, Ariss, and Weill (2015)
South Africa	• Calculate liquidity creation before and during the financial crisis of the late 2000s	• Esterhuysen, Vuuren, and Styger (2012)

Non-US country	Topics	Authors
25 OECD countries	• Effect of competition on liquidity creation	• Joh and Kim (2014)
Gulf Cooperation States	• Comparison of liquidity creation across Islamic, conventional, and hybrid banks	• Mohammad and Asutay (2015)

a. Countries that do not have explicit deposit insurance typically have implicit deposit insurance provided by the government that protects depositors to some degree.

As can be seen, very limited research has been done on large developed countries outside the US. Many nations around the world – both developed and developing – and numerous research topics are left as fertile grounds for future research. In some countries, it is difficult to garner data as detailed as in the US, but data that is sufficiently detailed to estimate liquidity creation should be available to central bank economists and others around the world.

15.3   EFFECTS OF BANK MERGERS AND ACQUISITIONS ON LIQUIDITY CREATION

There is a large literature studying many effects of mergers and acquisitions (M&As) in banking. However, only two studies investigate issues related to M&As and liquidity creation. Pana, Park, and Query (2010) examine liquidity creation at acquirers and targets using US data from 1997 to 2004. They find that small acquirers create more liquidity normalized by assets than their targets, large acquirers create as much normalized liquidity as their targets, and liquidity creation increases after merger completion. Baltas (2013) investigates the liquidity creation implications of M&As in Greece and the United Kingdom using data from 1993 to 2010, and also finds generally positive effects of these merger activities on bank liquidity creation.

There are many unanswered questions. For example, while these studies suggest that liquidity creation increases after mergers and acquisitions, it would be interesting to examine whether these results differ by the deal type: how is liquidity creation affected by intrastate and interstate consolidation in the US, domestic M&As in nations around the world, and in cross-border deals. Furthermore, it is possible that commercial bank M&As within US states and within small countries reduce liquidity creation as overlapping operations are closed. In addition, M&As may either increase or decrease liquidity creation depending on their effect on competition, as discussed in Section 15.4.

M&As may also affect liquidity creation of competitors to the merging banks (i.e., it may have external effects), just as M&As are found to affect small business lending of such competitors (e.g., Berger, Saunders, Scalise, and Udell, 1998; and Avery and Samolyk, 2004). In addition, these M&As may result in additional *de novo* entry in the local market, potentially offsetting any cutbacks or augmenting increases in liquidity creation by the consolidating banks, just as it does for bank lending (e.g., Berger, Bonime, Goldberg, and White, 2004).

15.4 EFFECTS OF BANK COMPETITION AND MARKET POWER ON LIQUIDITY CREATION

Competition and its inverse, market power, may have important effects on liquidity creation. For convenience, the discussion here focuses on a reduction in competition, which has the same effects as an increase in market power.[1]

The theoretical literature suggests that a reduction in competition may decrease or increase liquidity creation. Under the structure-conduct-performance hypothesis (Bain, 1959), reduced competition induces banks to offer less favorable pricing to customers (e.g., higher interest rates and fees on loans, lower interest rates and higher fees on deposits, and higher fees on off-balance-sheet guarantees), resulting in lower quantities being transacted and hence lower liquidity creation.[2] In contrast, some of the relationship banking literature argues that reduced competition enables banks to enforce implicit or explicit contracts in which relationship customers receive favorably-priced services in the short-term and pay less-favorable prices in later periods (e.g., Petersen and Rajan, 1995), allowing the banks to create more liquidity.

Most empirical studies focus on lending and find mixed evidence. Some find that reduced competition increases lending (e.g., Petersen and Rajan, 1995; Cetorelli and Gambera, 2001; and Bonaccorsi di Patti and Dell'Ariccia, 2004), while others find it decreases lending (e.g., Black and Strahan, 2002; Karceski, Ongena, and Smith, 2005; Cetorelli and Strahan, 2006; and Canales and Nanda, 2012).

Only two empirical papers to our knowledge look at the more general issue of the effect of competition on liquidity creation. Joh and Kim (2013) use a panel dataset of commercial banks in 25 OECD countries over the period 2000–2010 and find that banks create more liquidity as the banking industry becomes more concentrated. Consistent with this, Horvath, Seidler, and Weill (2015) use Czech banking data from 2002 to 2010, and find that competition is associated with reduced liquidity creation. Both studies provide support for the relationship banking perspective. Clearly, much remains to be done to extend this literature.

---

1. The effects are opposite in case of an increase in competition or a decrease in market power.
2. An assumption here is that the on- and off-balance sheet items that contract most have positive effects on liquidity creation. Shrinking of liquidity-destroying items, such as securities, would actually increase bank liquidity creation.

15.5   EFFECTS OF BANK DEREGULATION ON LIQUIDITY CREATION

It is useful to understand how deregulation of the banking sector affects liquidity creation by banks. Since deregulation of the banking sector typically results in M&As that may either increase or decrease competition,[3] it may seem that a separate analysis of deregulation is not needed. This is not correct: the M&As and changes in competition from deregulation generally start from very different initial conditions for at least two reasons. First, prior to deregulation, local banking markets are often insular and cut off from competition. Second, the deregulation may have additional effects, such as the existing banks in the market responding to threat of new competition.

The literature on the geographic deregulation of the US banking in the period from 1978 to 1994 finds real effects on the economy, such as higher state growth rates (Jayaratne and Strahan, 1996), new business formations (Black and Strahan, 2002), and reduced income inequality (Beck, Levine, and Levkov, 2010). Two studies find conflicting effects of deregulation on firm innovation (Chava, Oettl, Subramanian, and Subramanian, 2013; and Cornaggia, Mao, Tian, and Wolfe, 2015).

There may be an intermediate step in which the deregulation affects bank liquidity creation, which leads to these real economic outcomes, but this step has yet to be examined in the research literature. A few papers examine how deregulation affects one component of liquidity creation: credit supply. Rice and Strahan (2010) find that after deregulation, more firms use bank debt, but this does not result in an overall increase in the credit supply. Tewari (2014) finds that following removal of geographic restrictions on banks, mortgage-lending increases.

Much of the banking deregulation literature focuses on the effects in the United States, but it is just as interesting to study deregulation elsewhere. One example is the European Union's Second Banking Directive, which became effective in 1993 and created a "single passport," meaning that any bank licensed in the EU was allowed to open branches in any EU country, subject only to the supervision and regulation of the bank license issuing country. Another example is the opening up of Eastern European nations to foreign banks after the fall of the Soviet Empire.

15.6   EFFECTS OF DEPOSIT INSURANCE ON LIQUIDITY CREATION

Deposit insurance may have important effects on liquidity creation and its causes and consequences. As discussed in Chapter 10, the capital – liquidity creation relation depends in part on the presence of uninsured depositors who monitor

---

3. An M&A may reduce competition if it involves two banks with significant local market overlap. Such a deal increases local market concentration, meaning that the new entity has more market power. These kinds of deals are normally investigated carefully by regulators and may be blocked for antitrust reasons. An M&A may increase competition if it involves an aggressive bank expanding into local markets in which it did not have a prior presence.

the bank and can take their money out at any point in time. The introduction or strengthening of explicit deposit insurance changes the mix of insured and uninsured deposits and therefore may alter the capital – liquidity creation relation. Fungacova, Weill, and Zhou (2010) focus on the introduction of explicit deposit insurance in Russia and find that it exerts a limited impact on the relation and does not change the overall effect of capital on liquidity creation.

Related to this issue, deposit insurance has the capacity to reduce depositor panic, which directly affects bank stability and the ability to create liquidity, since the withdrawal of deposits directly reduces liquidity creation. This topic is investigated by Lakstutiene, Krusinskas, and Rumsaite (2011) for Lithuania, but more investigations using data from other nations are needed to provide a complete picture.

Presumably, the effects of monetary policy on bank liquidity creation, the effects of bank liquidity creation on the likelihood of financial crises, and other relations studied in this book may be affected by different deposit insurance schemes. More evidence on these topics is needed using data from multiple countries.

15.7 EFFECTS OF BANK CORPORATE GOVERNANCE – OWNERSHIP, EXECUTIVE COMPENSATION, AND BOARD AND MANAGEMENT STRUCTURE – ON LIQUIDITY CREATION

There is a large literature on corporate governance issues in banking and how they differ from those in other industries due to regulation of who may own a bank and how banks may compensate executives (for reviews, see Adams, 2010; Laeven, 2013; and Hagendorff, 2015).[4] Some of this literature focuses on risk taking and whether poor corporate governance was a proximate cause of the subprime lending crisis (2007:Q3-2009:Q4) or bank failures during the crisis (e.g., Kirkpatrick, 2009; Laeven and Levine, 2009; Gropp and Kohler, 2010; Beltratti and Stulz, 2012; Erkens, Hung, and Matos, 2012; and Berger, Imbierowicz, and Rauch, forthcoming). Extending this research to examine how bank ownership, executive compensation, and board or management structure affect liquidity creation would be helpful, given the links between liquidity creation and future financial crises discussed in Chapter 9.

15.7.1 Effects of Ownership on Liquidity Creation

Examination of the effects of different types of bank ownership on liquidity creation is important. Banks may have dispersed or concentrated ownership, with one or more blockholders being present. Existing studies have studied the effects of these different ownership types on bank risk taking and find that risk taking is higher in the presence of institutional owners (e.g., Beltratti and Stulz, 2012; Erkens, Hung, and Matos, 2012), blockholders (Laeven and Levine, 2009), and

---

4. For a review on the governance of bank holding companies, see Adams and Mehran (2003).

when ownership is more concentrated (Gropp and Kohler, 2010). This higher risk taking may involve greater liquidity creation, since more liquidity creation generally increases liquidity risk (the risk that the bank cannot meet its short-term financial demands) and possibly also credit risk (the risk that borrowers default on their debt by failing to make required payments).

Nations around the world also differ in the extent to which they have state-owned, foreign-owned, and private domestically-owned banks. Existing research finds that these different bank types tend to differ in terms of their efficiencies (e.g., Berger, DeYoung, Genay, and Udell, 2000; Claessens, Demirguc-Kunt, and Huizinga, 2001; Berger, Clarke, Cull, Klapper, and Udell, 2005; and Berger, Hasan, and Zhou, 2009) and lending (e.g., Sapienza, 2004; and Berger, Klapper, Martinez Peria, and Zaidi, 2008), so it may be expected that they may differ in their liquidity creation as well. Limited evidence on this exists to date. Fungacova and Weill (2012) examine how bank ownership affects liquidity creation in Russia, and find that state-controlled banks create the most liquidity per dollar of assets, while the ranking of domestic and foreign banks depends on the liquidity creation measure used. Lei and Song (2013) examine how capital affects liquidity creation in China and find that the effect is negative and significant for domestic and state-owned banks, but not significant for foreign banks.

There is also research on the effects of privatization – the dynamics of moving from state ownership of banks to private ownership (e.g., Berger, Clarke, Cull, Klapper, and Udell, 2005; and Clarke, Cull, and Shirley, 2005) – but no research on the effects of privatization on bank liquidity creation.

Banks may also have different operating models. One study examines how this affects liquidity creation. Mohammad and Asutay (2015) compare the liquidity created by Islamic, conventional, and hybrid banks in the Gulf Cooperation States, and find that Islamic banks create more liquidity than the other two types.

15.7.2 Effects of Executive Compensation on Liquidity Creation

Executive compensation has traditionally received limited attention in the banking literature. There are several general studies on the effects of executive compensation on bank risk taking and performance (e.g., Crawford, Ezzell, and Miles, 1995; Houston and James, 1995; Hubbard and Palia, 1995; Mehran and Rosenberg, 2008; and DeYoung, Peng, and Yan, 2013). During and after the subprime lending crisis of 2007:Q3 – 2009:Q4, executive compensation has received a lot more attention, and some studies specifically focus on claims that misaligned incentives were a potential cause of the crisis (e.g., Fahlenbrach and Stulz, 2011; Cheng, Hong, and Scheinkman, 2015; and Chu and Ma, 2015).

Banks can take more risk by increasing their liquidity creation, since this increases bank liquidity risk and may also increase credit risk. No research to date, however, has directly linked executive compensation at banks to their liquidity creation.

15.7.3   Effects of Board and Management Structure on Liquidity Creation

There are also studies that examine the effects of board and management structure on bank risk taking (e.g., Laeven and Levine, 2009; Becht, Bolton, and Roell, 2011; Beltratti and Stulz, 2012; and Berger, Imbierowicz, and Rauch, forthcoming). Some of the issues include the effects of the degree to which boards are shareholder-oriented, whether the CEO is also chairman of the board, board size, the proportions of outside versus inside directors (i.e., those not in versus those also in management). Diaz and Huang (2013) construct a shareholder protection measure (which includes board of director characteristics, bylaws, etc.) and examine how bank risk taking and this shareholder protection proxy affect liquidity creation at US bank-holding companies. They find that better governed firms create more liquidity.

More work seems warranted in this important line of research. General open questions include the following: Are the effects of corporate governance similar during normal times versus (different types of) financial crises? Do some governance aspects affect liquidity creation more than others? Do these results hold worldwide? Is there truly causation or are these merely interesting correlations?

15.8   LIQUIDITY CREATION AND RISK

As discussed above, normalized liquidity creation is positively associated with liquidity risk and may be positively associated with credit risk if the high liquidity creation is caused by high business loans and commitments. There is little research to date on this topic. An exception is Imbierowicz and Rauch (2014), who investigate the relationship between liquidity risk (measured as "cat fat" liquidity creation normalized by assets) and credit risk (loan charge-offs minus recoveries normalized by lagged loan loss allowances) and their joint impact on banks' default probability. To some extent, the literature on the effects of bank capital on liquidity creation in Chapter 10 also deals with this issue. For example, Berger and Bouwman (2009) include three measures of risk as control variables, but do not focus on them, and do not deal with their endogeneity.

A potentially promising line of future research would be to examine the relations between normalized liquidity creation and different types of risk. This would also help inform the policy issue of the optimal scale of normalized liquidity creation discussed in Section 15.10.

15.9   EFFECTS OF LIQUIDITY CREATION ON REAL ECONOMIC ACTIVITY

Well before the first liquidity creation theories, it was alleged that liquidity creation is vital for economic growth. However, little empirical evidence currently exists. Berger and Sedunov (2015) find that higher per capita "cat fat" liquidity creation in individual US states is associated with significantly more GDP per capita in these states, and it beats traditional output measures (per capita TA and GTA) in "horse races" to examine which better predicts GDP per capita. More research is needed to confirm and extend these links between liquidity creation and real economic activity.

15.10   IS THERE AN OPTIMAL SCALE OF BANK LIQUIDITY CREATION FOR THE INDUSTRY AND FOR INDIVIDUAL BANKS?

One of the most important open questions is whether there is an optimal scale of liquidity creation for the banking industry. As discussed in Chapter 1 and in Section 15.9, liquidity creation is believed to support economic growth, and the research summarized in Section 13.1 suggests that banks that create more liquidity are valued more highly. However, the analysis in Chapter 9 suggests that from a social viewpoint, too much liquidity creation may be bad because it might increase the probability of a financial crisis. Research on whether there is an optimal scale for the industry that trades off these outcomes would be useful.

In addition, there is the question of an optimal scale for individual banks. Some argue for breaking up the biggest banks, indicating that the large scale of individual banking institutions may raise the likelihood and severity of financial crises (e.g., Johnson and Kwak, 2010).[5] The question of whether there is an optimal scale in banking has been addressed before in the literature on bank economies of scale. This literature typically specifies multiple different outputs of banks (e.g., different categories of assets) and examines how costs change as these outputs increase proportionately or in some other combinations. The early literature using this approach suggests that scale economies in banking run out at relatively small scale (e.g., Berger, Hanweck, and Humphrey, 1987). However, more recent research suggests that scale economies exist beyond even the current scale of the largest banking institutions in the US for two reasons: first, technological progress and deregulation may have increased actual scale economies; and second, larger banks may be better at diversifying risk, and the more recent studies take this into account (Berger and Mester, 1997; and Hughes and Mester, 2013). One potential fruitful research area may be to examine scale economies when total bank liquidity creation or its individual asset-side, liability-side, and off-balance-sheet components are considered as bank outputs.

---

5. In the aftermath of the subprime lending crisis of 2007:Q3–2009:Q4, several politicians tried to push legislation to break up the largest banks. In April 2010, Senators Sherrod Brown and Ted Kaufman unveiled the "Safe, Accountable, Fair, and Efficient (SAFE) Banking Act," which proposed to put ceilings on the size of banks (e.g., New York Times, April 21, 2010). It would reinforce the Riegle-Neal Act of 1994, which prohibits any bank from gaining more than 10% of the total deposits of all insured banks and thrifts in the US through M&As of commercial banks (organic growth is permitted). After 1994, several large banks obtained waivers to exceed the ceiling. In 2010, three banks (Bank of America, Wells Fargo, and JPMorgan Chase) were above the limit. The proposal failed on the Senate floor.

In addition, there may be an optimal scale of normalized liquidity creation, that is, liquidity creation divided by assets. As discussed in Section 13.1, high normalized liquidity creation is associated with higher bank value. However, normalized liquidity creation is an inverse indicator of bank liquidity (see Chapter 6), suggesting that excessive normalized liquidity creation may be associated with dangerous levels of liquidity risk. Thus, there may be an optimal scale of liquidity creation normalized by assets that balances these costs and benefits, which could be investigated in future research.

15.11 LIQUIDITY CREATION DYNAMICS

Another striking omission from the existing research on liquidity creation is a study of its dynamics. It has been emphasized that liquidity is created on the asset- and liability-sides of the balance sheet as well as off the balance sheet, but there is currently little understanding of the dynamics of what happens when one of these components changes and affects one or more other components.

For example, if there is a $1 increase in transactions deposits, the effect on total bank liquidity creation depends on what is done with that dollar. According to the "cat fat" formula in Chapter 4, it will create the maximum of $1 of liquidity if it is invested in new business loans because business loans increase liquidity creation. It will also have the full $1 effect if it is used to retire subordinated debt or equity because these items reduce liquidity creation, so reducing them increases liquidity creation. However, the $1 of new transactions deposits will have no effect if it is invested in Treasury securities, which reduce liquidity creation by the same amount.

The situation is more complicated if off-balance-sheet activities are involved. For example, if a $1 unused loan commitment is taken down and turned into a $1 business loan, funds have to be taken from other assets or liabilities and these have very different implications for the total liquidity creation of the bank. According to the "cat fat" liquidity creation formula, the exchange of an unused loan commitment for a business loan of the same amount has a neutral effect on total bank liquidity creation, but the funds must be drawn from another source. If the bank sells $1 of securities, then total bank liquidity creation is increased by $\frac{1}{2} \times \$1 = \$0.5$ by releasing these liquid assets to the public. As well, if an additional $1 in transactions deposits is raised, bank liquidity creation goes up by $\frac{1}{2} \times \$1 = \$0.5$. However, to the extent that the bank does not renew or replace an existing loan that made a final payment of $1 and these funds go directly to the new commitment loan (with the bank only holding the extra cash for an instant), then total bank liquidity creation declines by $-\frac{1}{2} \times \$1 = -\$0.5$. The same holds when the bank issues $1 in equity to fund the loan. It seems likely that there was a combination of all of these effects during the subprime-lending crisis (2007:Q3 – 2009:Q4), when many businesses drew down their existing commitments.

New research on what the changes actually are may be very illuminating, and may help with the understanding of the dynamics of liquidity creation.

15.12 LIQUIDITY CREATION BY BANKS IN DIFFERENT FINANCIAL AND LEGAL SYSTEMS

Financial systems differ significantly across the globe. Most financial systems are bank-based, relying more on bank financing, including Japan, Germany, and developing nations, while others are market-based, relying more on stock and bond markets for sources of funding, like the United States and the United Kingdom. There is some research on the effects of bank-based versus market-based financial systems on external financing of firms, but the issue is not settled (e.g., Demirguc-Kunt and Maksimovic, 2002). Bank liquidity creation may differ between these two types of financial systems. It might also be expected that bank liquidity creation would be more important to economies in bank-based systems. These issues would also make for interesting future research.

In addition, there is a significant literature begun by Demirguc-Kunt and Maksimovic (1998) and La Porta, Lopez-de-Silanes, Shleifer, and Vishny (1998) which demonstrates that different types of legal systems with different protections for creditors have implications for financial systems and economies. Presumably, one mechanism for the effects they document may be differences in bank liquidity creation in these different legal systems, but there is currently no information on this mechanism. This may prove to be a fruitful line of future research.

15.13 LIQUIDITY CREATED BY OTHER TYPES OF FINANCIAL INSTITUTIONS AND MARKETS, AND HOW THEY INTERACT WITH BANK LIQUIDITY CREATION

Liquidity is created not only by commercial banks, but also by other financial institutions and markets. As discussed in Chapter 2, thrift institutions, credit unions, shadow banks (such as investment banks, hedge funds, private equity funds, and other financial firms that engage in bank-like activities), and stock, bond, and other capital markets likely create significant amounts of liquidity, while insurance companies likely destroy significant amounts of liquidity (although they do provide valuable risk-reduction services to their policyholders).

The tools for measuring bank liquidity creation can be adapted to measure the liquidity created or destroyed by these other financial institutions and markets. However, this has rarely been done, with the notable exceptions of Pana and Mukherjee (2012), who measure liquidity creation by credit unions, and Choi, Park, and Ho (2013), who measure the liquidity destroyed by insurance companies. The opportunities for more research like this are thus wide open.

It would also be interesting and policy relevant to examine how bank liquidity creation interacts with liquidity created by these other institutions and markets. As discussed in Chapter 9, abnormally high-bank liquidity creation tends to be followed by financial crises, and the evidence suggests that this occurred in the subprime lending crisis of 2007:Q3-2009:Q4. While the mechanism is difficult to pin down, it may be the case that excessive bank liquidity creation leads to bubbles elsewhere in the financial system that burst and cause financial crises (Rajan, 1994; Acharya and Naqvi, 2012; and Thakor, forthcoming). This could be tested by future researchers by examining whether high bank liquidity creation is followed by high-liquidity creation in stock, bond, and other financial markets.

Finally, the liquidity creation methodology can also be applied to nonfinancial firms. This is done by Gopalan, Kadan, and Pevzner (2012), who construct four alternative measures of firms' asset liquidity in order to examine the relation between firms' asset liquidity and their stock liquidity in the US. Charoenwong, Chong, and Yang (2014) examine this same topic in an international setting, covering 47 countries. It will be interesting to study the relation between liquidity creation by banks and firms' asset liquidity.

15.14 SUMMARY

This chapter briefly looks back on the issues addressed in earlier chapters of the book, and then looks forward to how others can address open research questions regarding bank liquidity creation and financial crises in the future. The existing research is mostly centered on the US and a few other nations, but should be expanded to many nations around the world. The unanswered research questions which need to be addressed include how liquidity creation is affected by bank mergers and acquisitions, bank competition or market power, bank deregulation, different types of deposit insurance, and differences in corporate governance. It is also interesting to study whether there is an optimal scale of liquidity creation for the banking industry and for individual banks (in dollar terms and normalized by assets), how bank liquidity creation and its effects differ across financial and legal systems, and how liquidity creation by banks and other parts of the financial system interact. The key takeaway is that there are many interesting questions left to address using the liquidity creation data and methodology.

Chapter 16

Links to Websites Containing Data, Documents, and Other Information Useful for US Bank Performance Benchmarking, Research, and Policy Work

To benchmark bank performance and to conduct banking research and policy work, it is important to know what banking datasets are available, where to find them, and have some information about them. This chapter contains information that serves these purposes. It describes and provides links to key websites containing commercial bank and Bank Holding Company (BHC) data, documents, and other types of relevant data and information. The focus here is on US data sources.

16.1 LIQUIDITY CREATION DATA

Quarterly liquidity creation data for US commercial banks from 1984:Q1 to 2014:Q4 (to be updated regularly thereafter) are available on this book's website: http://booksite.elsevier.com/9780128002339
The data include:

1. Key liquidity creation measures discussed in this book: the preferred "cat fat" measure, "cat nonfat," "mat fat," "mat nonfat," takedown probability-adjusted "cat fat," and securitization-adjusted "cat fat."
2. The components of the preferred "cat fat" measure: liquidity created on the balance sheet, on the asset side, on the liability side, and off the balance sheet.
3. Each bank's identifier, name, and alternative measures of bank output (assets and loans).

16.2 COMMERCIAL BANK CALL REPORT DATA

Quarterly Call Report data (which include the balance sheet, the off-balance-sheet activities, and the income statement) for every US commercial bank can be downloaded in bulk and/or for individual institutions from different data sources.

1. The Federal Reserve Bank of Chicago provides SAS files with quarterly bulk downloads of all Call Report items (one SAS file per quarter) for all banks from 1976:Q1 to 2010:Q4:
   https://www.chicagofed.org/banking/financial-institution-reports/commercial-bank-data

2. The Federal Financial Institutions Examination Council (FFIEC) provides zip files with quarterly Call Report bulk data (one zip file per quarter) for all banks from 2001:Q1 to present. Each zip file contains a large number of text files, corresponding to the different schedules in the Call Report, which have to be merged by bank identifier (RSSD9001):
   https://cdr.ffiec.gov/public/PWS/DownloadBulkData.aspx

3. The FFIEC also allows one to download the filled-in quarterly Call Reports for individual institutions at:
   https://cdr.ffiec.gov/public/ManageFacsimiles.aspx
   For example, to get the 2014:Q4 Call Report for JPMorgan Chase Bank, National Association and Community Bank of El Dorado Springs used as examples in Chapter 3:
   a. Select Report "Call\TFR,"
   b. Indicate Report Date "Single Date" "12/31/2014," and
   c. Institution Name "JPMorgan Chase Bank, National Association" or "Community Bank of El Dorado Springs"
   d. Click on Search – a pdf with the completed Call Report can now be downloaded.

4. Wharton Research Data Services (WRDS):
   http://wrds.wharton.upenn.edu/
   A WRDS subscription is required to access its website. After logging into the WRDS website, go to: Bank Regulatory. As can be seen, the quarterly financial statement data can be downloaded for all institutions or for individual institutions from 1976:Q1 to the present (with roughly a one-year lag). The data can be accessed in different ways:
   a. By schedule:
      - Balance Sheet Data
      - Income Statement
      - Off-Balance-Sheet Items
      - Risk-Based Capital
   b. By data series:
      - RCFD Series (Consolidated Foreign and Domestic data)
      - RCFN Series (Foreign data)
      - RCON Series (Domestic data)
      - RIAD Series (Report of income data)

16.3   COMMERCIAL BANK REPORTING FORMS

The FFIEC website contains the reporting forms to be filled out by banks. Over time, commercial banks have had to fill out different Call Report forms, depending on their size and geographic scope. Following are the links to the web pages that contain the most recent and historical versions of Call Reports and Instructions, which have detailed information on what is included in each Call Report entry over time.

1. FFIEC 031: filled out by banks with domestic and foreign offices from 1996:Q4 onward:
   https://www.ffiec.gov/forms031.htm
2. FFIEC 041: filled out by banks with domestic offices only from 2001:Q1 onward:
   https://www.ffiec.gov/forms041.htm
3. FFIEC 032: filled out by banks with domestic offices only and total assets of $300 million or more from 1996:Q4 to 2000:Q4:
   https://www.ffiec.gov/forms032.htm
4. FFIEC 033: filled out by banks with domestic offices only and total assets of $100 million–$300 million from 1996:Q4 to 2000:Q4:
   https://www.ffiec.gov/forms033.htm
5. FFIEC 034: filled out by banks with domestic offices only and total assets of less than $100 million from 1996:Q4 to 2000:Q4:
   https://www.ffiec.gov/forms034.htm
6. Christa Bouwman's website contains some historical Call Report forms filled out by banks between 1978 and 1995:
   http://people.tamu.edu/~cbouwman/

16.4 BANK HOLDING COMPANY (BHC) DATA

Quarterly financial statements (which include the balance sheet, the off-balance-sheet activities, and the income statement) for all BHCs are available from 1986:Q3 onward and can be downloaded from different data sources.

1. The Federal Reserve Bank of Chicago has financial statement data for holding companies from 1986:Q3 to present. All the bank structure and geographical information are included. The downloadable datasets contain data for three types of BHCs (described later) combined. This means that variables such as "total assets" appear in the dataset multiple times, but as indicated later, they all have a different prefix to identify the type of holding company for which total assets are reported. For most research purposes, FR Y-9C data are used:
   https://www.chicagofed.org/banking/financial-institution-reports/bhc-data
   a. FR Y-9C: consolidated financial statements filled out by all large and some small domestic BHCs.
      - All Y-9C variables are available quarterly and have the prefix BHCK.
      - The asset size threshold for filing the FR Y-9C has increased over time: it was increased from $150 million to $500 million effective

2006:Q1, and to $1 billion effective 2015:Q2. Smaller BHCs that meet certain criteria may also be required to file the FR Y-9C.[1]

b. FR Y-9LP: parent company only financial statements for all large and some small domestic BHCs.

- All LP variables are available quarterly and have the prefix BHCP.
- The asset size threshold for "large" has increased over time: it was increased from $150 million to $500 million effective 2006:Q1, and to $1 billion effective 2015:Q2. As discussed in the previous footnote, smaller BHCs that meet certain criteria may also be required to file the FR Y-9LP.

c. FR Y-9SP: parent company only financial statements for most small domestic BHCs.

- All SP variables are available semiannually and have the prefix BHSP.
- The asset size cap for "small" has increased over time: it was increased from $150 million to $500 million effective 2006:Q2, and to $1 billion effective 2015:Q2. As discussed in the previous footnote, smaller BHCs that meet certain criteria may be required to file the FR Y-9LP.

2. WRDS also has financial statement data available for holding companies from 1986:Q3 to the present (with roughly a 1-year lag).

http://wrds.wharton.upenn.edu/

A WRDS subscription is required to access its website. After logging into the WRDS website, go to: Bank Regulatory, and select Bank Holding Companies. Data can be downloaded separately for the three sets of holding companies (Y-9C, Y-9LP, and Y-9SP).

16.5   BANK HOLDING COMPANY REPORTING FORMS

The FFIEC website also has the reporting forms to be filled out by BHCs. Following are the links to the web pages that contain the most recent and historical versions of the reporting forms and instructions, which have detailed information on what is included in each entry over time.

1. FR Y-9C: consolidated financial statements filled out by all large and some small domestic BHCs (the reporting criteria are given in Section 16.4):

http://www.federalreserve.gov/apps/reportforms/reportdetail.aspx?sOoYJ+5BzDal8cbqnRxZRg==

a. Reporting forms and instructions are available from 1996:Q2 onward.

---

1. The Federal Reserve uses several criteria to assess whether smaller BHCs should submit the FR Y-9C and FR Y-9LP. The criteria include (but are not limited to): the holding company engaging in sizeable nonbanking activities; having major off-balance-sheet activities, including securitizations; or having a material amount of debt or equity securities outstanding that are registered with the Securities and Exchange Commission (SEC).

2. FR Y-9LP: parent company only financial statements filled out by all large and some small domestic BHCs (reporting requirements are given in Section 16.4): http://www.federalreserve.gov/apps/reportforms/reportdetail.aspx?sOoYJ+ 5BzDYeK/+NsOyV7PkVi3bV1QrX
   a. Reporting forms and instructions are available from 1996:Q2 onward.
3. FR Y-9SP: parent company only financial statements filled out by most small domestic BHCs (reporting requirements are given in Section 16.4): http://www.federalreserve.gov/apps/reportforms/reportdetail.aspx?sOoYJ+ 5BzDZA8/Yg6ycgR4lNYKgjqJz+
   a. Reporting forms are available from 1995:Q2 onward and instructions are available from 1996:Q2 onward.

16.6 MICRO DATA REFERENCE MANUAL (MDRM)

The Micro Data Reference Manual (MDRM) contains a Data Dictionary, which briefly explains each Call Report and BHC reporting variable as well as other micro data collected on banks, and indicates how long each variable has been collected: http://www.federalreserve.gov/reportforms/mdrm/

16.7 STRUCTURE AND GEOGRAPHICAL DATA

Useful structure and geographical data (including information on the ownership structure, location, regulators, BHC status, and highest holder) are available for banks and BHCs. An overview of all the variables can be found on the Federal Reserve Bank of Chicago website: https://www.chicagofed.org/banking/financial-institution-reports/structure-and-geographical-variables

1. Bank-level bank structure and geographical data are available from 1976:Q1 onward and can be obtained from two sources:
   a. The Federal Reserve Bank of Chicago:
      From 1976:Q1 to 2010:Q4, these data are conveniently included in its quarterly bulk download of all Call Report items for all banks (see Section 16.2, list 1).
      https://www.chicagofed.org/banking/financial-institution-reports/commercial-bank-data
      From 2011:Q1 onward, it provides these data separately on its website (and they have to be merged with the quarterly Call Report bulk data provided by FFIEC – see Section 16.2, list 2).
      https://www.chicagofed.org/banking/financial-institution-reports/commercial-bank-structure-data
   b. WRDS:
      http://wrds.wharton.upenn.edu/
      A WRDS subscription is required to access its website. After logging into the WRDS website, go to: Bank Regulatory. The structure and

geographical data are available under Other Variables. The data are available from 1976:Q1 to the present (with roughly a one-year lag).
2. BHC structure and geographical data are available from 1986:Q3 onward and can also be obtained from two sources:
   a. The Federal Reserve Bank of Chicago conveniently includes these data in its quarterly bulk download of all financial reporting items for BHCs from 1986:Q3 to present (see Section 16.4, list 1).
   https://www.chicagofed.org/banking/financial-institution-reports/bhc-data
   b. WRDS:
   http://wrds.wharton.upenn.edu/
   A WRDS subscription is required to access its website. After logging into the WRDS website, go to: Bank Regulatory. The structure and geographical data appear near the bottom of the page. The data are available from 1986:Q3 to the present (with roughly a one-year lag).

16.8 FDIC'S SUMMARY OF DEPOSITS (SoD) DATA

Data on total deposits and branches (including branch locations) are available as of June 30 every year.

1. The Federal Deposit Insurance Corporation's (FDIC) Summary of Deposits (SoD) website contains these data from 1994 to present:
   http://www2.fdic.gov/SOD/dynaDownload.asp?barItem=6
2. Christa Bouwman's website contains earlier deposit data from 1981 to 1993:
   http://people.tamu.edu/~cbouwman/

16.9 BANK AND BHC HISTORY (INCLUDING MERGERS AND ACQUISITIONS DATA)

Information about the history of a bank or BHC (including information on whether the institution was acquired) is available at:

1. The National Information Center's (NIC) "Institution Search" webpage:
   http://www.ffiec.gov/nicpubweb/nicweb/SearchForm.aspx
   To find a bank or BHC that may currently be open or closed, change Status to "Current and Non-Current" and include the entire (or partial) Institution Name, possibly with location information (City and/or State). For every bank with that name that is closed, it will indicate the "As of Date," the latest date on which information was still available. Clicking on the desired bank will give the latest available information. Clicking on "Institution History" will provide the full history of a bank or BHC that is still open and of institutions that failed and may have been acquired.
2. The Federal Deposit Insurance Corporation's (FDIC) "Find Banks" webpage:
   https://www5.fdic.gov/idasp/main.asp
   To find a bank that may currently be open or closed, change Institution Status to "All" and include the entire (or partial) Institution Name, possibly

with location information (City and/or State). For every bank with that name that is closed, it will indicate the Inactive Date. If the desired bank is Inactive, clicking on its name will give the latest available financial information plus Closing History (e.g., Merged without Assistance into bank X).

The Federal Reserve Bank of Chicago website contains information on all bank and BHC mergers and acquisitions since 1976:
https://www.chicagofed.org/banking/financial-institution-reports/merger-data

16.10   BANK FAILURES DATA

In its role as receiver for failed banks, the Federal Deposit Insurance Corporation (FDIC) compiles a list of banks that have failed since 2000:Q4:
http://www.fdic.gov/bank/individual/failed/banklist.html
The FDIC also provides detailed data on bank failures and assistance transactions, including the estimated loss to the FDIC, from 1934 to present:
https://www2.fdic.gov/hsob/SelectRpt.asp?EntryTyp=30&Header=1
Select "Failures & Assistance Transactions."
When the Deposit Insurance Fund (DIF) incurs a material loss (a loss exceeding the greater of $50 million[2] or 2% of an institution's total assets at the time the FDIC was appointed receiver), a Material Loss Review explains why the problems resulted in a loss and includes recommendations for avoiding such a loss in the future. When the loss is not material, but involves unusual circumstances, an In-Depth Review is written. Reviews are available from 2009 onward:
http://www.fdicoig.gov/MLR.shtml

16.11   FEDERAL RESERVE'S SENIOR LOAN OFFICER SURVEY (SLOS)

The Board of Governors of the Federal Reserve surveys, typically quarterly, up to 80 large domestic banks and 24 US branches and agencies of foreign banks. Questions focus on changes in the standards and lending terms. Senior Loan Officer Survey (SLOS) data are available from 1997:Q1 to present:
http://www.federalreserve.gov/boarddocs/snloansurvey/

16.12   AGGREGATE DATA ON THE BANKING SECTOR

The FDIC Quarterly summarizes the most current financial results for the entire banking sector (all FDIC-insured institutions), and alternatively split by asset size class and by geographic region from 2007:Q1 onward:
https://www.fdic.gov/bank/analytical/quarterly/

---

2. This threshold has changed over time. Section 38(k) of the Federal Deposit Insurance Act of 1950 originally defined it to be $25 million. The Dodd–Frank Act increased the threshold to $200 million for losses between Jan 1, 2010–Dec 31, 2011; to $150 million from Jan 1, 2012–Dec 31, 2013; and to $50 million for losses from Jan 1, 2014 onward.

The website also includes links to retired publications (FDIC Outlook and FDIC Banking Review) which contain similar data from the mid-1990s to 2006:Q4.

16.13   ST. LOUIS FEDERAL RESERVE'S FRED DATABASE

The Federal Reserve Bank of St. Louis maintains the Federal Reserve Economic Data (FRED) database, which includes macroeconomic and aggregate banking data:
http://research.stlouisfed.org/fred2/

16.14   CENTER FOR RESEARCH IN SECURITIES PRICES (CRSP) DATA FOR LISTED BANKS AND LISTED BHCs

The Federal Reserve Bank of New York has created an Excel file with both the regulatory identification numbers (RSSD9001 contained in Call Reports) and PERMCOs (contained in CRSP) of listed banks and listed BHCs from January 1, 1990 onward. It can be used to obtain CRSP data (stock returns, stock prices, and number of shares outstanding) for these institutions. CRSP can be accessed through subscription website WRDS (see Section 16.2, list 4):
http://www.newyorkfed.org/research/banking_research/datasets.html

16.15   EDGAR FINANCIAL INFORMATION ON PUBLICLY-TRADED INSTITUTIONS

Every listed financial and nonfinancial institution is required to disclose information to the Securities and Exchange Commission (SEC). It has to file registration statements, periodic reports (e.g., annually in 10-Ks and quarterly in 10-Qs), and other forms electronically through the SEC's Electronic Data Gathering, Analysis, and Retrieval (EDGAR) system. This information can be accessed online at:
http://www.sec.gov/edgar.shtml
To find Exxon Mobil Corp., whose 10-K data are used in Chapter 3:

1. Click on "search for company filings;"
2. Click on "company or fund name, ticker symbol, ..."
3. Enter "Exxon Mobil Corp" or "Exxon Mobil" in the Company Name search box. Alternatively, enter the firm's ticker symbol "XOM" in the Fast Search box. Click on "Search." A list containing all the company's filings appears.
   a. Entering "Exxon" in the Company Name search box yields a short list containing several names. The second entry is the desired company: Exxon Mobil Corp.

4. The example uses the 2014 10-K. To find this filing quickly, type "10-K" in the Filing Type box. A list of all the 10-Ks filed by the company appears. Since Exxon Mobil Corp's fiscal year ends on Dec 31, the filing date of the 2014 10-K will be early 2015. The desired 10-K has a February 25, 2015 filing date. Click on "Documents" for that entry.
5. A list of documents related to the 10-K appears. The first entry says "Form 10-K": click on the red link in the column next to it. Typically, this is the desired document. However, if it does not contain the full 10-K, check out the other links.

16.16 FEDERAL RESERVE'S MONETARY POLICY TOOLS

The Federal Reserve's website discusses its current and expired monetary policy tools:
http://www.federalreserve.gov/monetarypolicy/policytools.htm

1. Its current tools include, among others, the discount rate, that is, the rate charged to depository institutions including commercial banks on funds received from the discount window. Historically, only quarterly data aggregated at the Federal Reserve district level are available. In response to a Freedom of Information Act request, the Federal Reserve released daily discount window usage at the institution level from Aug. 20, 2007 – March 1, 2010. These data are largely in pdf format and can be found here:
https://publicintelligence.net/federal-reserve-financial-crisis-discount-window-loan-data/
Following the enactment of Dodd-Frank on July 21, 2010, the Federal Reserve releases daily discount window usage at the institution level quarterly with approximately a two-year lag. The data are in Excel format and can be found here:
http://www.federalreserve.gov/newsevents/reform_discount_window.htm
Current tools also include open market operations in which the Federal Reserve Bank of New York buys and sells treasury securities and engages in repurchase agreements for the purpose of influencing the federal funds rate, the main overnight interbank lending rate in the US. Data are available on open market operations starting with transactions conducted after the date of enactment of the Dodd–Frank Act, July 21, 2010, through September 30, 2010. Information for subsequent periods will be published quarterly, approximately two years after the transaction is conducted, and can be found here:
http://www.newyorkfed.org/markets/OMO_transaction_data.html
2. The Federal Reserve's expired policy tools include the tools used during the subprime lending crisis of 2007:Q3–2009:Q4, such as the Term Auction Facility (TAF) and the Term Asset-Backed Securities Loan Facility (TALF). A helpful overview site with links to the transaction data (in Excel format):
http://www.federalreserve.gov/newsevents/reform_transaction.htm

16.17   CAPITAL SUPPORT PROVIDED THROUGH THE TROUBLED ASSET RELIEF PROGRAM (TARP)

The US Treasury invested billions of dollars in the preferred stock of selected financial institutions to enhance their capital ratios during the subprime lending crisis of 2007:Q3–2009:Q4. It did so through the Capital Purchase Program (CPP) of the Troubled Asset Relief Program (TARP). Information and data are available on the Treasury Department's website:
http://www.treasury.gov/initiatives/financial-stability/Pages/default.aspx

16.18   HOME MORTGAGE DISCLOSURE ACT (HMDA) DATA

The Home Mortgage Disclosure Act (HMDA), enacted in 1975, requires that most mortgage lenders located in metropolitan areas gather data about their housing-related lending activity and make such data publicly available.

1. The HMDA website contains the most recent data: at the loan level from 2007 onward, and aggregate data summed by institution, geography (metropolitan area), and nationwide from 1999 onward:
   http://www.ffiec.gov/hmda/hmdaproducts.htm
2. The National Archives Online Public Access website has older data: at the loan level from 1981 to 2009 and aggregate data from 1990 to 2009:
   http://research.archives.gov/search?expression=2456161&pg_src=group&data-source=all

The HMDA data contain information on lenders, applicants, loans, and location. Key statistics often used in research include: lender identification (which can be used to match HMDA data with other databases), applicant income, gender, race, loan amount, the loan approval/disapproval decision, and location (to match the data with other economic conditions).

16.19   DEALSCAN SYNDICATED LOAN DATA

The Thomson Reuters Loan Pricing Corporation DealScan database contains detailed terms and conditions on loans made by bank and nonbank lenders to medium- and large-size private and public firms in the United States and other parts of the world. The data are collected from SEC filings and through direct queries to lenders and borrowers. The data start in 1988, but coverage in the initial years is relatively sparse. Key data items include the name and role of the lender, the name of the borrower, loan type, loan purpose, loan amount, fees, interest rate, collateral requirements, and covenants. The data can be accessed through WRDS:
http://wrds.wharton.upenn.edu/

A WRDS subscription is required to access its website. After logging into the WRDS website, go to: Thomson Reuters. The data can then be found under WRDS–Reuters DealScan. The data are split into five parts: company, facility, package, current facility pricing, and lenders. It also provides a Compustat linking table, which can be used to match DealScan data with Compustat.

16.20 FEDERAL RESERVE'S SURVEY OF SMALL BUSINESS FINANCES (SSBF) DATA

The Survey of Small Business Finances (SSBF) has survey data on US small businesses (less than 500 full-time-equivalent employees). The data include firm and owner characteristics, each firm's use of financial services, each firm's financial service suppliers, and financial statement information. The surveys were conducted in 1987, 1993, 1998, and 2003. The questionnaires, survey data, methodology, and more are available at:
http://www.federalreserve.gov/pubs/oss/oss3/nssbftoc.htm

16.21 KAUFFMAN FIRM SURVEY (KFS) DATA

The Kauffman Foundation conducts the Kauffman Firm Survey (KFS), a longitudinal survey that has information for a sample of 4928 start-ups that began operations in 2004 in the United States and were followed annually through 2011. The KFS contains detailed information on each firm's sources and amounts of financing, credit history, geographic location, industry, and information on the owners' experience, education, gender, race, and age.
http://www.kauffman.org/what-we-do/research/kauffman-firm-survey-series

16.22 FEDERAL RESERVE'S SURVEY OF CONSUMER FINANCES (SCF) DATA

The Survey of Consumer Finances (SCF), generally conducted every three years since 1983, contains information on individuals, their businesses, and finances. The data include information on families' balance sheets, pensions, income, and demographic characteristics:
http://www.federalreserve.gov/econresdata/scf/scfindex.htm

16.23 SUMMARY

This chapter describes important websites containing downloadable data, documents, and key information that are helpful for those interested in doing research on bank liquidity creation, financial crises, and many other banking topics using US data. The described websites have quarterly Call Report data of all commercial banks, blank Call Reports, filled-in Call Reports for individual banks, definitions of Call Report items, and much more. The key takeaway is that there are many easily accessible datasets for use in exploring liquidity creation, financial crises, and other research topics in banking.

References

Acharya, Viral V., Hamid Mehran, and Anjan V. Thakor., 2013, Caught between Scylla and Charybdis? Regulating bank leverage when there is rent seeking and risk shifting, Working Paper, Federal Reserve Bank of New York.

Acharya, Viral V., and Nada Mora, 2015, A crisis of banks as liquidity providers, Journal of Finance 70, 1–43.

Acharya, Viral V., and Hassan Naqvi, 2012, The seeds of a crisis: A theory of bank liquidity and risk taking over the business cycle, Journal of Financial Economics 106, 349–366.

Acharya, Viral V., Hyun Shin, and Tanju Yorulmazer, 2011, Crisis resolution and bank liquidity, Review of Financial Studies 24, 2121–2165.

Acharya, Viral V., and Tanju Yorulmazer, 2007, Too many to fail – An analysis of time-inconsistency in bank closure policies, Journal of Financial Intermediation 16, 1–31.

Adams, Renee. 2010, Governance of banking institutions, in: H.K. Baker and R. Anderson (Eds.), Corporate Governance: A Synthesis of Theory, Research, and Practice, pp. 451–467.

Adams, Renee, and Hamid Mehran, 2003, Is corporate governance different for bank holding companies?, FRBNY Economic Policy Review, 123–142.

Agarwal, Sumit, Efraim Benmelech, Nittai Bergman, and Amit Seru, 2012, Did the Community Reinvestment Act (CRA) lead to risky lending?, Working Paper.

Aiyar, Shekhar, Charles W. Calomiris, and Tomasz Wieladek, 2012, Does macro-pru leak? Evidence from a UK policy experiment, Working Paper.

Alhadeff, David A., 1954, Monopoly and competition in banking, Berkeley: University of California Press.

Allen, Franklin, Elena Carletti, and Robert Marquez, 2011, Credit market competition and capital regulation, Review of Financial Studies 24, 983–1018.

Allen, Franklin, and Douglas Gale, 2004, Financial intermediaries and markets, Econometrica 72, 1023–1061.

Allen, Franklin, and Douglas Gale, 2007, Understanding Financial Crises, Oxford: Oxford University Press.

Allen, Franklin, Aneta Hryckiewicz, Oskar Kowalewski, and Gunseli Tumer-Alkan, 2014, Transmission of financial shocks in loan and deposit markets: Role of interbank borrowing and market monitoring, Journal of Financial Stability 15, 112–126.

Allen, Franklin, and Anthony M. Santomero, 1998, The theory of financial intermediation, Journal of Banking and Finance 21, 1461–1485.

Amihud, Yakov, 2002, Illiquidity and stock returns: Cross-section and time-series effects, Journal of Financial Markets 5, 31–56.

Amihud, Yakov, and Haim Mendelson, 1986, Asset pricing and the bid-ask spread, Journal of Financial Economics 17, 223–249.

Amihud, Yakov, Haim Mendelson, and Beni Lauterbach, 1997, Market microstructure and securities values: Evidence from the Tell Aviv Exchange, Journal of Financial Econometrics 45, 365–390.

Avery, Robert B., and Allen N. Berger, 1991, Risk-based capital and deposit insurance reform, Journal of Banking & Finance 15, 847–874.

Avery, Robert B., and Katherine A. Samolyk, 2004, Bank consolidation and the provision of banking services: Small commercial loans, Journal of Financial Services Research 25, 291–325.

Bai, Jennie, Arvind Krishnamurthy, and Charles-Henri Weymuller, 2014, Measuring liquidity mismatch in the banking sector, Working Paper.

Bain, Joe S., 1959, Industrial Organization: A Treatise, New York, NY: John Wiley & Sons.

Baltas, Nicholas C., 2013, The Greek financial crisis and the outlook of the Greek economy, Journal of Economic Asymmetries 10, 32–37.

Basel Committee on Banking Supervision (BIS), 2010, Results of the Comprehensive Quantitative Impact Study, December.

Basel Committee on Banking Supervision (BIS), 2012a, Results of the Basel III Monitoring Exercise as of 30 June 2011.

Basel Committee on Banking Supervision (BIS), 2012b, Results of the Basel III Monitoring Exercise as of 31 December 2011.

Basel Committee on Banking Supervision (BIS), 2013, Basel III: The liquidity coverage ratio and liquidity risk monitoring tools, January.

Basel Committee on Banking Supervision (BIS), 2014, Basel III: The net stable funding ratio, October.

Becht, Marco, Patrick Bolton, and Ailsa Roell, 2011, Why bank governance is different, Oxford Review of Economic Policy 27, 437–463.

Beck, Thorsten, Ross Levine, and Alexey Levkov, 2010, Big bad banks? The winners and losers from bank deregulation in the United States, Journal of Finance 65, 1637–1667.

Bekaert, Geert, Campbell R. Harvey, and Christian Lundblad, 2007, Liquidity and expected returns: Lessons from emerging markets, Review of Financial Studies 20, 1783–1831.

Beltratti, Andrea, and Rene M. Stulz, 2012, The credit crisis around the globe: Why did some banks perform better?, Journal of Financial Economics 105, 1–17.

Berger, Allen N., Lamont K. Black, Christa H.S. Bouwman, and Jennifer Dlugosz, 2015, The Federal Reserve's discount window and TAF programs: "Pushing on a string?," Working Paper.

Berger, Allen N., Seth D. Bonime, Daniel M. Covitz, and Diana Hancock, 2000, Why are bank profits so persistent? The roles of product market competition, informational opacity, and regional/macroeconomic shocks, Journal of Banking and Finance 24, 1203–1235.

Berger, Allen N., Seth D. Bonime, Lawrence G. Goldberg, and Lawrence J. White, 2004, The dynamics of market entry: The effects of mergers and acquisitions on entry in the banking industry, Journal of Business 77, 797–834.

Berger, Allen N., and Christa H.S. Bouwman, 2009, Bank liquidity creation, Review of Financial Studies 22, 3779–3837.

Berger, Allen N., and Christa H.S. Bouwman, 2013, How does capital affect bank performance during financial crises?, Journal of Financial Economics 109, 146–176.

Berger, Allen N., Christa H.S. Bouwman, 2015, Bank liquidity creation, monetary policy, and financial crises, Working Paper.

Berger, Allen N., Christa H.S. Bouwman, Bjorn Imbierowicz, and Christian Rauch, 2015, Bank Value and Liquidity Creation, Working Paper.

Berger, Allen N., Christa H.S. Bouwman, Thomas K. Kick, and Klaus Schaeck, 2015, Bank risk taking and liquidity creation following regulatory interventions and capital support, Working Paper.

Berger, Allen N., Geraldo Cerqueiro, and Maria F. Penas, 2015, Market size structure and small business lending: Are crisis times different from normal times?, Review of Finance 19, 1965–1995.

Berger, Allen N., George R.G. Clarke, Robert Cull, Leora F. Klapper, and Gregory F. Udell, 2005, Corporate governance and bank performance: A joint analysis of the static, selection, and dynamic effects of domestic, foreign, and state ownership, Journal of Banking and Finance 29, 2179–2221.

Berger, Allen N., Robert DeYoung, Hesna Genay, and Gregory F. Udell, 2000, The globalization of financial institutions: Evidence from cross-border banking performance, Brookings-Wharton Papers on Financial Services 3, 23–158.

Berger, Allen N., Sadok El Ghoul, Omrane Guedhami, and Raluca A. Roman, 2015, Internationalization and bank risk, Working Paper.

Berger, Allen N., William Goulding, and Tara Rice, 2014, Do small businesses still prefer community banks?, Journal of Banking and Finance 44, 264–278.

Berger, Allen N., Gerald A. Hanweck, and David B. Humphrey, 1987, Competitive viability in banking: Scale, scope, and product mix economies, Journal of Monetary Economics 20, 501–520.

Berger, Allen N., Iftekhar Hasan, and Mingming Zhou, 2009, Bank ownership and efficiency in China: What will happen in the world's largest nation, Journal of Banking and Finance 33, 113–130.

Berger, Allen N., Bjorn Imbierowicz, and Christian Rauch, 2015, The roles of corporate governance in bank failures during the recent financial crisis, Working Paper.

Berger, Allen N., Leora F. Klapper, Maria Soledad Martinez Peria, and Rida Zaidi, 2008, Bank ownership type and banking relationships, Journal of Financial Intermediation 17, 37–62.

Berger, Allen N., Margaret K. Kyle, and Joseph M. Scalise, 2001, Did U.S. bank supervisors get tougher during the credit crunch? Did they get easier during the banking boom? Did it matter to bank lending?, in: Frederic S. Mishkin, (Ed.), Prudential Supervision: What Works and What Doesn't, National Bureau of Economic Research, University of Chicago Press, Chicago, IL, pp. 301–349.

Berger, Allen N., and Loretta J. Mester, 1997, Inside the black box: What explains differences in the efficiencies of financial institutions?, Journal of Banking and Finance 21, 895–947.

Berger, Allen N., Nathan H. Miller, Mitchell A. Petersen, Raghuram G. Rajan, and Jeremy C. Stein, 2005, Does function follow organizational form? Evidence from the lending practices of large and small banks, Journal of Financial Economics 76, 237–269.

Berger, Allen N., and Raluca A. Roman, 2015, Did saving Wall Street really save main street? The real effects of TARP on local economic conditions, Working Paper.

Berger, Allen N., and Raluca A. Roman, forthcoming, Did TARP banks get competitive advantages?, Journal of Financial and Quantitative Analysis.

Berger, Allen N., Anthony Saunders, Joseph M. Scalise, and Gregory F. Udell, 1998, The effects of bank mergers and acquisitions on small business lending, Journal of Financial Economics 50, 187–229.

Berger, Allen N., and John Sedunov, 2015, Bank liquidity creation and real economic output, Working Paper.

Berger, Allen N., and Gregory F. Udell, 1994, Did risk-based capital allocate bank credit and cause a "credit crunch" in the United States?, Journal of Money, Credit and Banking 26, 585–628.

Berkovitch, Elazar, and Stuart I. Greenbaum, 1991, The loan commitment as an optimal financing contract, Journal of Financial and Quantitative Analysis 26, 83–95.

Bernanke, Ben S., and Mark Gertler, 1995, Inside the black box: The credit channel of monetary policy transmission, Journal of Economic Perspectives 9, 27–48.

Bernanke, Ben S., and Cara S. Lown, 1991. The credit crunch, Brookings Papers on Economic Activity 2, 205–239.

Berrospide, Jose M., 2013, Bank liquidity hoarding and the financial crisis: An empirical evaluation, Federal Reserve Board Finance and Economics Discussion Series 2013-03.

Berrospide, Jose M., and Rochelle M. Edge, 2010, The effects of bank capital on lending: What do we know, and what does it mean?, Working Paper.

Besanko, David, and George Kanatas, 1996, The regulation of bank capital: Do capital standards promote bank safety?, Journal of Financial Intermediation 5, 160–183.

Bhattacharya, Sudipto, and Anjan V. Thakor, 1993, Contemporary banking theory, Journal of Financial Intermediation 3, 2–50.

Bizer, David S., 1993, Regulatory discretion and the credit crunch, U.S. Securities and Exchange Commission Working Paper.

Black, Lamont K., and Lieu Hazelwood, 2013, The effect of TARP on bank risk-taking, Journal of Financial Stability 9, 790–803.

Black, Sandra E., and Philip E. Strahan, 2002, Entrepreneurship and bank credit availability, The Journal of Finance 57, 2807–2833.

Blackwell, Norman R., and Anthony M. Santomero, 1982, Bank credit rationing and the customer relation, Journal of Monetary Economics 9, 121–129.

Board of Governors of the Federal Reserve System, 2015, Dodd-Frank Act stress test 2015 Supervisory stress test methodology and results.

Bonaccorsi di Patti, Emilia, and Giovanni Dell Ariccia, 2004, Bank competition and firm creation, Journal of Money, Credit and Banking 36, 225–251.

Boot, Arnoud W.A., and Stuart I. Greenbaum, 1993, Bank regulation, reputation and rents: Theory and policy implications, in: C. Mayer and X. Vives (Eds.), Capital Markets and Financial Intermediation, Cambridge University Press, Cambridge, MA, pp. 262–285.

Boot, Arnoud W.A., Stuart I. Greenbaum, and Anjan V. Thakor, 1993, Reputation and discretion in financial contracting, American Economic Review 83, 1165–1183.

Boot, Arnoud W.A., Anjan V. Thakor, and Gregory F. Udell, 1987, Competition, risk neutrality and loan commitments, Journal of Banking and Finance 11, 449–471.

Boot, Arnoud W.A., Anjan V. Thakor, and Gregory F. Udell, 1991, Credible commitments, contract enforcement problems and banks: Intermediation as credibility assurance, Journal of Banking and Finance 15, 605–632.

Bordo, Michael D., Barry Eichengreen, Daniela Klingebiel, and Maria Soledad Martinez Peria, 2001, Is the crisis problem growing more severe?, Economic Policy 32, 51–75.

Bordo, Michael D., and Anna J. Schwartz, 2000, Measuring real economic effects of bailout: Historical perspectives on how countries in financial distress have fared with and without.

Bailouts, Carnegie-Rochester Conference Series on Public Policy 53, 81–167.

Bouwman, Christa H.S., 2015, Liquidity: How banks create it and how it should be regulated, in: A.N. Berger, P. Molyneux, and J.O.S. Wilson (Eds.), The Oxford Handbook of Banking, 2nd edition, Oxford University Press, Oxford, pp. 184–218.

Boyd, John H., and Edward C. Prescott, 1986, Financial intermediary-coalitions, Journal of Economic Theory 38, 211–232.

Brown, Craig O., and I. Serdar Dinc, 2011, Too many to fail? Evidence of regulatory forbearance when the banking sector is weak, Review of Financial Studies 24, 1378–1405.

Brown, Stephen J., and William N. Goetzmann, 1995, Performance persistence, Journal of Finance 50, 679–698.

Brown, Stephen J., William N. Goetzmann, Roger G. Ibbotson, and Stephen A. Ross, 1992, Survivorship bias in performance studies, Review of Financial Studies 5, 553–580.

Brunnermeier, Markus K., Gary B. Gorton, and Arvind Krishnamurthy, 2011, Risk topography, in: D. Acemoglu and M. Woodford (Eds.), NBER Macroeconomics Annual 26, University of Chicago Press, Chicago, IL, pp. 149–176.

Brunnermeier, Markus K., Gary B. Gorton, and Arvind Krishnamurthy, 2014, Liquidity mismatch measurement, in: M.K. Brunnermeier and A. Krishnamurthy (Eds.), Risk Topography: Systemic Risk and Macro Modeling, University of Chicago Press, Chicago, IL, pp. 99–112.

Bryant, John, 1980, A model of reserves, bank runs, and deposit insurance, Journal of Banking and Finance 4, 335–344.

Butler, Alexander, Gustavo Grullon, and James Weston, 2005, Stock market liquidity and the cost of issuing equity, Journal of Financial and Quantitative Analysis 40, 331–348.

Calem, Paul, and Rafael Rob, 1999, The impact of capital-based regulation on bank risk-taking, Journal of Financial Intermediation 8, 317–352.

Calomiris, Charles W., Florian Heider, and Marie Hoerova, 2013, A theory of bank liquidity requirements, Working Paper.

Calomiris, Charles W., and Charles M. Kahn, 1991, The role of demandable debt in structuring optimal banking arrangements, American Economic Review 81, 497–513.

Calomiris, Charles W., and Berry Wilson, 2004, Bank capital and portfolio management: The 1930s 'capital crunch' and scramble to shed risk, Journal of Business 77, 421–55.

Campbell, Tim S., 1978, A model of the market for lines of credit, Journal of Finance 33, 231–244.

Campello, Murillo, Erasmo Giambona, John R. Graham, and Campbell R. Harvey, 2011, Liquidity management and corporate investment during a financial crisis, Review of Financial Studies 24, 1944–1979.

Canales, Rodrigo, and Ramana Nanda, 2012, A darker side to decentralized banks: Market power and credit rationing in SME lending, Journal of Financial Economics 105, 353–366.

Caprio, Gerard, Jr., and Daniela Klingebiel, 1996, Bank insolvencies: Cross country experience, World Bank Policy Research Working Paper No. 1620.

Cetorelli, Nicola, and Michele Gambera, 2001, Banking market structure, financial dependence and growth: International evidence from industry data, Journal of Finance 56, 617–648.

Cetorelli, Nicola, and Philip E. Strahan, 2006, Finance as a barrier to entry: Bank competition and industry structure in local U.S. markets, Journal of Finance 61, 437–461.

Charoenwong, Charlie, Beng S. Chong, and Yung C. Yang, 2014, Asset liquidity and stock liquidity: International evidence, Journal of Business Finance and Accounting 41, 435–468.

Chava, Sudheer, Alexander Oettl, Ajay Subramanian, and Krishnamurthy V. Subramanian, 2013, Banking deregulation and innovation, Journal of Financial Economics 109, 759–774.

Cheng, Ing-Haw, Harrison Hong, and Jose A. Scheinkman, 2015, Yesterday's heroes: Compensation and risk at financial firms, Journal of Finance 70, 839–879.

Choi, Byeongyong P., Jin Park, and Chia-Ling Ho, 2013, Liquidity creation or de-creation: Evidence from U.S. property and liability insurance industry, Managerial Finance 39, 938–962.

Chordia, Tarun, Richard Roll, and Avanidhar Subrahmanyam, 2001, Market liquidity and trading activity, Journal of Finance 56, 501–530.

Christie, William G., and Paul H. Schultz, 1998, Dealer markets under stress: The performance of NASDAQ market makers during the November 15, 1991, market break, Journal of Financial Services Research 13, 205–229.

Chu, Yongqiang, 2013, Asset fire sale and regulatory capital requirements: Evidence from commercial REO sales, Working Paper.

Chu, Yongqiang, and Tao Ma, 2015, How does executive compensation affect bank risk taking: Evidence from FAS123R, Working Paper.

Claessens, Stijn, Asli Demirguc-Kunt, and Harry Huizinga, 2001, How does foreign entry affect the domestic banking market?, Journal of Banking and Finance 25, 891–911.

Clarke, George R.G., Robert Cull, and Mary M. Shirley, 2005, Bank privatization in developing countries: A summary of lessons and findings, Journal of Banking and Finance 29, 1905–1930.

Cole, Rebel A., and Jeffery W. Gunther, 1995, Separating the timing and likelihood of bank failure, Journal of Banking and Finance 19, 1073–1089.

Cole, Rebel A., and Lawrence J. White, 2012, Déjà vu all over again: The causes of U.S. commercial bank failures this time around, Journal of Financial Services Research 42, 5–29.

Cornaggia, Jess, Yifei Mao, Xuan Tian, and Brian Wolfe, 2015, Does banking competition affect innovation?, Journal of Financial Economics 115, 189–209.

Cornett, Marcia M., Jamie J. McNutt, Philip E. Strahan, and Hassan Tehranian, 2011, Liquidity risk management and credit supply in the financial crisis, Journal of Financial Economics 101, 297–312.

Coval, Joshua D., and Anjan V. Thakor, 2005, Financial intermediation as a beliefs-bridge between optimists and pessimists, Journal of Financial Economics 75, 535–569.

Cowan, Arnold R., and Valentina Salotti, 2015, The resolution of failed banks during the crisis: Acquirer performance and FDIC guarantees, 2008–2013, Journal of Banking and Finance 54, 222–238.

Crawford, Anthony J., John R. Ezzell, and James A. Miles, 1995, Bank CEO pay-performance relations and the effects of deregulation, Journal of Business 68, 231–256.

Deep, Akash, and Guido K. Schaefer, 2004, Are banks liquidity transformers?, Working Paper.

Degryse, Hans, Nancy Masschelein, and Janet Mitchell, 2011, Staying, dropping, or switching: The impacts of bank mergers on small firms, Review of Financial Studies 24, 1102–1140.

Dell'Ariccia, Giovanni, Deniz Igan, and Luc Laeven, 2012, Credit booms and lending standards: Evidence from the subprime mortgage market, Journal of Money, Credit and Banking 44, 367–384.

Demirguc-Kunt, Asli, and Enrica Detragiache, 1998, The determinants of banking crises in developing and developed countries, Staff Papers - International Monetary Fund 45, 81–109.

Demirguc-Kunt, Asli, and Vojislav Maksimovic, 1998, Law, finance, and firm growth, Journal of Finance 53, 2107–2137.

Demirguc-Kunt, Asli, and Vojislav Maksimovic, 2002, Funding growth in bank-based and market-based financial systems: Evidence from firm-level data, Journal of Financial Economics 65, 337–363.

Demsetz, Rebecca S., and Philip E. Strahan, 1997, Diversification, size, and risk at bank holding companies, Journal of Money, Credit and Banking 29, 300–313.

Department of the Treasury, Federal Reserve System, and Federal Deposit Insurance Corporation, 2014, Liquidity coverage ratio: Liquidity risk measurement standards – Final Rule, Federal Register 79(197), 61440–61541.

DeYoung, Robert, William C. Hunter, and Gregory F. Udell, 2004, The past, present, and probable future for community banks, Journal of Financial Services Research 25, 85–133.

DeYoung, Robert, Emma Y. Peng, and Meng Yan, 2013, Executive compensation and business policy choices at U.S. commercial banks, Journal of Financial and Quantitative Analysis 48, 165–196.

Diamond, Douglas W., 1984, Financial intermediation and delegated monitoring, Review of Economic Studies 51, 393–414.

Diamond, Douglas W., and Philip H. Dybvig, 1983, Bank runs, deposit insurance, and liquidity, Journal of Political Economy 91, 401–419.

Diamond, Douglas W., and Raghuram G. Rajan, 2000, A theory of bank capital, Journal of Finance 55, 2431–2465.

Diamond, Douglas W., and Raghuram G. Rajan, 2001, Liquidity risk, liquidity creation, and financial fragility: A theory of banking, Journal of Political Economy 109, 287–327.

Diaz, Violeta, and Ying Huang, 2013, Bank Liquidity Creation: The role of risk taking and governance, Working Paper.

Dietrich, Andreas, Kurt Hess, and Gabrielle Wanzenried, 2014, The good and bad news about the new liquidity rules of Basel III in Western European countries, Journal of Banking and Finance 44, 13–25.

Distinguin, Isabelle, Caroline Roulet, and Amine Tarazi, 2013, Bank regulatory capital and liquidity: Evidence from U.S. and European publicly traded banks, Journal of Banking and Finance 37, 3295–3317.

Donaldson, Jason, Giorgia Piacentino, and Anjan V. Thakor, 2015, Warehouse banking, Working Paper.

Drees, Burkhard, and Ceyla Pazarbasioglu, 1995, The Nordic banking crises: Pitfalls in financial liberalization?, IMF Working Paper 95/61.

Duchin, Ran, and Denis Sosyura, 2014, Safer ratios, riskier portfolios: Banks' response to government aid, Journal of Financial Economics 113, 1–28.

Erkens, David H., Mingyi Hung, and Pedro P. Matos, 2012, Corporate governance in the 2007-2008 financial crisis: Evidence from financial institutions worldwide, Journal of Corporate Finance 18, 389–411.

Esterhuysen, Ja'nel N., Gary V. Vuuren, and Paul Styger, 2012, Liquidity creation in South African banks under stressed economic conditions, South African Journal of Economics 80, 106–122.

European Banking Authority (EBA), 2012a, Results of the Basel III Monitoring Exercise Based on Data as of 30 June 2011.

European Banking Authority (EBA), 2012b, Results of the Basel III Monitoring Exercise Based on Data as of 31 December 2011.

European Central Bank, 2015, The list of significant supervised entities and the list of less significant institutions.

Evanoff, Douglas D., George G. Kaufman, and Anastasios G. Malliaris, 2012, Asset price bubbles: What are the causes, consequences, and public policy options?, Chicago Fed Letter 304, 1–4.

Fahlenbrach, Rudiger, and Rene M. Stulz, 2011, Bank CEO incentives and the credit crisis, Journal of Financial Economics 99, 11–26.

Farhi, Emmanuel, and Jean Tirole, 2012, Collective moral hazard, maturity mismatch, and systemic bailouts, American Economic Review 102, 60–93.

Federal Deposit Insurance Corporation, 2012, FDIC community banking study.

Feinman, Joshua N., 1993, Reserve requirements: History, current practice, and potential reform, Federal Reserve Bulletin June, 569–589.

Flannery, Mark J., 1994, Debt maturity and the deadweight cost of leverage: Optimally financing banking firms, American Economic Review 84, 320–321.

Flannery, Mark J., 1996, Financial crises, payments system problems, and discount window lending, Journal of Money, Credit and Banking 28, 804–31.

Focarelli, Dario, and Fabio Panetta, 2003, Are mergers beneficial to consumers? Evidence from the market for bank deposits, American Economic Review 93, 1152–1172.

Francis, William, and Matthew Osborne, 2009, Bank regulation, capital and credit supply: Measuring the impact of prudential standards, Working Paper.

Freixas, Xavier, and Jean-Charles Rochet, 2008, Microeconomics of banking (2nd edition), Boston, MA: MIT Press.

Fungacova, Zuzana, Rima Turk Ariss, and Laurent Weill, 2015, High liquidity creation and bank failures, International Monetary Fund Working Paper 15/103.

Fungacova, Zuzana, and Laurent Weill, 2012, Bank liquidity creation in Russia, Eurasian Geography and Economics 53, 285–299.

Fungacova, Zuzana, Laurent Weill, and Mingming Zhou, 2010, Bank capital, liquidity creation and deposit insurance, Bank of Finland BOFIT Discussion Papers 17.

Gambacorta, Leonardo, and David Marques-Ibanez, 2011, The bank lending channel: Lessons from the crisis, Economic Policy 26, 135–182.

Gatev, Evan, Til Schuermann, and Philip E. Strahan, 2009, Managing bank liquidity risk: How deposit-loan synergies vary with market conditions, Review of Financial Studies 22, 995–1020.

Glick, Reuven, and Michael M. Hutchison, 2001, Banking and currency crises: How common are twins?, in: R. Glick, R. Moreno, and M.M. Spiegel (Eds.), Financial Crises in Emerging Markets, Cambridge University Press, Cambridge, UK.

Goetzmann, William N., and Roger G. Ibbotson, 1994, Do winners repeat? Patterns in mutual fund return behavior, Journal of Portfolio Management 20, 9–18.

Gopalan, Radhakrishnan, Ohad Kadan, and Mikhail Pevzner, 2012, Asset liquidity and stock liquidity, Journal of Financial and Quantitative Analysis 47, 333–364.

Gorton, Gary B., and Andrew Winton, 2000, Liquidity provision, bank capital, and the macroeconomy, Working Paper.

Greenbaum, Stuart I., 1967, Competition and efficiency in the banking system – Empirical research and its policy implications, Journal of Political Economy 75, 461–479.

Greenbaum, Stuart I., Anjan V. Thakor, and Arnoud W.A. Boot, 2016, Contemporary Financial Intermediation, 3rd edition, Elsevier Science.

Greene, Jason, and Scott Smart, 1999, Liquidity provision and noise trading: Evidence from the "investment dartboard" column, Journal of Finance 54, 1885–1899.

Gropp, Reint, Matthias Kohler, 2010, Bank owners or bank managers: Who is keen on risk? Evidence from the financial crisis, Working Paper.

Hackethal, Andreas, Christian Rauch, Sascha Steffen, and Marcel Tyrell, 2010, Determinants of bank liquidity creation, Working Paper.

Hagendorff, Jens, 2015, Corporate governance in banking, in: A.N. Berger, P. Molyneux, and J.O.S. Wilson (Eds.), The Oxford Handbook of Banking, 2nd edition, Oxford University Press, Oxford, pp. 139–159.

Hancock, Diana, Andrew J. Laing, and James A. Wilcox, 1995, Bank balance sheet shocks and aggregate shocks: Their dynamic effects on bank capital and lending, Journal of Banking and Finance 19, 661–677.

Hasbrouck, Joel 2009, Trading costs and returns for U.S. equities: Estimating effective costs from daily data, Journal of Finance 64, 1445–1477.

Hasbrouck, Joel, and Duane J. Seppi, 2001, Common factors in prices, order flows, and liquidity, Journal of Financial Economics 59, 383–411.

Hasbrouck, Joel, and Saar, 2002, Limit orders and volatility in a hybrid market: The Island ECN, Working Paper.

Hester, Donald D., 1967, Competition and efficiency in the banking system: Comment, Journal of Political Economy 75, 479–481.

Ho, Thomas S.Y., and Anthony Saunders, 1983, Fixed rate loan commitments, take-down risk, and the dynamics of hedging with futures, Journal of Financial and Quantitative Analysis 18, 499–516.

Hodrick, Robert J., and Edward C. Prescott, 1997, Postwar U.S. business cycles: An empirical investigation, Journal of Money, Credit and Banking 29, 1–16.

Holmstrom, Bengt, and Tirole, Jean, 1997, Financial intermediation, loanable funds, and the real sector, Quarterly Journal of Economics 112, 663–691.

Holmstrom, Bengt, and Jean Tirole, 1998, Public and private supply of liquidity, Journal of Political Economy 106, 1–40.

Hong, Han, Jing-Zhi Huang, and Deming Wu, 2014, The information content of Basel III liquidity risk measures, Journal of Financial Stability 15, 91–111.

Horvath, Roman, Jacob Seidler, and Laurent Weill, 2014, Bank capital and liquidity creation: Granger-causality evidence, Journal of Financial Services Research 45, 341–361.

Horvath, Roman, Jacob Seidler, and Laurent Weill, 2015, How bank competition influences liquidity creation, Working Paper.

Horvitz, Paul M., 1963, Economies of scale in banking, Private Financial Institutions, Englewood Cliffs, NJ: Prentice Hall, 1–54.

Houston, Joel F., and Christopher M. James, 1995, CEO compensation and bank risk: Is compensation in banking structured to promote risk taking?, Journal of Monetary Economics 36, 405–431.

Huberman, Gur, and Dominika Halka, 2001, Systematic liquidity, Journal of Financial Research 24, 161–178.

Hubbard, R. Glenn, and Darius Palia, 1995, Executive pay and performance: Evidence from the U.S. banking industry, Journal of Financial Economics 39, 105–130.

Hughes, Joseph P., and Loretta J. Mester, 2013, Who said large banks don't experience scale economies? Evidence from a risk-return-driven cost function, Journal of Financial Intermediation 22, 559–585.

Imbierowicz, Bjorn, and Christian Rauch, 2014, The relationship between liquidity risk and credit risk in banks, Journal of Banking and Finance 40, 242–256.

Ioannidou, Vasso, and Steven Ongena, 2010, "Time for a Change:" Loan conditions and bank behavior when firms switch banks, Journal of Finance 65, 1847–1877.

Ivashina, Victoria, and David S. Scharfstein, 2010, Bank lending during the financial crisis of 2008, Journal of Financial Economics 97, 319–338.

James, Christopher M., 1981, Self-selection and the pricing of bank services: An analysis of the market for bank loan commitments and the role of the compensating balance requirements, Journal of Financial and Quantitative Analysis 16, 725–746.

Jayaratne, Jith, and Philip E. Strahan, 1996, The finance-growth nexus: Evidence from bank branch deregulation, Quarterly Journal of Economics 111, 639–670.

Jimenez, Gabriel, Steven Ongena, Jose-Luis Peydro, and Jesus Saurina, 2012, Credit supply and monetary policy: Identifying the bank balance-sheet channel with loan applications, American Economic Review 102, 2301–2326.

Jimenez, Gabriel, Steven Ongena, Jose-Luis Peydro, and Jesus Saurina, 2014, Hazardous times for monetary policy: What do twenty-three million bank loans say about the effects of monetary policy on credit risk-taking?, Econometrica 82, 463–505.

Joh, Sung W., and Jeongsim Kim, 2013, Does competition affect the role of banks as liquidity providers?, Working Paper.

Johnson, Simon H., and James Kwak, 2010, 13 Bankers: The Wall Street takeover and the next financial meltdown, Pantheon Books, New York.

Kamara, Avraham, and Jennifer L. Koski, 2001, Volatility, autocorrelations, and trading activity after stock splits, Journal of Financial Markets 4, 163–184.

Kaminsky, Garciela L., and Carmen M. Reinhart, 1996, The Twin Crises: The causes of banking and balance-of-payments problems, International Finance Discussion Paper No. 544 (Washington: Board of Governors of the Federal Reserve System, March).

Kaminsky, Graciela L., and Carmen M. Reinhart, 1999, The twin crises: The causes of banking and balance-of-payments problems, American Economic Review 89, 473–500.

Karceski, Jason, Steven Ongena, and David C. Smith, 2005, The impact of bank consolidation on commercial borrower welfare, Journal of Finance 60, 2043–2082.

Kashyap, Anil K., Raghuram G. Rajan, and Jeremy C. Stein, 2002, Banks as liquidity providers: An explanation for the coexistence of lending and deposit-taking, Journal of Finance 57, 33–73.

Kashyap, Anil K., and Jeremy C. Stein, 1994, Monetary policy and bank lending, in: G. Mankiw (Ed.), Monetary Policy, University of Chicago Press, Chicago, IL, pp. 221–261.

Kashyap, Anil K., and Jeremy C. Stein, 1997, The role of banks in monetary policy: A survey with implications for the European Monetary Union, Economic Perspectives, Federal Reserve Bank of Chicago, September/October, 3–18.

Kashyap, Anil K., and Jeremy C. Stein, 2000, What do a million observations on banks say about the transmission of monetary policy?, American Economic Review 90, 407–428.

Khwaja, Asim Ijaz, and Atif Mian, 2008, Tracing the impact of bank liquidity shocks: Evidence from an emerging market, American Economic Review 98, 1413–1442.

Kirkpatrick, Grant, 2009, The corporate governance lessons from the financial crisis, OECD Financial Market Trends 2009/1, 1–30.

Kishan, Ruby P., and Timothy P. Opiela, 2012, Monetary policy, bank lending, and the risk-pricing channel, Journal of Money, Credit and Banking 44, 573–602.

Koehn, Michael, and Anthony M. Santomero, 1980, Regulation of bank capital and portfolio risk, Journal of Finance 35, 1235–1244.

La Porta, Rafael, Florencio Lopez-de-Silanes, Andrei Shleifer, and Robert W. Vishny, 1998, Law and finance, Journal of Political Economy 106, 1113–1155.

Laeven, Luc, 2013, Corporate governance: What's special about banks?, Annual Review of Financial Economics 5, 63–92.

Laeven, Luc, and Ross Levine, 2009, Bank governance, regulation and risk taking, Journal of Financial Economics 93, 259–275.

Laeven, Luc, and Fabian Valencia, 2013, Systemic banking crises database, IMF Economic Review 61, 225–270.

Lakstutiene, Ausrine, and Rytis Krusinskas, 2010, Lithuanian banks liquidity creation in 2004-2008, Economics and Management 5, 986–991.

Lakstutiene, Ausrine, Rytis Krusinskas, and Dalia Rumsaite, 2011, Effect of depositor panic on the financial stability of banks, Economics and Management 16, 1154–1163.

Lee, Hyung Min, 2014, The impact of financial crisis on the economic values of financial conglomerates, Working Paper.

Lei, Adrian C.H., and Zhuoyun Song, 2013, Liquidity creation and bank capital structure in China, Global Finance Journal 24, 188–202.

Lesmond, David A., Joseph P. Ogden, and Charles A. Trzcinka, 1999, A new estimate of transaction costs, Review of Financial Studies 12, 1113–1141.

Li, Lei, 2013, TARP funds distribution and bank loan supply, Journal of Banking and Finance 37, 4777–4792.

Lindgren, Carl-Johan, Gillian G. Garcia, and Matthew I. Saal, 1996, Bank soundness and macroeconomic policy, International Monetary Fund Working Paper.

Lo, Andrew W., 2012, Reading about the financial crisis: A twenty-one-book review, Journal of Economic Literature 50, 151–178.

Loutskina, Elena, 2011, The role of securitization in bank liquidity and funding management, Journal of Financial Economics 100, 663–684.

Martinez Peria, Maria S., and Sergio L. Schmukler, 2001, Do depositors punish banks for bad behavior? Market discipline, deposit insurance, and banking crises, Journal of Finance 56, 1029–1051.

Mehran, Hamid, and Joshua Rosenberg, 2008, The effect of employee stock options on bank investment choice, borrowing, and capital, Federal Reserve Bank of New York Staff Reports 305.

Mehran, Hamid, and Anjan Thakor, 2011, Bank capital and value in the cross-section, Review of Financial Studies 24, 1019–1067.

Melnik, Aries, and Steven Plaut, 1986, Loan commitment contracts, terms of lending, and credit allocation, Journal of Finance 41, 425–435.

Merton, Robert C., 1977, An analytic derivation of the cost of deposit insurance and loan guarantees: An application of modern option pricing theory, Journal of Banking and Finance 1, 3–11.

Mohammad, Sabri and Mehmet Asutay, 2015, Measuring liquidity creation and its determinants in banking sector: A comparative analysis between Islamic, conventional and hybrid banks in the case of the GCC Region, Working Paper.

Morgan, Donald P., 1994, Bank credit commitments, credit rationing, and monetary policy, Journal of Money, Credit and Banking 26, 87–101.

Morgan, Donald P., 1998, The credit effects of monetary policy: Evidence using loan commitments, Journal of Money, Credit and Banking 30, 102–118.

Herszenhorn, David M., and Sewell Chan, 2010, Financial debate renews scrutiny on banks' size, New York Times, April 21.

Ongena, Steven, Alexander Popov, and Gregory F. Udell, 2013, "When the cat's away the mice will play": Does regulation at home affect bank risk-taking abroad?, Journal of Financial Economics 108, 727–750.

Pana, Elisabeta, 2012, QEP and bank liquidity creation: Evidence from Japan, Working Paper.

Pana, Elisabeta, and Tarun K. Mukherjee, 2012, Credit unions as liquidity creators, Working Paper.

Pana, Elisabeta, Jin Park, and J. Tim Query, 2010, The impact of bank mergers on liquidity creation, Journal of Risk Management in Financial Institutions 4, 74–96.

Pastor, Lubos, and Robert F. Stambaugh, 2003, Liquidity risk and expected stock returns, Journal of Political Economy 111, 642–685.

Peek, Joe, and Eric Rosengren, 1995a, Bank regulation and the credit crunch, Journal of Banking and Finance 19, 679–692.

Peek, Joe, and Eric Rosengren, 1995b, The capital crunch: Neither a borrower nor a lender be, Journal of Money, Credit and Banking 27, 625–38.

Petersen, Mitchell A., and Raghuram G. Rajan, 1994, The benefits of lending relationships: Evidence from small business data, Journal of Finance 49, 3–37.

Petersen, Mitchell A., and Raghuram G. Rajan, 1995, The effect of credit market competition on lending relationships, Quarterly Journal of Economics 110, 407–443.

Puddu, Stefano, and Andreas Walchli, 2014, TARP effect on bank lending behaviour: Evidence from the last financial crisis, Working Paper.

Rajan, Raghuram G., 1994, Why bank credit policies fluctuate: A theory and some evidence, Quarterly Journal of Economics 109, 399–441.

Ramakrishnan, Ram T.S., and Anjan V. Thakor, 1984, Information reliability and a theory of financial intermediation, Review of Economic Studies 51, 415–432.

Reinhart, Carmen M., and Kenneth S. Rogoff, 2009, This time is different: Eight centuries of financial folly, Princeton University Press, Princeton.

Repullo, Rafael, 2004, Capital requirements, market power, and risk-taking in banking, Journal of Financial Intermediation 13, 156–182.

Rice, Tara, and Philip E. Strahan, 2010, Does credit competition affect small-firm finance?, Journal of Finance 65, 861–889.

Roll, Richard 1984, A simple implicit measure of the effective bid-ask spread in an efficient market, Journal of Finance 39, 1127–1139.

Roman, Raluca A., 2015, Shareholder activism in banking, Working Paper.

Romer, Christina D., and David H. Romer, 2004, A new measure of monetary shocks: Derivation and implications, American Economic Review 94, 1055–1084.

Saheruddin, Herman, 2014, Bank capital, reputation, and relationship lending: Evidence from bank loan announcements during normal times and financial crises, Working Paper.

Sapienza, Paola, 2004, The effects of government ownership on bank lending, Journal of Financial Economics 74, 357–384.

Saunders, Anthony, and Marcia Millon Cornett, 2014, Financial institution management: A Risk Management Approach, 8th Edition, New York: McGraw Hill.

Schandlbauer, Alexandar, 2013, How do financial institutions react to a tax increase?, Working Paper.

Shaffer, Sherrill, 1993, A test of competition in Canadian banking, Journal of Money, Credit and Banking 25, 49–61.

Sheng, Andrew, 1995, Bank Restructuring: Lessons From the 1980s, World Bank.

Shockley, Richard L., and Anjan V. Thakor, 1997, Bank loan commitment contracts: Data, theory, and tests, Journal of Money, Credit and Banking 29, 517–534.

Shrieves, Ronald E., and Drew Dahl, 1995, Regulation, recession, and bank lending behavior: The 1990 credit crunch, Journal of Financial Services Research 9, 5–30.

Smith, Adam, 1776, An inquiry into the nature and causes of the wealth of nations, edited by Edwin Cannan 1976, reproduced at http://www.econlib.org/library/Smith/smWN.html.

Sufi, Amir, 2009, Bank lines of credit in corporate finance: An empirical analysis, Review of Financial Studies 22, 1057–1088.

Temesvary, Judit, 2015, Foreign activities of U.S. banks since 1997: The roles of regulations and market conditions in crises and normal times, Journal of International Money and Finance 56, 202–222.

Tewari, Ishani, 2014, The distributive impacts of financial development: Evidence from mortgage markets during U.S. bank branch deregulation, American Economic Journal: Applied Economics 6, 175–196.

Thakor, Anjan V., 1996, Capital requirements, monetary policy, and aggregate bank lending: Theory and empirical evidence, Journal of Finance, 51, 279–324.

Thakor, Anjan V., 2005, Do loan commitments cause overlending?, Journal of Money, Credit and Banking 37, 1067–1099.

Thakor, Anjan V., 2014, Bank capital and financial stability: An economic tradeoff or a Faustian bargain?, Annual Review of Financial Economics 6, 185–223.

Thakor, Anjan V., 2015, The financial crisis of 2007-09: Why did it happen and what did we learn?, Review of Corporate Finance Studies 4, 155–205.

Von Hagen, Jurgen, and Tai-Kuang Ho, 2007, Money market pressure and the determinants of banking crises, Journal of Money, Credit and Banking 39, 1037–1066.

Von Thadden, Ernst-Ludwig, 2004, Bank capital adequacy regulation under the new Basel Accord, Journal of Financial Intermediation 13, 90–95.

Woodford, Michael, 1996, Loan commitments and optimal monetary policy, Journal of Monetary Economics, 37, 573–605.

Author Index

Subject Index

Printed in the United States
By Bookmasters